BY THE SAME AUTHOR

Optimism
Men in Groups
The Imperial Animal (with Robin Fox)
Women in the Kibbutz (with Joseph Shepher)
Female Hierarchies (ed.)

OPTIMISM

The Biology
of Hope

by LIONEL TIGER

SIMON AND SCHUSTER
NEW YORK

Designed by Stanley Drate
Manufactured in the United States of America

1 2 3 4 5 6 7 8 9 10

Library of Congress Cataloging in Publication Data

Tiger, Lionel, 1937–
  Optimism: the biology of hope.

  Bibliography: p.
  Includes index.
  1. Sociobiology. 2. Optimism. I. Title.
GN365.9.T53   301.2   78-31328

ISBN 0–671–22934–6

Material from "Individual Mobility in a Stationary
Population" by Nathan Keyfitz is reprinted by
permission of the author.

Acknowledgments

If it is true that many writers conduct their transactions with words within the blight or blessing of isolation, for others the agreeable work of preparing acknowledgments reveals the intricacy and sturdiness of the community within which writing happens. I am happy to acknowledge here the contribution of people and groups to the life of this project, while also underscoring the real point that they are responsible only for being constructive, warm, helpful, advisory, or friendly, *not* for any errors of description or interpretation which the print which follows may make embarrassingly plain.

I'm grateful to the Harry Frank Guggenheim Foundation for its financial support and dignified yet always forceful commitment to expanding human understanding. It has been an abiding privilege to have had association with persons as provident and deft as Peter Lawson-Johnston, Chairman of the Board, Dr. Mason Gross, the late President of the Foundation, and Mr. George Fountaine, the Executive Director of the Foundation. Messrs. Joseph Koenigsberger and Paul Parren of the Foundation have cordially overseen the financial and associated factors of the work reported here.

Dean Kenneth Wolfson and his colleagues at the Graduate School of Rutgers University have consistently provided an academic ambience both tolerant yet responsive, and I hope work such as this provides them some sense of justification for their helpfulness over the years.

Steven M. L. Aronson was firmly involved in the origins of this project and has remained constructively coercive about its ontogeny since.

Alice Mayhew has been an editor and intellectual protagonist of vivacity and seriousness at once; she gave the book first a shelter, then a home. I am grateful to John Cox of Simon and Schuster for his contribution to the book's editing.

Robin Fox has been part of my working environment for so long that it is easy for me to forget except on occasions such as this how much I value his gleeful skepticism and rigorous intellection.

For some people, written words are especially sweet and tyrannical. Karyl Roosevelt is one such person. Of her contribution to this book only she can be clearly, and I dimly, aware.

It is a pleasure to thank Lynn Nesbit for generosity in professional duty beyond the call of friendship.

Not only am I grateful to Richard Gilman for his helpful comments upon an early draft of part of the manuscript, but I am compelled to record for the sake of someone compiling an unnecessary book on literary coincidences that it surely means nothing whatever that he and I and our families shared a Tuscan vacation house in which I struggled with *Optimism* in a downstairs room while Gilman wrote his book *Decadence,* upstairs.

Several Rutgers students—some already, others soon to be professional anthropologists in their own right—have assisted me in this work: Barbara Blei, Jay Callen, Heather Fowler, Susan Fox, Paul Heyer, and Terrence O'Keefe.

The following people have all been directly generous and helpful to the work of this book but have not been specifically mentioned in the text: Ian Bowers, Karen Colvard, Maggie Curran, David Easton, Abraham Edel, Edward Jay Epstein, Erving Goffman, Donald Griffin, David Hamburg, Adrienne Harris,

Oscar Hechter, Beatrice Indursky, Arthur Kling, Alexander Marshack, Roger Masters, Jack Nessel, Herman Roiphe, Jonathan Rubinstein, Edward Sachar, Erica Spellman, Sherwood Washburn, Edward O. Wilson, and Jonathan Winson.

This book seems to demand a dedication to close people, and it is dedicated to three. Martin Tiger fathered and raised me with as much enthusiasm and ardor as he wished me to have in my life. Virginia Tiger has been consistently knowing about this book during its history and I always admire her sensibility and wisdom. Sebastian Tiger is my son and my sun, and I look forward to and crave his every tomorrow.

To Martin Tiger
  Virginia Tiger
    Sebastian Tiger

Contents

1

As Necessary as Air

In the stairwell of a Montreal hospital, my father and I stood talking with the surgeon who had operated on my mother. The tumor that had prospered in her belly remained to be discussed. There was about the surgeon a kind of central stillness—I remembered him as a grand and haloed figure a couple of years ahead of me at McGill University. That he was married to the daughter of the doctor who had reached into my mother and delivered me ten thousand days before was not a very pacifying irony.

The doctor reviewed my mother's case history with a firm lack of nonsense—I realized of course that he was helpless not to give us the hard news, because he knew that whatever he said would have for us the force of law. Everything that could be done had been done, he pronounced, the tumor would just have to run its course, the rest was up to . . . Here he pointed his index finger upward and shrugged.

The gesture seemed to me to be directed to my father, whose loneliness lay just ahead of him to be borne. He was the one who needed hope the most. And if that hope was beckoning, it was also false. I knew by the doctor's eyes that my mother would die soon, and once again I was dumb with astonishment at the poverty of the circumstances in which people almost always have to conduct their transactions with infinity.

A short while later, in another hospital, my mother was being operated on again. During the nausea of the long wait, in a room furnished with old magazines and plastic chairs and lithographs of mountain scenery, my father, aunt, and wife huddled together as my mother's light went down. Late at night, there was a flurry of action: orderlies wheeled the patient, swaddled in sheets and unaware of her kin, down the long length of the hospital corridor. Moments later, the surgeon, an alchemist in green, strode from the operating theater to the disrobing room.

We waited, paced; presently, flushed with fatigue, he came in to speak to us. The charade was over. He said flatly that my mother was riddled with cancer, he'd done the best he could without killing her on the table. My father, like me a petty gambler concerned with small odds, asked how long she had. The machinery of the terminally ill is an uncertain thing; the doctor said two weeks, at most a month . . .

My wife was at the time ten weeks away from giving birth to our first child. The question was, which belly would conclude its business first—my mother's in death or my wife's in birth.

In the event, my mother lived long enough to have her first grandchild brought to her. Somewhere she found the strength to rise out of her bed and take him, who had surely been the youngest Air Canada passenger from New York to Montreal that night, in her shriveled arms—holding him for the first, and, when the weekend was over, the last time. And having held him, she sank back, releasing him to the future.

The contrasts between hope and despair are bewildering and stark. Even buildings may express the human passions which are revealed at the poles of the dichotomy. Tourists visiting the fortified colonial castle, now a national monument, on the shore at Cape Coast in Ghana, may be guided to the dungeon in which slaves awaiting shipment overseas were held. It is a ghastly place with low ceilings, small windows near the ceiling, and when the sea is rough the South Atlantic ocean splashes in. Sometimes slaves drowned there.

An opposite image is the Statue of Liberty on the other side of the Atlantic, which rises from the water to welcome free people to elaborate and rich lives. It symbolizes an attitude, a process, a gigantic assertion about the human condition. In this essay I shall examine the latter symbol, though the glisten of liberty remains gravely shadowed by the gloom of many dungeons.

This book is a tour of the forms and functions of personal optimism and of the social groups and patterns that it nourishes and sustains. As mood, attitude, and mode of perceiving life optimism has been central to the process of human evolution; it determines to a degree not yet charted the way humans think, play, and respond to birth and death. I think it is a force which can be a lever in the hands of statesmen and a bludgeon in the hands of dictators; it is a part of doctors' kits and ensures employment for priests as well as croupiers. It permitted us to attack intimidating wild animals when we hunted and to have some confidence in seeds, soil, water and sun when we planted. We know that people may stimulate their own deaths, as in voodoo or among recently retired men, and that recoveries may follow the administration of pills of simple sugar. When investors are confident fortunes are made, and when they are not the negotiable value of a community's wealth falls like a stone though no real wealth has been stripped from the factories and shops. Shrines, lotteries, strawberry desserts and the movie's happy ending share a benign sense of the future. Its absence in the long run is foreign to human beings and in the short run is as awkward as cactus. A hopeful sense of the promise of the future may be as important to communities' welfare as yeast to rising bread.

I am saying that making optimistic symbols and anticipating optimistic outcomes of undecided situations is as much part of human nature, of the human biology, as are the shape of the body, the growth of children, and the zest of sexual pleasure. This optimism is related to our general confidence in social arrangements which a mammal with a lengthy phase of dependence will develop, but also with a kind of cognitive overdrive associated with our past as a hunting primate. When we acquired our huge cerebral cortex this elaborate organ started producing an ever more complex and imaginative stock of optimistic schemes and varyingly plausible adventures. Neither the consciousness of mortality nor a cold sense of human frailty depresses the belief in desirable futures. The strategists of modernization, the generals on both sides, each of them certain of victory, the revolutionaries committed to human perfection, believers devoted to salvation in the future through good works now—all such students of glowing possibility enjoy a cheering legacy from their genetic forebears. By and large they do not know this common legacy nor do they know—beyond the parochial imperatives of jobs, time, and place—what the reasons may be for their firm assumptions about the future's promise. To attribute such fabulous confections as theories of the future to the gene pool of the human species may seem curious. Yet I think that we know how complex these genes are and how affected by them are our lives and bodies to begin to estimate the connection between the Infinite and evolution, between Salvation and bodily states. I propose to try, knowing what we do not know. We are as yet uncertain about the precise relationship between the brain and its ideas, between actions and thoughts about actions, about how healthy bodies affect what we think of the present and diseased ones what we fear in the future. We do not know firmly why some communities believe in a glad hereafter which is almost inevitable, while others are convinced they must either earn their sojourn in heaven through good works on earth or lose all peace of mind and body in some hell-like place. Why do some human societies prefer to cherish secular beliefs, such as the importance of the coming of communism or socialism, while others look forward to a happy millennium? We do not know why some people are grumpy when they are idle while others are exhilarated. We do not know how much the brain contrives to make its own reality and how much it over- or underestimates the reality conveyed to it by our senses. It is difficult to pinpoint when visionaries become mad and when skeptics become paralyzed. It is baffling why in some places joy is a just desert while in others it must be spirited away from the colorless rigamarole of dour civility. We will never quite know why the threats of the prophet Ezekiel were so dispiriting while the promises of Isaiah formed such a sturdy offer. There is a provocative matter here at hand and we cannot escape scrutinizing how we make our futures, with what, and why. Artists have frequently depicted the haze of heaven and the future as a cloudlike form floating above the people it concerned and who were concerned with it, ranging from the prophetic inhabitants of clouds in William Blake's illustrations to the wretched man of Al Capp's, whose cloud followed him everywhere. I want here to understand that haze, that cloud, and the reason for our upward look.

First let me limit the field of inquiry, before it threatens to encompass all of human existence. Visualize the range of human social behaviors and see it as composed of discernibly different behavioral elements, in the way that the physical universe is composed of elements or the alphabet is composed of individual letters and the musical scale of particular notes. While we may define connections between the elements, the letters, the notes, because they work together though on a scale of variation, it is also possible to perceive them as discrete units or phenomena. Just as certain elements will be more pervasive in some compounds than in others, for example, the two H's to the one O in water, H_2O, so in behavioral terms, some elements will obviously be more significant in one set of circumstances than another. So, optimism will be more dominant in certain systems of action and not others—for example, in praying or buying a lottery ticket, compared with selecting grapefruits at a fruit stand or painting a bedroom wall beige or ivory. My proposal is that even though it varies in its importance in particular situations, from being overwhelmingly predominant in some to negligible in others, we can see optimism as an isolatable element—as an attitude, mood or strategy—and that understanding its origins, functions, incidence and characteristics will make us aware of a surprisingly neglected feature of behavioral patterns and outcomes.

This is essentially a psychological assertion. I am saying that one can isolate optimism (without for a moment equating this work with theirs) as Theodore Adorno (1964) and his colleagues sought to isolate authoritarianism, or David McClelland (1967) the need for achievement, or Erik Erikson the factor of trust in individual lives. But, necessarily, an effort at a natural history of the element of optimism must fall not only within psychology but within a wide spectrum of the sciences of living systems. Such an excursion must be highly selective, but the focus of concern—the hard, pervasive and complicated reality of human optimism—must unite the parts. A modern biologist who studies a particular behavioral pattern of another animal will be concerned not only with overt behavior but also with the social setting in which it takes place, its physiological and cognitive correlates, and possibly its function in the evolution and survival of the animal. In a similar way I will argue that an analysis of such a central and unique characteristic of man requires a synthetic approach.

More important here than a defense of method is a definition of the subject matter. Optimism I take to be a mood or attitude associated with an expectation about the social or material future—one which the evaluator regards as socially desirable, to his advantage, or for his pleasure. The attitude is both variable and complex: how optimism is defined in a particular situation depends on what the particular optimist regards as desirable. In essence there can be no objectively obvious optimism. It is always subjective and exists in the context of an individual's purposes as it is described or assumed by that individual. It may be as optimistic (if also gruesome) for a person to pray for the death of an enemy as it is for a cancer researcher to be convinced that a series of experiments will solve the mystery of why cancer conquers doctors. It is as optimistic (if gruesome again) for a Hitler to assert that killing Jews and gypsies will purify Aryan communities as for a donor of a collection of art to expect the gift to enrich and please the population. It is as optimistic for a friendly person to open a simple restaurant serving good food pleasantly at reasonable prices, to make diners happy, as it is for a private detective to set up shop to make a living invading privacy at the will of clients. Visiting Mecca, going on a diet, and selling short on the stock market share the element of optimism. So do planning to have a baby, buying a dress in the latest fashion, and anticipating an island vacation. Though the social and economic consequences of these actions will differ enormously for the people involved, a serious and recurrent element of the chemistry of their behavior is the calculation that what they are doing will win gain, pleasure, or safety. Achieving these may hinder or aid the commonweal—that is another matter. But while optimism is of itself morally neutral, there seems to be a considerable likelihood that people will make the claim that satisfying their private optimisms will be to the general benefit of everyone—often indeed more so than there may be benefit to themselves.

Such a comfortable attitude to one's own selfishness seems particularly pronounced among political and economic leaders and the occasional Robin Hood-like criminal, though the principle applies to ideologues and enthusiasts in a wide spectrum of activities. The "fit" between private goals and public needs, insofar as it revolves around the problem of optimism and how the future is to be approached, provokes frequent uncertainty, not only in political theories about the nature of representative systems, but also among real politicians and real constituents. We will have to examine later how the moral neutrality of attitudes to the future stimulates very intense, morally founded controversy and why it is precisely its quality as a force awaiting harness which makes the management of optimism so critical in social life. Many communities have strong rules to inhibit people who spread panic and hysteria and who incite their fellow citizens to extremes of distress, fear, or despair. Purveyors of optimism may be as extreme in their offerings—heaven is extreme after all—but they appear to be much more acceptable than doomsayers. This is an argument to which we will return after a discussion of the properties of optimism.

For various reasons, among them perhaps the zeitgeist of a crowded species and considerable new data about our pasts, there have been serious changes underway in how humans understand their origin as a species and their destiny as biological creatures. The consequences of these new notions and facts have yet to be fully appreciated. In particular, we do not know or feel their implication clearly. I became interested in optimism and its relation to cognition only in the latter phases of research for a book called *Men in Groups,* which was published in 1969. I did not think of this study as an investigation of human ideas and their function, but rather of relatively straightforward social patterns. I was interested in current and prehistoric male relationships in various contexts. I focused on what was then new information about the predominantly hunting-gathering history of evolving man—we have been hunters and gatherers for 99 percent of our existence. What seemed significant was how the change from vegetarian primate life to omnivorous human life affected social and sexual patterns, and hence our genetic heritage. The relationships between males in politics, but especially in food gathering or the hunt were, I argued, as important for genetic selection as the relationships between males and females were in intimate, personal terms. I tried to examine the characteristics of the male bond as part of a speculative reconstruction of what was going on among males during the formative two to three million years of the human species. Apart from what resulted from this study about males in particular (which was in any event speculative and controversial), what became plain was that there was some elaborate connection between the evolution of the hunting-gathering way, the subsequent development of the large cerebral cortex, and presumably therefore of the emergence of ways of using the brain and body in conjunction with this new, powerfully successful way of living and making a living.

There is even evidence to think that there was an evolutionary advantage gained by people who thought well of the future or of their immediate prospects. In particular, work on the relationship between systems of reproduction during that evolutionary phase when we increased our brain size most rapidly suggested how we may have had to inhibit present responses in order to achieve future goals. This was called "equilibration." Our existence, in other words, became augmented by an elaborate ability to think things through and think ahead. Surely the workaday hazards of hunting large animals—the record shows that our predecessors secured larger and presumably more dangerous prey as the archeological record unfolds— would have given some impetus and advantage to persons willing to entertain the idea of a successful foray and to act on the basis of that idea rather than on the spectre of injury and failure. As I noted at the end of *Men in Groups*, "Being a hunting species, humans must have hope. There must even be a program for hope springing eternally in our innards."

There are scores of hunting species in the world. Even if many others employ the optimistic scenario in a strategic way in their hunting work, an important distinction between humans and other hunters lies in the capacity of the power of the cerebral cortex to produce nightmarish symbolic impediments and countless imaginative reasons for failure; we must presume that other animals are markedly less burdened with complex renditions of the process of failure or disaster. Part of the problem of developing the new and imaginative cortex was in disciplining it, in somehow reducing the possible demoralizing effects of a grim and fertile imagination for defeat and death.

The consequences were not merely private, they were social. However newly well-armed we might be with the weapons we made to subdue dangerous animals we were also surely, if slowly, increasing our numbers and achieving a more complex social organization. While these new social groups reduced our personal sense of fragility and loneliness, they could also become enemies, a potential threat if groups should split and enmities result. For social as well as economic and ecological reasons it became useful, if not essential, to employ symbolic skills for evaluating the future. Optimists were more likely to cope and reproduce than pessimists, other things being equal; an important root of social cohesion and economic innovation is as biologically understandable as the sweating that accompanies fear, though far less tangible and immediate. I will also return to a full discussion of the development of the optimistic state of mind and the social process arising from it which permits people alone and people in groups to feel glad and confident about their forthcoming experiences. I think both these evolved in biological terms as materially as the plumage of the peacock, or the quail's protective color, or the crow's announcement.

I'm not as yet making a distinction between what could be called "little optimism" and "big optimism." The former has to do with personal and intimate wishes—I will get to be law clerk to Judge Brandeis, my child will smile sunnily at morose people, my party will be fun, the combination of this tie and that shirt will be of artful interest—while big optimism is concerned with such matters as the transsubstantiation of souls, the enhancement of communities by greater expenditure on education or on computerized missiles, the proposition that technology yields progress with the revision of the economic order to release the energy of the poor.

There is, of course, a connection between all these facets; sometimes assertions or distortions of one kind of optimism will promote or inhibit the other. For the time being I will try to define the subject in general while alluding to both its complexity and integrity. Because it is such an obvious and general characteristic of so many aspects of social and psychological life, it is difficult to define optimism or even discuss it usefully and with precision. Yet this is precisely why it is so important as a phenomenon, and why reviewing optimism in the context of social behavior will constructively crosscut conventional perspectives. For there is an underlying unity of human experience; people in apparently diverse cultures and with varying dilemmas approach the problem of their futures with comparable concern and a common mood at their disposal: optimism.

Perhaps the most obvious way of seeing this is negatively, trying to imagine what human social life would be without a general optimism. Even if the biblical assertion is incorrect that "where there is no vision, the people perish," it is difficult to think what could be the engine or stimulus for social behavior in a nihilistic system committed only to the certainty of the passage of time, without any energetic relationship to another principle or purpose. Would pleasure be the goal? Would power? Would the alteration of consciousness? Would the salvation of one's soul in classical religious terms? Would the birth of children? Would making love or money, or monuments, or revolution? I will try to show that all such motives acquire teleological or purposeful implications once they become the focus of social behavior; an additional ingredient, the ingredient of promise, is eventually added to these other elements. Even the existentialism of Jean-Paul Sartre was tempered by his personal Marxism. The perpetual void postulated in his early works, for example, in *Being and Nothingness,* was later mitigated by his effort to endow the human situation with hope and meaning through political action. In *Critique of Dialectical Reason* the notion of formal and unending nothingness yields to the desire for a more humane human future achievable through revolution; even from violence springs the ingredient of hope. It is even the fashion in some political circles to assert that violence against society will expose that society's moral poverty and inequity and thus hasten the replacement of contemporary social forms with the ones of a revolutionary dream. Whatever the grisly means, optimistic ends survive pain, destruction, fear, and gratuitous intervention into the routines of social life. Even terrorism adopts optimism as its justifying coloration. A star of hope, if not of wonder, orients the stage directors of disjointed times. The austere agnosticism and atheism of Soviet Communism were spiced by an impending triumph of the Communist system over others which were decaying and fatally marked without a purifying revolution. A similar present constraint in the name of future largesse is urged by modernizers of poor countries, and more recently by leaders of rich ones concerned with profligate use of scarce natural resources. A comparable restless certainty that *however good or bad experience is, it can be better*, routinely infects even the most thoroughgoing secularisms.

Even the decay of the body through the life cycle, the most stately, dismal, and immediate of trajectories, has been mitigated and soothed by the promise of drastic renewal in a

Heaven, a Valhalla, a Nirvana—some blessed place immune to mortal suffering.

The basic problem remains: why do happy ideas about their destiny appear to make people feel better in their bodies? How can ideas have such power even over metabolism? What are the tangible consequences of optimistic thoughts? How do they get made, interpreted and sustained? Who is most influential in making them, manipulating them and evaluating them? Who consumes them, from horoscopes to think-tank blueprints? Why, indeed, be concerned about the future at all? What work does the past do for the future? Who produces the future? Who consumes it? Where do moods come from? Such questions of deliberate naïveté are important to answer; naïve questions may often be poorly answered for the very reason that they straddle central and unexamined phenomena of social life.

This is not a wholly academic or theoretical exercise. There are direct reflections of the optimistic urgency in numerous practical social policies. The notion of progress, both social and personal, in important measure underlies contemporary political and economic programs as well as the therapeutically relevant psychological sciences. Conceptions of personal salvation which have been historically important in the great religions find their modern counterpart in programs of political and economic modernization. These may involve improved material circumstances very directly—better food, housing, sanitation, clothing, government services. Modernization may also connote contact with the symbolic system of the modern, represented by such things as airplanes, sophisticated electronic equipment for communications, office work, and rapidly diffused fashions in personal decoration. The ritual production of economic development plans, particularly in poor countries, appears to serve political functions in response to "the revolution of rising expectations" as much as they are concrete blueprints for action. Governmentally stimulated or tolerated inflation of currency provides a purely cognitive substitute for real increase in wealth. Until inflation becomes grossly evident and thus outrageous it has enjoyed a relatively congenial reputation among economists and government officials, many of whom see it as a necessary corollary of economic growth and vitality. (There are also some prominent exceptions who are critical of any legitimated economic inflation.) The contemporary stress on education involves a similar underlying notion of personal growth—as opposed to simple enjoyment or the benign passage of time. Activity comes to assume a self-improving quality no longer restricted to young people but increasingly the recurrent concern of all people through adulthood into old age. (Historically, religious study has always offered a certain promise of increased personal value and morality, a concern particularly keen among older people for whom the issue of mortality assumes relatively pragmatic characteristics. Will "senior citizen" extension education be able to replace this in the secular age?) Changes in aesthetic forms, so that newer ones replace older ones, come to imply improvement and personal advance; when older art forms and styles are rediscovered, as in the rebellion against strict modernist architecture or the fascination with décor of the 1920's, then the rediscovery of quality in what was held to be passé is regarded as surprising. How could those old-fashioned people possess such skill and sense of the human measure? goes the critics' question. Almost ceaselessly, an amalgam of design and novelty proves an extremely effective basis for economic activity; new designs, new models, the latest shape, the next year's form, stimulate purchasers to part with money even to replace items providing reasonable satisfaction to their users. The success of advertising in this respect is neither accidental nor solely the result of a conspiracy by advertisers against consumers (though that it is in part, as well); it is a sophisticated manipulation of a propensity firmly rooted in the human conceptual repertoire. Mammon didn't exist so humans found it necessary to invent him.

We will have to come to Mammon as well as to God. The basic emphasis of this book is to explore why human beings are made happier by optimistic *thoughts* than despairing ones. Happy thoughts make us feel good. This is at once obvious and problematic. It is obvious because it is so deeply familiar as an aspect of life. But it is problematic because it raises the question of how the cortical events which comprise optimistic thoughts can produce general feelings of well-being elsewhere in the bodily system. It also introduces the cognitive problem of the manner in which encouraging ideas are distinguished from threatening ones and under what circumstances thoughts that might otherwise be threatening or neutral become defined as hopeful.

And it poses two other apparently disparate questions: How does the sense of the future become manifested in sexual and reproductive activity—the source of family life? And how does it stimulate the persistence of systems of heavens, hells, and other thereafters—the cornerstones of religion? All of them are provoked by the behavior of an animal full of turbulence, of repose, of mastery in work, harassed by mortality, by urgency in love, and by uncertainty about strangers.

Fear of the future and flair for confronting it are complexly intertwined; I want to pick away at the threads, to explore the tangle.

This study has its general intellectual roots in a variety of sources, and I should discuss the principal ones here, if only briefly. Not only are these not exotic sources but they have either created or helped formalize several of the critical scientific assertions of our time, so I base my case on an insistence that the obvious must be reexamined, and that sometimes not only trees, but woods and whole forests, require a fresh look to see why rivers sometimes run dry and sometimes flood and why colonies of people or armies of odd mites or fungi destroy or abet a natural system in ways no planner had ever planned.

As much for its compassionately skeptical tone as for its analysis, approach and information, William James's *The Varieties of Religious Experience* has provided a gilt bench mark. Though prepared three-quarters of a century ago in 1901–02 as the Gifford Lectures at the University of Edinburgh, James's scientifically and medically based anatomy of experience related to the supernatural remains vital—a secular scholarly inspiration. As he commented at the end of his lectures, "For practical life at any rate, the *chance* of salvation is enough. No fact in human nature is more characteristic than its willingness to live on a chance." (1958:397.) James's effort to connect the matter of the supernatural with the phenomenon of human nature was made at a time when important scientific tools were lacking—tools which are now readily at hand—and his accomplishment is all the more startling for its invention and importance, in view of the crude scientific materials with which he had to work. One drastically more complex understanding which James did not have was of how genetic processes were involved in the daily lives of even the most developed animals. The new insights and data of contemporary genetics have been powerfully analyzed by Jacques Monod, whose *Chance and Necessity* (1971) approaches both genetic unity and variation in species, and their reflection in general patterns of human behavior. While Monod's concern for change is somewhat different than James's, his commitment to finding material causes and components of even the most arcane and exotically frivolous of behaviors is similar. Most importantly he was willing to argue that on the basis of what is known now about the complexities of the genetic codes, even the instructions or rules for language can be contained in the codes. Such a judgment is very encouraging if one is seeking to make a similar comment about a much broader, more general and phylogenetically older behavioral pattern—in this case, optimism.

And there is indeed reason for encouragement as a consequence of recent work in comparative linguistics—another of the intellectual sources of my inquiry. Though he does not discuss Noam Chomsky's effort in his book, Monod's genetic suppositions are given support by Chomsky's striking if controversial success in asserting that all human languages are relatively similar in their basic form and process. This implies there is a "universal grammar" marking human speech in the same way as relatively standard processes of human digestion are "universal." Chomsky's demonstration of human similarity even in the genetically recent acquisition of the language contradicts at once two important groups of theorists about behavior; those who would take a cultural relativist position that all cultures differ because environments differ and there is no common behavioral nature, and secondly those who on biological grounds argue that some races or groups are more developed than others and hence superior. Indeed, it will be a theme of this book that there are relatively great similarities in how apparently different cultures symbolize the future, that there is a common human approach to these matters which unites rather than divides us. Just as it can no longer be crudely asserted that people with gods are pagan but those with God are civilized, so, after Chomsky, it is foolhardy to make evaluative judgments about the major instrument of cultural expression, language.

All cultures possess the same remarkable instrument and appear to use it with comparable complexity, zest and effectiveness. In terms of the fundamental character of linguistic expression, we all fundamentally speak the same language.

The third source of guidance for this study of optimism emerges from the proposition of Claude Lévi-Strauss, who has argued that human symbolic life shares with language a common-core unity. Among other things, Lévi-Strauss has sought to explore the ideas which humans find easy to entertain. Just as some foods are, and are defined as being, "good to eat," so some thoughts are "good to think." What is good to think is, by implication, what is more natural for humans—more natural in the way the universal grammar of language is natural. At its most general, this is a variation and refinement of Freud's "pleasure principle," which was a method of defining people's choices by what gave them (basically) physical pleasure. Lévi-Strauss's extrapolation of the pleasure principle to cognition, so that some *thoughts* provide pleasure, of course reduces the traditional distance between mind and body and encourages an assimilation of thinking with behaving. It also raises rather portentous general questions about the evolutionary implications of what is good to think; just as sexual intercourse, for example, is presumably pleasurable as an inducement toward reproductive success, so then what is pleasurable to think may well be similarly linked to human evolution.

The middle third of the twentieth century has seen the development of the final main source of this inquiry, the ethological method of approaching behavior and analyzing it. This involves investigating the behavior of animals, now including humans, in a Darwinian framework so that the sociology of an animal's behavior is studied in the context of what is known about its own and similar animals' evolution. Through this comparative method, the relating of behavior with biology and bodies with brains loses improbability and absurdity. Indeed, there has been an enormous shift in the quality and sophistication of discussion of the relationship between biology and society. While in one sense this has been an unfortunate product of a frequently redundant and irrelevant controversy, for example, about the political implications alleged to inhere in biological discussion of social behavior, it has also had the most significant stimulus from new evidence of fact and new refinement of theory. There is a sociological equivalent of the secular trend, the trend toward a biological perspective on behavior. The location of social reality has been driven deeper and deeper into the processes both of fundamental genetics on one hand and its expression in physiology and behavior on the other. Even the emergence of a conspectus of human symbolism—the Lévi-Straussian initiative—has grown to depend increasingly on an awareness of the neurophysiological and other cognate processes which must underlie human understanding, feeling, and evaluating.

Not only has the nature-culture barrier proved highly porous as far as humans are concerned, but our understanding and appreciation of other animals has developed very rapidly. The refinement of modern biology's knowledge of animal behavior is in its way as spectacular for its complexity and sense of adventure as the explorations of space and rocketry have been. (For an example of the sophistication of even an introductory treatment of this material, see the biology textbook by Peter Marler and William Hamilton, *Mechanisms of Animal Behavior* [1966]. And now, even the first breach in the curtain of animal muteness has been pierced by Griffin's *The Question of Animal Awareness* (1976)—a bold step toward approaching vigorously the matter of human uniqueness in the animal kingdom as far as complex consciousness is concerned.

No longer do biologists presuppose that biology coerces society and not sometimes or often the other way around. For example, as Niko Tinbergen stated in his Nobel-Prize acceptance paper (1974), it is increasingly successfully asserted that not only does the body have a guiding effect on social behavior—in a sense rather like the effect of the id on behavior in classical Freudian terms—but the pattern of social life may significantly affect the conduct of physiological existence. Thus biology is no longer the science which narrowly seeks the source of social patterns in physiological ones, but the one which will increasingly become preoccupied with the contrary process—if only because the effect of a crowded and needy species' social circumstances on its thoughts will be of paramount political and humanitarian consequence. And, under these conditions, what humans think about their futures and whether or not thinking about the future will be good to think is likely to be a matter as important to societies as what people want to buy is to economists and what they fear is to soldiers, priests, and politicians.

I want to focus on thinking about and dealing with the future, which must be discussed in the context of a broad, sturdy apparatus of comparative biology. I do this not only because this is of interest in itself, but because for too long—despite even Darwin—it has been assumed that the biological sciences have no business interfering with such exalted matters as human thought and that they should confine themselves to relatively mechanical operations and systems, of course, principally those of other animals. In relation to man, the injunction has been to exercise the most severe austerity in applying general biological findings to this specific animal. The injunction has for too long been punitively severe; the insights of biology have grown too powerful, and their pertinence to humans too plain, for the many lines of separation between the human and natural sciences to remain firmly etched. It is my view, and of course the view of many others, that the broad outlines of a human behavioral biology have already been defined in a preliminary but secure way and that the next decades will see a fundamental resetting of data about human behavior in the context of nature. In a real sense the Darwinian revolution about the study of social behavior begins to reach its conclusion, and human self-consciousness has been irrevocably changed.

What has not yet been forthrightly begun is a biology of human thought, expression, art, and fantasy and their relationship to both public and private social events. While there is a considerable literature which pertains to this, which we will refer to as we proceed, there remains a general barrier and even impasse in the work of approaching biologically what has for so long been seen as quintessentially and specially human. No book can alone offer a firm enough analytical bridge. But as the camel discovered, each straw makes a difference.

Nor should this endeavor be so startling. Rousseau long ago was concerned with a "speciational consciousness" and (as the intellectual genealogy is traced by Stanley Diamond) so also was Karl Marx committed to understanding that human nature which must properly be fundamental to enlightened social reformation. (Diamond, 1974.) As far as the specific relationship between Marx and Darwinism as well as with Darwin himself is concerned, the study by Paul Heyer (1975) shows the extensive effect of biological thought on Marx's perception of social life in general and human social life in particular. It is significant that at the graveside oration in Highgate Cemetery at Marx's funeral Friedrich Engels explicitly compared Darwin's and Marx's work, noting no disconnection or disharmony between their approaches and results. That the eventual outcome of Marxist social theory was a rather stringently anti-biological perception of the bases of human social behavior—expressed most starkly in the Lysenkoist tradition—would probably have been of great surprise and very likely disappointment to Marx. Nevertheless, as I will try to show, such an attitude to human nature was as inevitable in the Communist east as in the capitalist west, both of which predicated major social policies on human malleability. (See also Tiger, 1978a.) Both, in effect, assumed a programmatic optimisim as the basis for their policies and assumed further that the unit of social action, the individual human being, was in broad terms available to policy makers for the purposes political leaders decided were appropriate for the community at large. I think that this is an extremely handy working tool for political leaders if they are interested in maintaining the status quo and the privileges they presumably enjoy under it. Rather like priests, in another form of manipulating the future, not this time the sacred one, political managers of human optimism must be uncomfortable with notions of nature which may limit their freedom of social decision. That both American and Soviet theories of human nature owe a very great deal to the psychology of operant conditioning descended from the work of Pavlov is not at all accidental, in my view, nor has the subject been adequately investigated by scholars.

Whatever its political context, there is a recurrent paradox in the discussion of the human nature problem. On one hand it is confidently asserted by those who see no continuity between humans and other animals directly, (1) that humans are biologically different from other animals by virtue of their cultural accomplishments and then (2) that these cultural accomplishments (which are presumably a species-specific characteristic and hence almost inevitable productions of mankind) are exempt from scrutiny from a biological perspective. But if biology allows us to have operas, then operas and what they describe and mean must bear some close relationship to the biology of the animal that performs them. Of course most operas deal with a limited set of processes, so the analytical task is undaunting; love and reproduction, honor and aggression, vanity and political dominance, families and misunderstanding, competition— these are the problems of many operas. Only an art form dealing in obvious human characteristics could be successful despite the artificial mode of the operatic drama, its frequently clumsy and unconvincing actors, and the problem that most hearers of most operas are listening to a language they do not or poorly understand. Plainly, the glory of the singing and the easy recognizability of the human issues in operas overcome these obstacles.

Shielding human nature from the incursions of a predatory biology may be protecting it from an important challenge. It may also represent a shrewd understanding of the forces of scientific rigor. But I think the notion of human cultural uniqueness is no stronger an explication on its own than is the

notion of the soul as a theory of human motivation and response. If humans are unique culturally, and of course they are,
then this is a feature of their biology and therefore subject to
both the rules of biological events and of biological sciences. I
do not accept the essentially theological conception of man as a
base beast turned away from horror and incivility by the persuasion of cultural norms and legal codes. People make cultural
norms as inevitably as they make love and, as Piaget has discovered, when they are old enough, *i.e.*, biologically ready,
even children invent legal codes on their own. Human culture
is not optional though its specific forms usually are. In this
book I am proposing that one set of forms, pertaining to optimism and the future, are hardly optional at all and that they are
as natural to man as his eyes that see and as irreplaceable as air.

But why be strident or skeptical about a habit of mind which
may give people relief, joy, and a serious chance (because of
their innocent enthusiasm) in their endeavors? Because the
most important function of the natural sciences is to reveal pro-
gressively more subtle, arcane and sophisticated orders of nature and relationships between them. William Harvey's discovery of the circulatory system was a transaction very similar to
the modern identification of the neuro-transmitters and what
role they play in thought and feeling. Galileo's adventurous
proposal conferred a benefit similar to Sir Peter Medawar's discovery of the mechanisms of immune reactions in the body. In
all these cases, an ordered and regular process was discovered
where either none was expected or, it was feared, one could not
go much beyond randomness as a description or explanation of
what happens. A similar process of defining regularities occurs
in the social sciences. So Freud argued there was a specific
process of contact between adolescents and their parents, or
Charles Booth in London (1902) and William F. Whyte in Boston
(1955) described the intricate social order of slums which outsiders had formerly defined as chaotic and without significant
structure. Yet, making connections between biophysiological
events, such as feelings, thoughts, the life cycle, and responses
to drugs, and small and large-scale systems of behavior is on
the face of it no less legitimate if perhaps more scientifically

perilous than seeking these now recognized forms of social order.

This in turn raises a major issue at the core of the problem of sociological analysis—the understanding of why and how people behave. One important reason for the historical dichotomy between the natural and social sciences has been an assumption raised to an assertion by sociological scientists that facts of society should only be analyzed in terms of other facts of society —that, for example, employing psychological, biological, or physiological argument is reductionist and is as fruitless as arguing from astrology to the law of supply and demand. This sociological separatist effort was given its most significant boost by the French sociologist Émile Durkheim, whose *The Rules of Sociological Method* is one of the most influential and yet inhibiting theoretical texts of the Euro-American social scientific tradition. In part because of his long-term concern with the sociological study of religion, Durkheim approached social phenomena in an almost directly opposite manner than James—the latter integrated behavior into nature, from which the former sought to distinguish it. Though Durkheim was a student of the biologist Espinas, and clearly derived a strong sense of how behavior could occur in systems from Espinas, the root of social systems—nature—was a subject which he shunned. It has remained, in a day-to-day sense, largely taboo among sociologists or is at the very least treated as tangential to the day-to-day conduct of their research.

Durkheim and his successors sought to answer the basic social scientific questions: Where does society exist, why do people form communities, what is the basis of the social order, and where do the impulses for changing social order come from? The Durkheimian answer was that society itself was the cause of society and that the form, texture and pace of human social interactions were governed by extant social circumstances. Of course this is on the face of it an incontestable position to take, since social behavior is so clearly and inextricably linked with other social behavior. However, there appears to be a more interesting, sophisticated, and contemporary answer to this question emerging from the thinking and research of persons

concerned with the social behavior of animals and the relationship of this to genes. The proposition of the biosociologists,
ethologists, sociobiologists—call them what you will—is that
the Durkheimian answer is not only obviously tautological but
that the answer must be biological; since other animals have
society then society must be, in varying ways and degrees,
located in the gene pool. The discussion of this proposition has
turned out to be extremely controversial, often for reasons
closer to ideology than to scientific analysis. Nevertheless the
long-range outcome of the dialogue is likely to offer a synthetic
perspective in which there is a constructive awareness implicit
in the sciences of behavior of the predisposing—predisposing,
not coercing!—role of genes in structuring behavior.

If a broad readiness for society in general is a reflection of our
special human genetic inheritance, then the next question is,
what specific readinesses are there? What social behaviors are
people more, rather than less, likely to undertake and complete
easily?

I've already begun to claim that optimistic practices may be
easy for people to learn, pleasurable to engage in, and indeed
may often be necessary for the conduct of long-term social relationships. Thinking rosy futures is as biological as sexual fantasy. Optimistically calculating the odds is as basic a human
action as seeking food when hungry or craving fresh air in a
dump. Making deals with uncertainty marks us as plainly as
bipedalism.

This has very practical outcomes. It is relatively easy to cater
to and exploit this "psychological sweet tooth." I believe that
optimism, not religion, is the opiate of the people. Religion is
only one expression of the optimistic impulse. As well, exploitation based on optimism occurs in a wealth of places, not only
religious ones; it occurs as much in betting shops as cathedrals
and stock brokerages as confessionals. It has as much to do
with health as with pilgrimages.

It has also to do with politics, and later we will have to consider the possible relationship between civility and equity in
government and optimism as well as despair when we confront
the problems of morale, demagoguery, the "realpolitik," as

they affect the conduct of governors and governed. For the moment, it is sufficient to remark that an important thrust of contemporary scholarship and idealism has been to demystify leaders and leadership and hence force the consumers of government to recognize the fragility of their leaders. Or their humanness, to put it another way. As George Bernard Shaw remarked about females—the comment is appropriate from either side—"love consists in overestimating the difference between one woman and another." The comment is also surely applicable to political figures (and many of the same processes of exaggerated estimation are involved in both spheres of political taste and sexual passion). The promises of politicians are an important if legendarily risible component of their stock-in-trade; why such insubstantial creations should so significantly affect the often remarkably important matter of which candidate is elected demands scrutiny and an answer.

We will expand the argument later on. Now I want to turn very briefly to another matter. The chief business of the book which follows is an analytical encounter with research findings and speculation. However, the approach to the material and its organization are possibly idiosyncratic and thus an outgrowth of the author's person more directly than usual. Therefore a brief personal comment may be in order about my own temperamental biases and intellectual roots as they pertain to this work. These intimations are not placed here because they are of interest in their own right but only insofar as they may suggest a context within which the work of the book can be seen to occur and to be considered.

As a relatively optimistic person, I might be a prejudiced accountant of the material. In general I find it difficult to understand, temperamentally, why people commit evil actions which are against either the public interest or the welfare of those who are relatively without power. I assume that matters will turn out well rather than badly, and am generally optimistic about personal and professional matters of my own. I am thus emotionally naïve and trusting about structural processes of societies and also assume "the best" of the people with whom I

interact directly and indirectly. I am readily able to be sentimental; I enjoy happy endings of dramatic pieces and savor the
noise and glory of large major conclusions of symphonies. At
the same time, having grown up in a cynical ghetto community
(in Montreal, a riven city in which everyone feels himself a
member of a minority, including the French Canadian majority), I am suspicious of people's motives—a suspicion which
was of course enhanced and elaborated by training as a social
scientist. The more experience I have with the observation of
large power and the use of petty power the more aware I become of the fragility of reason and thus the effect of caprice or
inadvertence on the conduct of social affairs. As an analyst of
social processes, I am as pessimistic as I am the contrary about
personal ones because the tools and scope of human mischief
have swollen decidedly more rapidly than the means to understand and (certainly) control them. The prognosis for burgeoning congeniality and agreeable human improvement appears to
be a depressing one. I have a sentimental commitment to the
analysis of illusion.

The Past of an Illusion

For a moment let us assume God exists and that He attended to the development of Homo sapiens. In that case His management of human creation would have to be judged parochial and inept. No God with a thoughtful plan could have or should have permitted such a paradoxical and conflicted form to represent the essence of His divinity. It is also unlikely that a God with a desire to connect generously with Earth would have focused on one species. If He did, it was an ungodly, inefficient, and elitist decision.

The only possible explanation of a divine origin of man which takes seriously the wisdom and compassion frequently associated with God is that having created man and having failed to represent Himself thereby with dignity, the project was abandoned as altogether too perilous. This style of explanation would then continue: having made this one major mistake too many, God abandoned human beings to their own devices. But He cruelly endowed us with skill enough to sense the spice and incense of divinity and mind enough to recall the episode of creation and our part in it. Forever after, from the

Fall, we have struggled with the memory of God's patronage and love at the same time as we have been bludgeoned by the intricate power of ceaseless mortality. Only strong and excellent personal action and obedience to the memory of lost divinity will enhance a person's access to heaven.

Of course many people believe in such a description of man's place in nature. It is likely that nearly all human beings on earth embrace or at least do not reject the strong possibility that other forces than obvious ones affect their lives. Most people behave as if this were so. I think it is easy to understand why such arcane forces could be accepted as real when they produce malign results—when they cause disease, floods, death, heartbreak, war, the suffering of children. What is more difficult to understand is why human beings accept the possibility that there are *benign* forces acting on their behalf which, like some slim, strong wind at a regatta, will propel them. My personal assumption about my own life and my community's, and also my working assumption in this book, is that there are neither such pleasing nor gruesome forces. The challenge is to find out why people think there are.

I have already claimed that optimism is a biological phenomenon; since religion is deeply intertwined with optimism, clearly I think religion is a biological phenomenon, rooted in human genes, which is why it keeps cropping up. This is not a new perception, and it has been reported in various forms by many students of the matter ranging from Freud to James to Weston LaBarre. As LaBarre has written, ". . . *the understanding of religion may be the key to an understanding of the nature and function of culture at large and hence the survival of our species.*" (1972:40. Italics in original.) Or, as Alice Kehoe has said, ". . . phylogenetically ancient mechanisms of formalized behavior persist, changing semantic content and behavioral details. Ethology predicts that rituals will last as long as the race." (1973:13.) In this view, religion is as predictable and normal among humans as that we will have five fingers on each hand and eyeballs that rotate to some extent. Given this context, the work of theology and liturgical disputation becomes not a search for truth or falsehood but rather an historical or ethnographic study of the varieties of bio-religious form. If there is a common biological stimulus or a root for religious behavior then this provides the logical basis for asserting the equivalent validity of all religious systems. Some may be more elaborate, colorful, vengeful, militant or egalitarian than others. There may be great differences in the relative power of religious laymen and functionaries. The cost in money and time to particular communities of sustaining their religious apparatus may vary considerably. However, they all do the same work in supporting communal social bonds and they all offer individual people opportunities to organize their fears about their futures. As a result they can act as if these fears were trivial or manageable.

A perspective rooted in the biological sciences yields a view of religion which is both humane and respectful of religion's function. Perhaps it will seem ironic that the science particularly feared by the protectors of religious orthodoxy, biology, should contain the basis for such a view of religion. On the other hand, the matter becomes less strange when one recognizes that the principal source of religious/biological acrimony came from the religious camp, whose proponents insisted that the efficacy of religious schemes depended on their exemption from general laws of nature. But surely divine operations gain importance and power from association with nature. Did not countless theologians intuit this when they claimed that their particular religious belief was self-evidently the true one that in effect reflected nature? The function of God was not to defy or contradict nature, but to supervise it and form its central principle. Nature could be seen as powerfully implicit in the idea of God. Theologians nevertheless clung to their traditional claim that the realm of theological exploration is superior to nature, not immersed in its forces.

However difficult it may be for religious authorities to redefine themselves as participants in the biological system, empirical evidence about the function and nature of religion may persuade them to do so. Perhaps the apparent decline of religious belief reflects primarily not profound social change but the diminished effect of theologians themselves, who as a group have failed to identify, and tap, the true source of their potential power.

I am not advocating that they should exploit this power, merely stating that someone can and usually does, and that it is likely that religious protagonists will enjoy an advantage in "winning souls." We assume from the record that their once confident scorn of skepticism lent their case energy, not weakness. Why, then, is this apparently no longer true?

We have to approach the problem through an understanding of the function of the brain in producing futures and calculating lives. The brain produces notions of the future, what has been called "imaginal thinking," almost as the endocrines produce secretions which affect behavior. As Galanter and Gerstenhaber say, "imaginal thinking is neither more nor less than constructing an image or model of the environment, running the model faster than the environment, and predicting that the environment will behave as the model does." (Quoted in Miller, Galanter and Pribram, 1960:173.) Both religious and scientific thought are concerned with imaginal thinking; that is, with prediction and testing, however disparately the testing may occur in the separate cadres of thinkers.

From the perspective of the study of optimism, what is the relationship between religious thought and scientific work? Until science, religion was the most ambitious scheme of imaginal thinking and it was immensely and practically implicated in the conduct of individual and community life. Though science is a more precise and effective manager of life's procedures, it may be too easily converted to an ethic of enlightenment or efficiency or some other supervening value (other than just finding things out) for it to become a broadly effective source of general social (as opposed to technological) action. Perhaps this is so because religion is forceful even among the very young, whereas science seems to be an effective moral force later in life. This may represent the relative primacy and generality of the two methods of "imaginal thinking" (here caricatured). The brain is more likely to plan and structure behavior in a religious than scientific manner. One reason for this may be that the scientific method is more tentative and ambiguous—it demands a willingness to be wrong with as much equanimity as right. Religion taps political responses of acceptance of authority central to evolution, while science is often anti-political and critical of the powerful. Science tends to query the sources of authority by evidence and argument. Religion asserts that authority belongs to those who hold it, even though it is by delegation.

A description of science and religion as distinct and often opposed processes may suggest they have nothing in common. This is not the case. Religious organizations have frequently taken advantage of some of the skills and rigamaroles which scientists use in their work. Developing the intellect, gathering information, and disputing evidence are often part of the initiation of religious devotees. In monasteries, yeshivoth, seminaries and similar environments, there is a continuing and elaborate effort to understand the manifestations of the divine through scrutiny of the mundane.

I stress the importance of religious observance in human evolutionary survival because I think that the role of emotional display and related aesthetic factors in the persistence of religious and religious-like social groups becomes clearer in this perspective. The realm of religion is not autonomous and was so linked with critical processes of human development that aspects of religious behavior continue to emerge in unexpected places. It becomes understandable why even the first full flush of development of science in the late nineteenth century was accompanied by notions of progress—several almost millennial in scope—which appear to contain as much wishful thinking about the ultimate potential of human beings as their judgments about technical and scientific capacities. Not that utopian or millennial thinking is restricted to scientifically informed people or eras. But the contrasts are intriguing. The existence of millennial thinking suggests the power of religion with its accompanying open-endedness even over people who have performed major tasks of will and intellect, which is science with its associated technology and industry. We will have to come back to this crucial relationship between religious thought, scientific knowledge, and social progress. Meanwhile it may be useful to keep in mind the problem represented by the source of the idea not only of heaven, but intermediate heavens—utopias, better cities, excellent nations, or peaceful worlds—so often offered to those with worldly, not divine, discontents. Why, on earth, was the first human step on the moon a giant step forward for mankind? Who said so? Who believed it?

Before we trace any footsteps to the moon, we should step back for a moment, very far back, to consider the evolution of optimism as a way that we have had of coping with material and social environments. I have chosen a chapter title which plays ironically on the title of Freud's important statement about religion and traditional belief, *The Future of an Illusion*, first published in English in 1927 (Freud, 1964). Freud wished to determine the relationship between basic "instinctual" patterns of human existence and the various formulae for social life that are created and maintained by communities. He proposed, for example, that art and religion "offer substitutive satisfactions for the oldest and still most deeply felt cultural renunciations . . ." (p. 18) and he regarded religion as ". . . what is perhaps the most important item in the cyclical history of a civilization. This consists in its religious ideas in the widest sense—in other words . . . in its illusions." (Freud, 1964:18.) One can see plainly the connection in Freud's thought between survival and illusion.

Now I shall quote from several important paragraphs: "It is true that nature would not demand any restrictions of instinct from us, she would let us do as we liked: but she has her own particularly effective method of restricting us. She destroys us—coldly, cruelly, relentlessly as it seems to us and possibly through the very things that occasion our satisfaction. It was precisely because of these dangers with which nature threatens us that we came together and created civilization, which is also, among other things, intended to make our communal life possible. For the principal task of civilization, its actual raison d'être, is to defend us against nature . . . thus a store of ideas is created, borne for man's need to make his helplessness tolerable and built up from the material of memories of the helplessness of his own childhood and the childhood of the human race. It can clearly be seen that the possession of these ideas protects him . . . against the dangers of nature and Fate and against the injuries that threaten him from human society itself. Here is the gist of the matter. . . . Over each one of us there watches a benevolent Providence which is only seemingly stern and which will not suffer us to become a plaything of the over-mighty and pitiless forces of nature. This itself is not extinction, is not a return to inorganic lifelessness but the beginning of a new kind of existence which lies on the path of development to something higher." (*Ibid.:* 20–26.)

Here Freud is emphasizing the relationship between illusion and early familial experience, not only illusion but some general attitudes of trust, stubbornness, persistence and continuity. When we discuss the relationship between early experience and adult perceptions of the future, then Freud's and his successors' and critics' contributions will be salient as psychological analyses. Here, I want to emphasize the phylogenetic/evolutionary, not ontogenetic/psychological aspects of the development of remedies for helplessness. Clearly Freud understood the implication of man's inherited biology. Even though he had extremely scant data on which to work he foresaw clearly (in *Totem and Taboo,* as well as elsewhere) some of the significant developments in contemporary primatology. He did not have the material now available which describes the extent and process of human evolution and the importance of social behavior to it. Freud was, of course, profoundly concerned with the function and process of consciousness and it would be critically important for him were he alive now to know about the significant variations in the rates of development of various parts of the human brain, and their various contributions to survival and to consciousness. Although he was a neurophysiologist, Freud was unable—there was no good evidence—to clearly identify the relationship between our contemporary behavior and our neurophysiological evolution. Even so, his broad predictions were correct. Freud's expectation was that eventually all human behavior would be explained by understanding chemical processes in the brain. His own contributions to the

study of the effects of cocaine on human bodies and consciousness fall into his general pattern of scientific exploration. (Byck,
1975.) While this estimate of Freud is duly noted by his successors in psychoanalysis, the notation is formal, and the implications of Freud's commitment to neurochemistry get lost in the
hash of hagiographic psychoanalytic disquisition.

Freud had to speculate on these matters at a time when the
extent of the trajectory of human evolution was not appreciated,
when the significance of the hunting-gathering way of life was
not understood and when the likely mode of human adaptation
resulting from this evolution could not be clearly surmised.
Furthermore he could not have been aware of the precise or
even general manner in which selection for particular behaviors
could show results in the gene pool—even today population
geneticists grapple with this issue—and reflect anew in each
generation the minor but cumulative variations which produce
distinctive species.

He could not have known a great deal since not a great deal
was known about the evolution of that critical organ in the
production of optimism, the brain. Because of his inability to
approach the problem of how and why brain tissue evolved he
was not able to appreciate why the process of human neurophysiological evolution made illusion more likely and complex
rather than decreased its importance. The conceit of Homo sapiens is that the evolution of our brain produced a greater capacity for rational, technical and logically formal thought rather
than confusion, oceanic moods, private inefficiencies and public selfishness. Yet, in effect, a direct consequence of adding
cortical tissue to the human brain—*and of the continuing evolution of the lower centers of the brain as well*—was an enhanced
capacity for producing illusionary notions. It is even possible
that the role of mechanical and other realistic modes of thought
is reduced. Far from human evolution restricting the play of
illusion, the greater capacity of the brain and its increasingly
complex control over behavioral processes yielded an augmented armamentarium of illusion. Plainly inadequate for the
big-brained human was the one-to-one relationship of cat and
mouse, paw and fruit, male and female, mother and child. *We*

rode to hounds in red jackets, served baked Alaskas surrounded by glazed berries, made up stories of Isolde and the
Madonna, sought modes of joy from circuses to family chamber
music groups, and nourished petulances of evidently endless
form and inexhaustible energy. If one pattern of our evolution
was toward science and formal rigor, the major patterns of the
tapestry were fancy, dreams, fears, and eschatological theories
about this world and life's forces.

The very essence of human cultural accomplishment depends
upon achieving distance in time and space between people and
their real worlds. In this sense, literalness is the enemy of culture. It is the formidable characteristic of the species to routinely seek the improbable, the difficult, even the impossible,
as a source of pleasure and self-justification. This perception
enjoys kinship with William James's mordantly paradoxical one
about "instincts," which was that since humans were such
complicated animals, they were plainly creatures with more,
not fewer, instincts than other animals. Of course the conception of "instinct" here is relatively simple-minded, but the
analogy remains tight. With augmented capacity in the brain
more ideas and hence more illusions, not fewer, were made
possible. These were not only ideas about nature and things,
but, more dynamically, ideas about people and groups, cooperation and strife. Ideas about things and ideas about people
become, also, complexly connected so that particular illusions
become translated into specific actions involving human bodies
and property. For example, the frailest of illusions about glory
and supremacy, supported by the notion of finding the Grail,
stimulated the Crusaders to kill and destroy property as they
ran helter-skelter across their continent and the Middle East.
These pious men of Europe and England displayed a quintessentially preposterous version of the relationship between illusions about ideas and about things. Similarly, more recently, a
group of Nazi Germans were able to broadcast successfully the
illusion that many values of civilization and German honor depended upon the military steel and shot of the German people.
We are now aware of the set of special circumstances which
applied in Nazi Germany, for example the pathologies of Hitler

and some of his associates as described by Fest (1974), and the development of particular techniques for mass persuasion and mobilization—here the books of Albert Speer are a chilling but instructive guide (Speer, 1970, 1976). Millions of Germans believed or accepted reluctantly promises of their leaders. Despite the generally high level of education, cultural activity and social welfare in Germany, the country embarked on a catastrophic course of violating and destroying portions of the physical and human universe in the name of human perfection and the allegedly special German role in securing it.

How can all this be explained? How did the human cognitive apparatus become able to undertake and complete such violent, massive, unlikely cooperative work? Obviously it was not the development of better teeth, fiercer nails, more leathery skin, or other bodily structures patently devoted to the conduct of bellicose encounter. The growth of the brain and the enlargement of the top of the skull produced no fearsome weapon able to butt down enemies and their barricades. No, the evolution was not external and mechanical, it was internal, cognitive, and social. And also unexpectedly complex. We know confidently how the rapid increase of the cortex accompanied a rapidly increased sophistication of weaponry, social behavior, economic life and presumably symbolic life. Less well known is the fact that just as the cortex was evolving and expanding so were the more "primitive" parts of the brain. For example, proportionate to their relative sizes, the cerebellum has expanded more rapidly in the past million years than the cerebral cortex. The evolution of brain tissue involved more than the augmentation of the means to process information of a very sophisticated kind. It also meant that the brain was better able to process and respond to "primitive" information.

Based on his pioneering neurosurgical research on brain mechanisms, Wilder Penfield concluded as early as 1938 in his Harvey Lecture at the New York Academy of Medicine that the *indispensable substratum* of consciousness lies outside the cerebral cortex, probably in the diencephalon.

"The realization that the cerebral cortex, instead of being the 'top,' the 'highest level,' was an elaboration level divided sharply into areas for distinct functions (sensory, motor, or cycle) came to me like a bracing wind. It blew the clouds away and I saw certain *brain-mechanisms* begin to emerge more clearly, and they included those of the mind." (Penfield, 1975:18.) This conclusion was arrived at because ". . . it became quite clear in neurosurgical experience, that even large removals of the cerebral cortex could be carried out without abolishing consciousness. On the other hand, injury or interference with function in the higher brain-stem, even in small areas, would abolish consciousness completely." (*Ibid.:*18.) In other words the development of the vaunted cerebral cortex not only permitted the improvement of our abilities for rational exposition and analysis, which we would broadly regard as modern, it also appears to have improved the capacity of the brain to engage in what Paul MacLean, Chief of the Laboratory of Brain Evolution and Behavior at the National Institute of Mental Health, has called "paleo-psychic" processes. Broadly, these are functions of the brain performed, modulated or affected by portions of the brain of great ancientness in the scheme of brain evolution (MacLean, 1978). Thus, behavior which marks the reptiles or other animals remains rooted in portions of brain tissue which humans have not only retained but which, provocatively, have increased in size in recent evolution. Have we here a physical rendition of a relatively unchanged or even diminished "balance of power" within the brain between the higher cognitive processes and those less characteristically human ones associated with other animals, not usually with people?

Rudolfo Llinas has suggested that the distribution of tissue in the brain reflects the contribution of the various parts to the successful survival of the species. This becomes truly significant when we learn that in the last million years the human cerebellum has "enlarged between three-fold and four-fold," suggesting the importance of the functions performed by the cerebellum. (Llinas, 1975.) The cerebellum is an organic structure about a hundred million years old. Its explosive expansion in the last million years appears to be related principally to the role of hands in behavior and to orientation in time. The possibility exists that the expanded capacity of the cerebellum provides a neuromechanical basis for the ability to prepare symbolic forms of the future. In Llinas's view (pers. comm.) this sudden expansion was very likely abetted by the hunting-gathering ecology, by the shift to a more committed attention to hunting, and by the development of a rich and complex connection between past experience of the behavior of animals and their predictable behavior in the future. Llinas has postulated further that a consequence of the hunting adaptation is the development of a strong potential for mimesis, or empathic identification with the hunted animal. This would promote a rapid development of the ability to plan or at least predict the behavior of an external phenomenon—and a complicated one at that—the prey.

Now pieces of the puzzle may seem less isolated from each other. For example, the social functions of the cave life which we will discuss later may be relevant here, given its forceful emphasis on hunted animals. Also related to this process of expansion of the cerebellum would be the ability to predict and coordinate. Was the development of language connected with this? The consensus reached at a conference of the New York Academy of Sciences on the Evolution of Language (Harnad and Steklis, 1977) is that it is very old, perhaps a million to three million years old, rather than the earlier estimate of fifty thousand years, suggesting that the cerebellum and language are intertwined with hunting. This even presents us with the possible basis for the future tense as a linguistic form. An additional intriguing phenomenon, which we will discuss later, is that ingesting intoxicants and other mind-altering substances affects people's orientation not only in space but also in time. The discoordination of body may be similar to the discoordination of one's control of time. I will try to show later that these phenomena are related and that a function of intoxicants is to make futures benign, to exaggerate agreeable anticipations of the future, to make the future sing, or hum at least.

It is widely remarked that humans are the only animals aware of their own deaths; this seems to be a subform of the overall fact that humans may be the only animals informed in a relatively formal way about mortality itself. Insofar as the notion of mortality contains an inherent requirement for a future, this knowledge of the future may stimulate not only the manufacture of religions but also encouragement of a habit of mind which is "easy to think," in which there is a trading system, as it were, in which current activities are conducted against a sense of the future. Many humans may do this very badly. For example, the millions of people who continue to smoke cigarettes while knowing the clear relationship between smoking and hastened death are presumably relying on the statistical likelihood that they will not be included in the proportion of the smoking population plainly afflicted by smoking-related disease.

My suggestion is that there is a neurophysiology for a sense of the benignity of the future. It is an imperfect sense, a design defect really, and I will try to show how and why it evolved in the past and what it does in the present. That there may be such a neurophysiology for the future offers intriguing guidelines as we explore the evolution of speaking, planning, and recording. There are also immediate practical implications, such as coping with manic-depressives and compulsive gamblers, as well as the formal proposals of planners and the usually more elegant schemes of dreamers. As for the relevance of our species-past for our individual lives, perhaps that nostalgia for the future which is reverie has its origins long ago.

I want now to make some specific comments about the phenomenon of optimism, to suggest why it became "good to think" and why it became "easy to learn." The consequence of the new biology is that scientists can ask about the behavior of animals, why have particular patterns evolved? in the same way as they have for so long been able to ask why did this or that physical structure evolve, such as a long neck, a particular kind of shell, a certain scaly skin, or a particular kind of paw. As dog breeders and other practical students of the genealogies of animals have always known, it is possible to breed animals to achieve certain behavioral results just as it is well known how to produce physical specimens of a certain size, color, shape and pelage. Behavioral genetics is a highly practical and effective science for people interested in the evolution of the animals with whom they work and play.

Behavior evolves. Human behavior evolved. Thinking is a human behavior and the constellation of our ways of thinking, ideas, may also have evolved. Now we have to turn to this area to explore if and how ideas about the future which we had in the past remain sufficiently useful to affect our survival as a species and hence, our present state of natural being.

To do so we have to begin rather simply at the beginning. I want to make the following argument, which I will outline first: all animals, certainly complex ones, have a "stop-go" choice in their behavioral repertoire. They "go" when there seems advantage in action. They "stop" when it seems prudent to do nothing. Built upon this basic structure in the human is an infinitely more complex set of motivations and inhibitions as well as capacities which are available to be used. One of the significant features of the human pattern of "stop-go" depends upon the use of an elaborate set of symbolic phenomena which appear to have consequences for the emotional pleasure or distress of the individual. Not only real things and events but ideas about real things and events make people feel good or bad. We have to assume that to early man this presented as much a problem as an opportunity. When the beaver slaps its tail on the water or the deer flashes its white tail the warning call is clear and all the members of the group respond immediately. Social coordination for both positive and evasive actions comes relatively easier in animals simpler than ourselves.

However, human beings differ considerably from each other. When this differentiation is added to our complexity it can produce a volatile amount of non-coordinated behavior. We lack the beaver's and the deer's simple signal. But we have symbols. In order to permit the social organization of human beings there was an advantage to be gained by having people coordinate their "stop-go" systems.

The use of symbols became particularly significant for this purpose. Thus, sharing the optimisms of the community, as well as its devils, needed a symbolic mechanism to maintain social ties. The matter of social cohesion was critically important—too important to permit idiosyncratic individual conceptions of what was desirable and frightening to threaten conventionalized, socially agreed-upon ones. To achieve this coordination of responses humans have added to the underlying primatological components of political behavior an extraordinarily important ingredient of political hope. Added to that has been an often surprisingly intense faith in leaders.

We faced—and solved—the problem of making two important and apparently contradictory responses. The first was to sustain and indeed encourage a considerable amount of human variability, plasticity, creativity, adaptability, so that we could successfully adapt to what is now an astonishing array of different habitats, climates, ecologies, social patterns, religious systems. And yet this plasticity had somehow to be overcome when coordination was necessary, so that individuals, however disparate their brains, skills, enthusiasms and threshholds of anguish, could still become coordinated into the community and with its action. The solution to the problem was to develop an extensive capacity to learn. *The function of the great human capacity for learning is to reduce the effect of the considerable individual variation which exists in the species.* Put another way, the function of human learning potential is precisely to reduce the operation of this potential—to conventionalize it and integrate it, so that coordinated social behavior becomes likely, not questionable. The particular function of ideas about the future and its possible benign character extends the control which governors may wield over people's present behavior. It gives them the ability to offer prospects of great agreeability to communities of a species prepared by thousands of generations of evolution for precisely such a trade-off. In effect I am saying that the very skill of evolving Homo sapiens in adapting to new circumstances created a possibility of great individual differences in communities—differences which might produce inadequately coordinated citizens. So a central function of symbols was precisely to reduce the amount of individual variation in the name of the collective unity. And in turn, one of the most effective of possible symbols was the future, which had not yet come, which was not yet tangible, but which could be anticipated by political and religious leaders for their and their communities' purposes.

The chimera of heaven is rooted in tissue. In Chapter Four, Hope Springs Internal, I will try to describe the existence and function of various mechanisms in the body which are related to feeling well and feeling bad. I think a strong case can be made for the existence and efficacy of these physiological mechanisms. Of course other animals have similar mechanisms which underlie their social and psychological behavior; I am not at all suggesting we are dealing with a solely human phenomenon. What is, however, I think, uniquely human are the various manifestations of possibly primitive mood states— "paleo-psychic processes"—in an array of social and symbolic situations. Humans have religions and as far as we know no other animals do, and this is the distinction which has got to be explained.

The distinction may become clearer if we consider what it meant to human beings to become hunters and gatherers of their food, so that unlike the other primates they lost exclusive dependence on vegetables and fruit and acquired the ability to secure increasingly large sources of animal protein. Apart from the obvious nutritional consequences perhaps the most important result of this ecological shift was that it permitted, perhaps forced, the collectivization of economic life and the enhancement of cooperative rather than selfish social systems. Unlike the other primates, who didn't have to cooperate to feed themselves and whose forms of social connection were through kinship, play, or the overriding political system, humans added economic life to the mix of interdependencies in terms of which they lived.

Is it possible to establish a "phylogenetic baseline" which would describe the most common pattern of economic activity of prehuman economic producers, and of the subsequent developments in the work of our immediate ancestors? In our book, *The Imperial Animal* (1971), Robin Fox and I tried with perhaps undue succinctness to characterize the link between the primate givens from which the human adaptations devel-

oped and then the pattern of the social adaptations as they
related to economic behavior. We tried to show the primate
beginnings of the human trajectory. We made a number of
assumptions which I will not repeat here. In the years since the
book was published new data and analyses of the issues it
treated obviously require that various assertions be changed,
enlarged, or abandoned. Where necessary I will spell out such
changes.

"The primate base provides for a) a rudimentary sexual division of labor, b) foraging by the males, c) cooperation of males
in the framework of b, d) competition between males." (Tiger
and Fox, 1971:155.) Were we writing that passage now we
would add that there was very likely extensive cooperation between females which occurred most commonly along the lines
of kinship networks involving three or more generations. There
may also have been competition between females which may
have been a form of competition primarily between lineages of
kin members rather than competition between individuals.
(For a discussion of some of these issues see Caspari, 1978.) We
went on to say about the primate economy that "It is based on
a sexual division of work requiring males to hunt and females
to gather." We did not imply by this bald statement any com-
parisons between the importance of the male and female contributions. However, we did imply—an implication that we
believed consistent with available evidence then, and largely
the scientific case still—that the addition of regular and organized hunting to the primarily vegetarian primate economy
was a critical innovation. The fact that this was almost everywhere a form of work principally done by males did not and
does not mean that, for example, any skills involved in adapting to hunting—cortical, linguistic, cooperative—would be retained in the male line only and not spread equally through the
female population. This untutored and silly argument, for example, made by Shapiro (1971), suggests that the component
skills associated with the ability to develop hunting—increasing intelligence, the ability to plan, to coordinate, to describe
and to perceive, etc.—are linked directly to the male chromo-
some. This is of course not so and reveals a crude misunder-

standing of the basic function of sexual reproduction, *which is to exchange characteristics between males and females.* A tall father is as likely to have a tall daughter as a tall son, with the same female partner.

Fox and I went on with our discussion of the hunting-gathering transition: "It is based on tool and weapon manufacture. It is based on a division of skills and the integration of these skills through networks of exchange (of goods, services and women). There are networks of alliances and contracts—deals—among men." We should have added what has become increasingly clear, that it also involved complex reciprocal interactions among females who plainly cooperated about using information and time in the gathering enterprise and in those less directly economic matters, such as nutrition, modes of child rearing, and welfare.

"It involves foresight, investment, judgment, risk taking—a strong element of gambling." This element we did not extensively discuss in that book, but it is clearly an important component of my discussion here.

"It involves a redistributive system, operating through the channels of exchange and generosity; exploitation is constrained in the interest of group survival.

"It bases status on a cumulative skill married to distributive control—again in the interest of the group as a whole.

"It is important to see all these factors as integrated into the hunt. They are social, intellectual, and emotional devices that go to make up an efficient hunting economy, in the same way that muscles, joint articulation, eyesight, intelligence, etc., go to make up the efficient hunting body. They are the anatomy and physiology of the hunting body social. It is a system of the savannas and the hunting range, and it is the context of our social, emotional, and intellectual evolution."

The effect of the transition to hunting was more than economic. The form of economic life of early hunting-gathering man certainly affected the way he organized his social life and affected how he thought, what he thought about, and how he felt about what he thought. Since symbols, thoughts, and cognition are critically important to humans it follows that the consequences of cognitive processes were as much genetic as immediately social, and that indeed the long-range effect of the particular hunting-gathering mode was to predispose humans to particular social and symbolic forms. Is this not a likely basis for the development of a concern with the future and a talent for managing it? Were not the coordination of complex society and the development of symbols both significantly stimulated by the economic change to future-oriented schemes of hunting and gathering?

Marshack has suggested (Marshack, 1971) our talents for calculation and notation are much older than earlier students of the matter assumed. Perhaps the schemes for ordering symbols which Marshack describes were as much related to anticipating the future as understanding the present and codifying the past. It would indeed not be unreasonable to suppose that the origin of "mind" is coincident with and related to the origin of the future as a phenomenon. Perhaps the innovation of the future permitted communities and their leaders to manipulate communities and their futures at once in a newly effective way— they could use symbols readily understood and enthusiastically embraced by an intellectually complex organism skillfully quizzical about its destiny.

So far the reconstructed plot is: a particular species of primates begins to find itself adapting to circumstances not solely by physical/physiological mechanisms but employs the techniques of social organization and intellectual analysis more effectively than its competitors. It is successful in expanding its populations and its ecological range. But this presents it with two new problems—first, how to organize itself internally in an effective way, despite larger numbers of members; and, second, how to coordinate successful pursuit of the meat-providing animals on which it has come, in part, to depend, the eating of which gives it a significant nutritional and energy-saving advantage over its competitor primates. A further refinement of its internal skill leads to the development of some division of labor. Some members of the group are either more interested in or more skilled with manipulation of symbols and more importantly of symbols of the future. It becomes their practice to understand and provide exegesis of the future. They tell it before it happens.

We do not know if this was in fact the case. However, there is some reason to believe it was, if only because the role of religious functionaries is very clear during the human transition from hunting-gathering to agriculture. Flannery, Braidwood, and other anthropologists concerned with the emergence of agriculture and urban life have said about this relatively recent stage of human history that the earliest managers of the new economy were also people who had performed the functions of the priesthood. One wonders why priests should gain such power were it not that they and the more important laymen were willing to believe that they could improve the odds in favor of the group. It seems as if the body politic had a particular vitamin deficiency which the priests overcame.

Surplus wealth, which resulted from increasingly efficient agriculture, permitted establishment of a formal class of religious functionaries—presumably the first group ever of leisured organisms. Not until the emergence of aristocracies would there be another group of persons who didn't have to work and whose principal function was to pronounce judgment on the present, to anticipate and mitigate the future, and in a complicated transaction between morality and production try to circulate agricultural surplus to ensure survival for everyone in the group, not just the most efficient producers. If giving tithes—a tenth of one's production—to the priesthood was plainly extremely useful for the priesthood, it was at the same time a powerful stimulus toward formalizing social systems. The system of accounting, recording, projecting and exchange which this demanded was novel.

Thus in one historical moment the apparatus for ramifying and energizing social systems in a structurally new way was created. Now they could produce surpluses and use these with some strategy, to even out the flows of success and failure in agriculture and animal husbandry and also to permit the beginning of the slow, inexorably important increase of human population, the results of which are so critical now.

So are other results. The innovation of linking the manage-

ment of the future with the emergence of a leisure class produced further elaborations which were presumably not the intention of the first priests. Presumably they did not anticipate
or seek their eventual destruction as the preeminent economic
class—as exemplified for example in England in the confisca-
tion after the Anglo-Catholic Reformation or in the far more
significant cataclysm of the Protestant revolution with its implicit stimulus to capitalism and the formal discrepancy between economic life and religious life (except, of course, from
the Calvinist viewpoint, which regarded the obvious results of
real work as the tangible proof of an unobvious religious favor).
Paradoxically, this discrepancy of Protestantism would be reduced or removed by the communist system, in which the goals
of the productive apparatus were subserved to the system of
statecraft and internal politics. Indeed, in a form of Calvinism
without the personal payoff and certainly without the religious,
work was redemptive in quality because it augmented the prosperity and moral validity of the state. Significantly, the center-
piece of economic action in the initial stages of Russian communism was the preparation of systematic plans for the
economic future, five-year plan after five-year plan—plans
which were themselves filled with moral content and which
symbolize that link between economy and the future which I
have suggested has always been of interest to an animal as
skilled at foreboding as the human.

The factors involved in all this are of course exceedingly complex. Work itself as a business of living is not universally recognized for what it is in the capitalist west and communist east.
As Godelier has noted (Godelier, 1977), a good many languages
lack a word for labor and have no representation corresponding
to it. The idea, furthermore, that nature is transformed is of
relative recency, though just when it first emerged no one precisely knows. In any event, ancient Greek and Latin lacked
words equivalent to "labor" and to "work." But even though
we are dealing with imponderables here, let us try to discuss
the social transitions involved in the major economic changes
and what they may have meant overall for the human pattern.
Fox and I argued that the movement from hunting-gathering to

pastoralism-agriculture was very precipitous and eventful for people's sense of economic behavior. Hunter-gatherers were and are now, for example, like the Bushmen, very circumscribed in the amount of material possessions they could carry with them, particularly if hunting patterns involved efforts to follow their prey animals. It is now widely accepted that there is not only a lack of incentive for personal gain in this system but certainly a lack of clear opportunity to create complex hierarchies based on ownership of material objects. Meat spoils. If for no other reason successful hunters would have to share their meat, insuring a lively amount of leveling of individual status. Despite the general economic egalitarianism, Lee has noted (1968) that among the San Bushmen of the Kalahari there appears to be a general, almost casual tendency for some males to become leaders more often than others, though there is little formalization of such a pattern. Lee has also argued for the affluence of early hominids based on the presumed typicality of the San Bushmen. However, the general validity of speculations about early man based on the particular group reported on by Lee has been importantly questioned by B. J. Williams, who in answer to his own question about why these particular Bushmen appear to be so pacific and egalitarian as well as to have plentiful resources on which to live, comments in a book review about the Bushmen that: "Cultural elaboration of these themes also brings into question the superabundant food hypothesis . . . the real clincher . . . was there from the beginning. The information does not appear in the book [*Kalahari Hunter-Gatherers*, Lee and Devore, eds., 1976] and has not, to my knowledge, been published elsewhere, but Lee noted in his Ph.D. dissertation of 1965 that two-thirds of the San population in the Dobe region had been removed from the region in a resettlement program only two to three years prior to his fieldwork. That there were superabundant gathered foods after two-thirds of the population had been removed is not surprising, nor is the superabundance relevant to general hypotheses concerning hunter-gatherer adaptations." (Williams, 1977.)

Lee *et al.* (1977) have replied, indicating that the matter is possibly more complex than Williams suggests, though they do not address the question of ill-health and low birthrates. On the critical historical fact described by Williams may also rest an explanation of the difference found between the Bushmen reported on by Lee and those by Eibl-Eibesfeldt (pers. comm.), who found a much less congenial and excellent situation among the particular Bushmen group he encountered.

Whatever the present situation, in general there appears to have been a relatively stable equilibrium of resources to people during the hunting-gathering phase, which was presumably reflected in the relatively low rate of population growth during this time and before the pastoral-agricultural phase of our history. This relatively stable population level suggests how well adapted the human species was to its ambient circumstances. Its patterns of behavior and the opportunity to employ these were sufficiently close that no violent changes in population occurred to affect the system overall. This belies the romantic view of ancestral hunter-gathers of some writers, such as Marshall Sahlins, who would argue in part on the basis of Lee's interpretations (which must now themselves be reinterpreted) that hunter-gatherers were and many still are members of the "original affluent society." If nothing more, one might have expected affluence to produce and support a greater rate of population growth than evidently occurred during the hunting-gathering phase. But population growth did not increase markedly until the rise of agriculture. Before then, what had plainly happened was that the human species increased its living area by exploring and colonizing rather than increasing its production by more efficient cultivation of available resources. I do not imply that the relatively stationary population density of the hunting-gathering stage of human evolution and the relatively slow population growth of the species were in themselves desirable; "no change" is surely not by definition preferable to "much change." But the hunting-gathering scheme persisted successfully for a long time; and even if we do not know the "quality of life" of the people living in this way we can assume that the relatively stable nature of their existence reveals a reasonable relationship of problems and solutions and hence needs and satisfactions.

As I will show later, not until the advent of agriculture and industry was the optimistic factor translatable into expectations of economic growth—more resources for individual people. Inflation, economic imperialism, rising growth curves of sales reports, and guaranteed annual increases in income are all post-hunting-gathering phenomena and all reflect a new concatenation of economic opportunity with psychological optimism which was not possible during the egalitarian days of hunting and gathering. "More" is new. Once the ecological stability of the hunter-gatherer was lost, the impetus to expand was unleashed—and we all know the consequences. It is of parenthetic interest that visionaries seeking to establish communes away from the clamor of industrial society usually adopt the agricultural ecology instead—a grievous error since, if anything, agricultural life is more tryingly ill-adapted to hunting-gathering Homo sapiens than industry is. This may explain the relatively poor success rate of agricultural communes unsecured by commitment to the service of God, such as the Hutterites, or the Bruederhoef or Mennonites. The major exception is the kibbutz, about which more later.

I want to add a brief note before going on about a notion which directly reflects the optimistic factor and is deeply imbedded in many anthropological, economic and sociological theories, the notion that there is a real development, evolution, or improvement in societies. I believe, on the contrary, that there isn't true progress or change as opposed to cosmetic or even regressive change in human social nature as it moves from one type of economy or government to another. Although in recent years the creative evolutionary view has been seen as something of a nineteenth-century conceit, still the anthropologist Fried, for example, has argued that there is a fundamental evolution of political forms and has implied that the very political nature of the persons living in these differing systems has changed. (Fried, 1968.)

In my view the patterns of social response have probably not changed very much, if at all, from the Paleolithic period and possibly even before. To be sure, there has been an immense number of interventions in the earlier arrangements of Homo sapiens, such as large, crowded aggregations of people, writing and reading, other forms of mass communication, rapid travel, and notions of personality and of justice independent of God. But such interventions probably have forced few major changes in the organism's social capacities over the past fifty thousand years. If this is true, MacLean's "paleopsychic processes" continue to provide the basic valences and ambivalences as well as perceptual formulae by which people live. It is interesting to observe parenthetically that Jaynes's ambitious and novel argument, that major shifts in intellectual capacity occurred some fifty thousand years ago as a result of illusions of divine communication, should itself contain this other-worldly component—literally a deus ex machina. (Jaynes, 1977.)

I am not implying that the circumstances of people do not improve, but I think it is a good argument from science and citizenship, and also humane and finally democratic, to see all the members of the human species forming a unity over time and space. The obvious differences between people in this scheme are not easily organized according to some made-up calculation. The traditional opposite notion to this is that there are some good people called Christians or Moslems or Jews, for example, and that all the rest are more or less imperfect to the extent they depart from the standards of the chosen group. We know too well the consequences of strident belief in the religious superiority of one's own group. There is also a technological version of this whereby certain societies possessing certain machines regard themselves as superior to others, and this has led to a variety of schemes of classification of societies which are fundamentally evaluative rather than diagnostic. There is also a psychological version of this notion of basic societal quality in which certain societies are deemed superior because they permit members to "express themselves" or "be free" in the psychological sense, or "be disciplined" or whatever, to the comparative disadvantage of members of less favored societies.

Let's return to the basic theme of this chapter, which is an examination of the way in which perceptions of the future evolved and were related to historic patterns of economic life and change. We saw that opportunities for economic differentiation under the hunting-gathering system were limited. Even if a group were to engage in the extreme form of exploitation by taking slaves, those slaves would still have to join in the hunt, would still have to consume the food necessary to permit them the energy outputs involved in hunting-gathering, and would not necessarily produce more wealth than they would themselves consume. Slavery appears to possess very different and more lucrative advantages for those who control pastoral and agricultural societies. But when we skip to large-scale industrial ones it is relatively rare for slave labor to be exploited for long periods of time, except under particular circumstances widely viewed as politically punitive, aberrant and grotesque, such as the Nazi or Soviet concentration camps or certain jail systems, *e.g.*, in the southern U.S., where convicts may be made to work for local entrepreneurs who are presumably in legal and illegal collaboration with prison authorities.

Assuming not only ethical but also economic forces underlie the reluctance of industrial society to maintain slavery, we can perhaps make certain inferences from studying parallels with the past. Archeological and anthropological research has clarified the relationship between hunting-gathering and agricultural-pastoral systems. To quote from Philip Smith's recent discussion of Paleolithic communities along the Nile, "With the benefit of hindsight we can now see that many late Paleolithic peoples in the Old World were poised on the brink of plant cultivation and animal husbandry as an alternative to the hunter-gatherer way of life. The new livelihood had its formal beginnings around the start of post-glacial times in Southwestern Asia and perhaps elsewhere as well. One current hypothesis about the origins of agriculture is that it was related to late Pleistocene population growth and increased pressure on food resources. This," according to the hypothesis, "led in some cases to the greater exploitation of foods that up to that time had been comparatively neglected. Particularly plants, smaller animals, birds, fish and mollusks." (Smith, 1976:37.)

Smith also notes that this trend of some nine to fourteen thousand years ago toward greater use of non-hunted sources was a preadaptation to " . . . a ready acceptance of food production later." From the hunting-gathering system the agricultural-pastoral transition occurred and with logical and formal appropriateness for the development of agriculture was abetted by the existence of an optimistic mood in the human—the necessary but not sufficient condition for the development of agriculture. Obviously ecological conditions were inextricably involved, such as population density and climate. However, at least with hindsight, it seems essential that there had to have existed a capacity to produce, maintain and make readily meaningful to large numbers of people a set of shared symbols purporting to deal with the future. This was vital in confronting the hiatus between sowing and reaping. If the harvest was a festival the period before it was a trial of nerves. I think that the energies and skills involved, for example, in making the cave paintings discussed hereafter were readily convertible into a set of non-animal symbols, and these represented the institutionalization of hope and control in non-hunting-gathering societies.

Here Moses' breakthrough was dazzlingly innovative and symbolically highly significant. His insistence on separating "graven images" from Godly forces prompted the transition to non-animal symbolism. Moses made the bleak, but for that time imaginative, assertion that it was inappropriate to show spiritual devotion to animals, and he succeeded for his group in breaking not only the complex ties between animals and people but between animals and the future, which there is reason to believe existed widely before then if only because of the apocalyptic nature of Moses' assertion about the need to put that form of observance into the past. But he was even more aggressively innovative about religious observance. Not only did he commit his people to a symbolic focus of worship but he took also the additional and at first seemingly peculiar step of prohibiting the utterance or writing of the true name of God. In a sense this was a brilliant extension of his radical act: he took from his people that which they could tangibly see and touch to worship and gave them that which they could neither see nor touch and furthermore prevented them from even referring to the symbol of that which they couldn't see or touch.

This was daring indeed. The intriguing question is, why did it work? How did such a difficult transition succeed?

First of all, it appears that, wonderfully, the brain could perform the necessary transactions and believe in their potency. Secondly, perhaps given the peripatetic circumstances of the Hebrews, an internalized approach to the religious experience rather than one that focused on words, artifacts, images fulfilled the particular needs at the time. But for whatever reasons, in a deft way the Mosaic injunctions appeared to have been successful at the time and appear to have remained so as the components of a durable system of religious belief and communal identification. The concern with one's personal and communal future became cerebralized. Was it the very uncertainty of this situation which was so energizing, as risk-filled situations often are? Was it the uncertainty which produced the commitment to at least scholastic if not intellectual analysis which marked the Hebrew tradition for such a long time? And has the practical effectiveness of members of the Judeo-Christian community resulted from facing a boldly stated and insoluble dilemma: *How can the optimistic factor be turned into a wholly theoretical possibility—perhaps its most effective rendition—and still have concrete effects on day-to-day life?*

As we have seen, the functions of religion are not served solely, or perhaps even primarily, by rational, logical argument. The information content of religious ceremonies is usually suffused with if not overwhelmed by nonverbal means of communication. In the great cathedrals of Europe it is often difficult to hear the specific words of the services as they are conducted; what is profoundly effective about communal worship in these places is the grandeur of the event—the improbable power of the architecture, the engulfing efficacy of the music, the richness of the costumes, and presumably the provocativeness of the contrast between the small, weak communicants and the towering, powerful vaults. Cathedrals are after all exceptionally improbable artifacts; that they exist at all, having been expensive and inconvenient to make, suggests the force of the emotional return (as well as the political benefits) which they provide. I do not want to get involved here with the problem of the beauty of cathedrals because it begs the questions what beauty is, how notions of it change, how it's identified, and what work it does in the human system. However, plainly, the function of cathedrals is to stimulate dramatically a connection between the worshiper and the wide forces of existence. While many people may find the bravado and expense involved in building major religious structures puzzling, the highly concrete fact of their existence indicates their importance to the communities which build and maintain them. The ubiquity of the pattern of religious construction—temples, mosques, cathedrals, synagogues and shrines—attests to the power of an irrational ambition. Individuals will differ in the amount of trust and fear they bring to the cathedral encounter but overall the buildings themselves are an unassailable witness to human passion. Even if there is a God, the existence of cathedral structures would be surprising—why would God require such offerings? But if there is no God the existence of great religious buildings can be shocking. How? Why? Using what demented calculation could an animal build such places? I think we know. An animal with a gorgeous genius for hope.

It is curious that Roman Catholicism and Judaism have until recently employed languages for their services which were not understood by most of their communicants. Latin and Hebrew continued to be used for centuries as a means of contact between worshiper, priest or rabbi, and God. No matter that there was not generally strict understanding; the connection was still made. It is by no means clear that the decision by the Roman Catholic hierarchy to conduct services in the vernacular has had the desired effect of making church teachings more accessible to parishioners and hence the church more persuasive over their lives. My own suspicion is that since people do not attend churches for information but rather for other reasons, the linguistic reforms will have the effect of trivializing the church experience and rendering less significant the forces held to reside in churches.

Religious buildings not only have direct effects on individuals within them but also evoke mythic recollections having to do with the buildings' origins and history. I once toured the

Temple Square in Salt Lake City, the central religious shrine area of the Mormon faith—its Vatican City. The woman guiding the tour group provided a full account of the choice of architecture and the history of a number of the features of the Temple. She remarked that a group of gilt seagulls set on top of a column had been erected to commemorate the miracle of the gulls' appearance from the coast at a particularly crucial time during the second season of the Mormons' plantation in the city, a time when their virgin crop was being attacked by crickets, which the gulls mercifully devoured. This the Mormons took to be a sign of deliverance and hence erected the gold seagulls to mark the miracle.

Explanation by miracle is a form of retroactive collective optimism. A community agrees that a highly improbable event occurred because it favored the best interests of the community, its importance and value. For example, to return to Temple Square in Salt Lake City, we were told this story: During construction of the Temple (a brooding gray stone tower which non-Mormons may not enter) Brigham Young, who designed the building, told his stone masons to leave holes in the thick walls from the roof to the foundation and also to provide a large square central aperture with no apparent function. At the time, according to the story, no one understood the purpose of these features; Young reportedly claimed God had inspired him to incorporate them in the design. But, subsequently, with the invention of electricity and the installation of plumbing, the wall ducts took on an immediate and appropriate use, and the central shaft now accommodates an elevator. Thus was Young's divine inspiration justified.

The building of cathedrals is no casual matter. In his novel *The Spire*, William Golding evokes the system and dilemmas in creating an effective and complex building—in this case, Salisbury Cathedral, with its spire evidently too large in practical terms for the structure. No one who has visited the highest passable level of the dome of St. Peter's basilica in Rome can fail to understand the cost, danger, difficulty, bravery, madness and passion involved in raising such a vast edifice.

But likewise it is impossible to be casual about using cathedrals, even when, as so often happens, they have been cast in the shadows of other structures. In any case, a direct consequence of the ambient secularization of industrial societies is that piety requires a more effortful, skilled and self-conscious process than faith and worship presumably required when faith was the order of the day and worship a thoroughly conventional act. For all the exotic interest of ancient and certain modern churches, it is the skyscraping monuments to work and money which provide the dramatic focus of our cities.

Given this, to sense the breezes of community in North America requires a special receptivity, which may even have to be learned or regained in adulthood. Perhaps the continuing importance of revivalist, "born again" religion in North America and to a lesser extent in England reveals how difficult it is for adults to remain sensitive to the meaning of divinity. Is there a contrast between adult religious energy which is newly derived and those certainties derived from childhood? And what happens to the children of those who are "born again"? How does the ruckus of new belief affect them? Indeed, the general questions stand posed—how does the way one is reared affect one's trust in social arrangements? How does one develop, on one hand, a healthy skepticism about the possible outcome of events and, on the other, an openness to what Peter Berger has called a "rumor of angels"?

Soon I will turn to a discussion of the relationship between (most generally stated) childhood and belief—the subject of the next chapter. But before doing so I wish to recall the principal concern of the present chapter. I suggested that the transitions from primate vegetarianism to human hunting-gathering and into agriculture have left their mark on the human cognitive apparatus. They encouraged a considerable expansion of imaginative capacity as well as judgment about the future. However, and this is, I think, a key point in what will be the development of a serious biology of symbolic life, *the overriding function of the development of individual differences in thought and feeling was precisely to make individuals receptive to common symbols. The function of the extensive apparatus for human learning was to take the individual differences which exist in this complex species and*

*turn these differences into common responses to the same things.
The function of learning is to reduce social differentiation not to
increase it;* the human being expresses gregariousness as much
by sharing symbols as by sharing food, sharing children, sharing beds, and sharing space.

Children learn; they learn what's around them, what they're
expected to learn, and what it is hoped they will not learn. The
manner in which children apprehend what the future is like
and what to expect of it they will presumably, to some extent at
least, recall and represent to their own offspring. Eventually I
will examine the childhood of the animal with the longest span
of dependency.

But before then it should be useful to look at a period of the
late childhood of the species, when some of us anyway lived in
caves, to try to learn what this period of history, and the records
it has left us, may mean in the context of a larger process of
evolution from nonhuman primate to big-brained human
being.

The Interlude in the Dark

Both the explosive growth of Florida, California and the Ri-
viera and the findings of archeology indicate that humans are
keener on warm than cold climates. Unprotected, they can tolerate only a narrow range of climatic conditions. In the absence
of warmth they make clothes and shelter and build fires in order
to escape from the weather.

From its inception, probably in East Africa, the human race
inexorably moved northward. Slowly but steadily it spread out
over the continent of Europe. Its early remains, both bodies
and artifacts, are still everywhere. Initially these emigrants
must have resisted going where they wouldn't be comfortable,
but such pressures as population and political challenge eventually forced some of them to the periphery. Their migrations
must have been as frightening and provocative as more recent
ones have been, and probably much more so, given the power
of the unknown then as compared to now. Finally, these people

confronted the crisis of the Ice Age. But when the ice descended through Europe, a number of them chose to stay where they were.

Thus they had to find shelter, not merely for comfort but for survival. Living in caves provided one way, probably not new but useful. Caves conserved the heat that bodies generated. Moreover, fires made in caves would not be rained out or snowed out and, through their judicious placement, would protect the cave dwellers not only from cold but from predators.

The caves of these hunters, rediscovered only in this century, are among the most critical markers of human history. I was privileged to explore some of them, in particular the caves of the Périgord region of France. These and the paintings within them are the first record we have so far of human beings' insistence that they can control their futures, that they are not random actors in a patternless universe and that they are not required passively to accept the vicissitudes of the social and material world without fighting back by thinking ahead. Presumably these prehistoric people derived satisfaction, perhaps even reassurance, from painting on cave walls. Painting on the walls may have helped them to believe that they were going to improve their circumstances, that they were going to be able to control others' circumstances, that they would no longer be at the mercy of animals. Apart from the fact that the caves are in themselves among the most amazing places on earth, they may reveal something of the turmoil and accomplishment of our ancestors' society and hence of the foundation and even construction of our own.

In planning my trip to the cave country in the Dordogne, I was fortunate to have the assistance of Alexander Marshack of the Peabody Museum at Harvard, whose work on the interpretation of prehistoric remains has been of major significance to our understanding of them. Marshack's use of the sophisticated techniques of microanalysis and infrared photography has enabled him and subsequently other investigators, arguing from solid evidence, to reach portentous conclusions. As a result, there exists now a considerable body of new theories about the meaning of the artifacts which have been found and their relationship to the people who produced them. In general I have relied on the expertise of professionals in these matters and used my own judgment only in interpreting the impact of the caves on one person's being, an impact which I confess I found shockingly contemporary and immediate—stunning beyond expectation. Thus, from my standpoint at least, the significant thing to keep in mind is that the art in the caves was produced by people living between ten and thirty thousand years ago—people without benefit of written language, of more than rudimentary technology, but quite likely of the self-conceptual ability which marks individuals in our own time. To my mind, the seeming modernity of this work, the clarity with which the artists realized their aesthetic intentions and the intense evocativeness of the results suggests how much we share with these people. By implication it suggests how consistent has been the thematic relationship between art—the assertion and description of life—and the mastery and living of life.

Before I left for France, Marshack advised me that I would be overwhelmed by a "sense of place." He was right. The caves are places of extraordinary potency—marvelous to some, nightmarish to others, fantastical and penetratingly damp and cold to all. It is not surprising to me that in their ambience were created works of art and symbolism of surpassing ambition and daring; the caves themselves are anything but ordinary. Rouffignac is one of the largest in the world. It contains some five miles of corridors (a small railway takes tourists through part of the complex). A walk from the mouth to the so-called Red Chamber takes almost an hour, provided one is shown the way by an experienced guide, in my case the cordial owner of the cave, and furnished with an efficient gas lamp. Prehistoric visitors to the chamber, who apparently came and went deliberately to make certain marks and images, must have taken at least forty-five minutes each way, with only a flickering oil lamp guarding them from total darkness and terror. The bodies of many of them, lost in Rouffignac, have already been found. As I walked, I marveled at the tenacity with which they carried out their observances—and, to a degree, at my own.

The center for prehistoric research in France is the town of

Les Eyzies de Tayac. A community of perhaps 800, it has a national museum of prehistory and affords close access to many of the most interesting caves. Several, in fact, are within walking distance. In Les Eyzies were discovered the remains of the creature called Cro-Magnon man; in 1868 laborers building a road there discovered the skeletons of two adults and three children at a site now occupied by a hotel. The neighborhood of Les Eyzies is softly beautiful and one can easily understand why the valleys of the Dordogne, Vézere and Lot attracted our ancestors. The Dordogne region offers a variety of terrain, access to water, and moderate extremes of temperature, the last presumably a most important consideration during the climatic changes preceding and during the Ice Age.

Near the village, in the Gorge d'Enfer, the image of a large male salmon, originally painted red, is carved into the ceiling of a cave opening toward the Dordogne. As Marshack has suggested, the image may have been a seasonal reminder of the return of salmon to the river in the spring. The image is solitary and powerful and suggests at least one function of art during this period—marking and defining sources of food and thus perhaps inviting them to the human table.

Images of animals predominate in the caves, giving rise to the assumption, or presumption, that the images served as magical aims, the supposed primitive theory being that by drawing animals man subjected them not only to physical mastery but to spiritual mastery as well. Certainly the depictions of bison, mammoths, reindeer, cows, horses and the other native animals of the period suggest a central concern with those creatures. One would expect nothing else of course from hunter-gatherers. The power of the renditions and the extraordinary care with which they were so frequently made seem appropriate when we imagine ourselves in the place of people whose lives depended on those animals and whose prosperity was associated with finding and controlling them in the hunt.

I wish to avoid discussing the artistic quality of the work and its variation in style from period to period and to concentrate instead on the implications of the work for understanding the lives of its creators. In this context the focus on animals is, as I have just suggested, very understandable. It may be unnecessary to determine whether the function of the paintings is to make sympathetic magic or to express fear of the animals or contempt for them. It seems more sensible to assume—human beings being complicated and multifaceted in their approaches to all important things—that the animal representations meant a variety of things to the people who made them. My earlier concern with the relationship between hunter-gatherers and human evolution caused me to reflect in an earlier book on the possibility that the Dordogne caves served as places of initiation for young males as they entered formally into the central hunting processes of their communities. (Tiger, 1969.) As well, drawing animals may have been associated with instruction about them, about their bodies, their vulnerabilities, their coloring, and their general nature as they related to humans and each other. However, in the major caves, such as Pech-Merle, Rouffignac and Lascaux, the purposes served by the artwork seem to go well beyond the requirements of initiation and instruction and appear to imply general communal assertion and possibly solidarity. In other words, the intensity and evocativeness of the work seem to connote wide concerns and generalized passions rather than a specific, time-limited problem, such as initiation.

Moreover, when we consider some of the other imagery in the caves, the notion of sympathetic magic is called into question, if only because many symbols themselves appear to bear no relationship to known phenomena of the time. An example of such confections is what the Abbé Breuil called "macaroni," a recurrent motif in the caves. These "macaroni" are basically a set of parallel lines obviously drawn with the fingers of one hand held together and following no apparent linear pattern but meandering, often for considerable distances, over the surfaces of the walls. Another example is the "red dots"—dabs of red paint applied to the walls of, for example, Pech-Merle and Cougnac, which, judging from analyses of pigments and the intensity of applications, apparently were put there by different persons. These tokens suggest social participation and ritual.

Perhaps the most extraordinary example of the genre is in the aforementioned Red Chamber of Rouffignac, whose approach I described through an extraordinarily beautiful yet frightening descending tunnel. After a long trek, suddenly one arrives at the Chamber. The approach is bare but the inside of the room is literally covered with macaroni markings. The shape of the room is itself perhaps ritually significant. The roof is domelike, leading to a series of natural arches where the roof meets the floor. These arches are about eight feet wide at the floor and have the appearance of separate "chapels" in a large cathedral. Moreover, the macaroni symbols appear to be related spatially to these chapelesque arches. In short, it is an amazing room, since nothing outside it prepares one for the intensity, intricacy and commitment that its embellishments obviously reflect. What do these macaroni-like inscriptions mean? Who made them? Were they the work of all members of the community, its senior members, its priests, its initiates, its aged? These questions may be partly answered by future analyses of the depths of impression, size of digits, etc., which may reveal at least whether the makers were old or young, male or female. But for the moment it is sufficient to say that this extraordinary embellishment reveals something of the elaborate and thought-out nature of the makers' social relationships or at least of their commitment to making assertions in a publicly recognized place. That this room was a shrine seems inescapable.

To add to the mystery, the ceiling contains numerous depictions of serpents, while in another part of the cave two figures, rather grotesquely drawn, have suggested to the French authorities who have studied the cave a kinship with representations of Adam and Eve. However conjectural—presumably the figures had no such meaning for the people who made them—that coincidence and the existence of the snake images, along with the macaroni markings, are an intriguing, if bizarre phenomenon. I myself had difficulty seeing the Adam and Eve because they are so inaccessible.

Equally inaccessible is a drawing of the head of a powerful male, at the bottom of a treacherous fissure in the lowest level of the cave. The face—looming, reflective, demanding—is drawn without any distortion or surrealism, but rather with rich and evocative force. That it is so difficult to reach and possesses such authority suggests that it may prefigure the commandment against making graven images. It almost appears that the artist was aware how strongly he had evoked the human face and wanted it hidden in an obscure and private place. In several of the other caves, for example Pech-Merle and, most markedly, Cougnac, there are human depictions, but in the great cave of Rouffignac, as in the paramount cave, Lascaux (where there is only one image of a human—the so-called Sorcerer), the implication is strong that representing the human face and figure was by no means trivial but on the contrary charged with psychic energy and consequence. There is, of course, the additional possibility that these human images were made for so-called black magic. Their reclusiveness may mean nothing more than that the artists who painted them had literally gone underground, had sought to have a magical effect on the life of the community without showing their hand.

And yet elsewhere such representations are common. At Cougnac there are a number, at least six sticklike figures impaled by arrows. The figures seem to be in flight, suggesting that the depictions may indeed represent some kind of sorcerer's enterprise. In any case, they clearly convey an understanding of human suffering and pain, of the human as prey in the midst of the far more pervasive rendering of animals as prey.

Nevertheless, the predominance of animals in the renditions in the caves is compelling. Robert Carniero of the American Museum of Natural History has studied the behavior and social system of the Amahuaca people of Peru. He comments on their hunting magic that "It has often been observed that supernaturalism came to surround those activities which are either uncertain or hazardous or both, while conversely little or no supernaturalism accompanied those spheres of life where security and predictability prevail. The Amahuaca certainly bear out this generalization. Almost no supernaturalism is connected with horticulture, which yields very opulently and reliably. On the other hand, hunting, whose outcome is never certain and often involves an element of personal danger, is attended by

considerable supernaturalism. . . . Amahuaca supernaturalism, as it relates to hunting, can best be summarized by saying
it is positive rather than negative. There is little or nothing that
a hunter must not do to have success in hunting, but there are
many things he can and does do. Positive kinds of hunting
magic vary considerably, some of it acts on the hunter himself
or on his weapons, helping him to find game sooner, to see
more of it or to make his arrow fly surer. Other hunting magic
acts on the game, making animals 'tamer' so they can be seen
and shot more readily." (Carniero, 1970: 338.) For a discussion
of several of these same issues with some additional emphasis
on charismatic and religious performances, see David Aberle's
important paper. (Aberle, 1966.)

The cave which most exemplifies the power of animal paintings is of course Lascaux, and it is worth describing in some
detail. Because of chemical deterioration caused by unlimited
visiting and/or atmospheric control used when it was first
opened, the cave has been closed to the public since 1963. A
very limited number of visitors with special permission may
visit the cave on application to the French government's cura-
tor. Once a day a resident guide escorts a group of not more
than five persons through the cave. On my visit the guide was
the very man who with a childhood companion discovered the
cave.

We entered the cave through a number of chambers which
are air-conditioned to moderate changes in pressure, moisture
and temperature. Thereafter we washed the soles of our shoes
in a chemical solution to prevent our transplanting spores into
the cave. Somewhere within a whirring machine asserted its
dominion over the atmosphere.

Another door was opened, a light switched on, we entered
the famous rotunda. Its effect is indescribable. The combination of cool, sepulchral air, the sheer size of the animal figures—some as long as 17 feet—and the breathtaking virtuosity
with which they are drawn all conspire to disarm even the most
carefully prepared visitor. Although I had read descriptions of
the cave and seen reproductions of its paintings, I hadn't begun
to anticipate the elaborateness and aesthetic power of the place.

One is allowed only thirty-five or forty minutes in the room, and the speed with which one moves through it heightens its drama and force. If it is a function of great art to shatter one's idea of the possible, the expectable, even the foreseeable, then Lascaux as a whole achieves this profoundly unsettling effect. The brilliance of the painting is so astonishing as to obliterate the lines between prehistoric, historic and contemporary.

The cave is managed and has been "produced" as far as its lighting is concerned with the painstaking éclat devoted to favored monuments of France, and in the carefully dimmed light the natural muds and dyes used for the colors appear lively and moving. One wonders what they must have looked like in the light of the oil lamps presumably used by the artists and how the animals must have loomed in the gloaming. The guide pointed out that the artist responsible for one of the drawings seemed to know exactly what he was doing, for one continuous line appears to contain the entire form of a very large animal. Certainty, confidence, a willingness to assert emanate from the figures. There is little evidence at Lascaux of the ambiguity, quest, perhaps even thoughtfulness that characterize the inscriptions of Gabillou or Rouffignac. Here is clear authority, of the kind associated with such apotheoses of their genre as the frescoes of the Sistine Chapel, the mosaics of San Marco and the total environment of Santa Sophia.

Apart from the thrill they awoke, the effect of the caves is to reinforce one's humility about the present state of accomplishment in art. The daring, scope and skill not to mention artistic integrity of the cave artists, inform us that we are not first or perhaps foremost in creating scenes from life. In this connection, I am reminded of a story told by Professor Sol Tax of the University of Chicago's Department of Anthropology. One day, according to his account, he was carrying his granddaughter on his shoulders. They met a friend who had seen the child only some months before. The friend looked at the child high on her grandfather's shoulders and observed, "My, my friend, how big you've grown," to which the child replied, "Not all of this is me." When certain early twentieth-century painters, such as Picasso and Giacometti, realized that African sculptural forms were not merely primitive but profoundly effective, they assumed that they had discovered the wellspring of artistic form. The quality of the cave art is much the same, although it relates to our own art not in an ethnographically comparative but in a chronological way. In both cases, however, the leap needs to be made: from viewing certain art forms as primitive—the false view of African art—to seeing them as natural.

But wherefrom come the connections between art and assertion? Why was it once and why is it now the case that things which look a certain way have an aesthetic impact? Perhaps, as in many things, the answer lies in observing the behavior of children. For example, I was once surprised to discover that my infant son showed aesthetic preferences when he was too young to distinguish the conventional preferences of the world around him or to know what was nutritionally advisable for him to eat. Why, I asked myself, would a three-month-old child prefer, for instance, spinach to squash or pureed chicken to eggs? Obviously an organism would prefer certain people to others, if only because certain people (as opposed to others) would give it more food, more pleasing sounds, more time, perhaps some greater sense of affection. But aesthetic preference? Of taste? Of texture? Of color? And aesthetic preferences which vary from infant to infant?

If these observations have meaning, then we have found the beginning of wisdom—to root formally in biology the precultural formation of the phenomena of taste and aesthetic choice. Moreover, such an approach would guide the work of the humanist professions of criticism, composition, performance, back toward a natural, inevitable expression rather than further into the vain experimentation so frequently associated with the artistic function today. In the prevailing view, art emerges from a particular and civilized cadre of relatively well-off members to become part of the formal high culture of society. In the minority view, which I share, it springs from human nature, which it reveals in a plethora of ways.

Perhaps what is revealed is not different in kind from what is shown by children when they display preference and create colorfulness. We know that children strive ceaselessly to become older and bigger, to find personal efficacy and mastery over their own incapacity and the rigors of their environment. We also know that in this endeavor the exercise of preference or taste is unremitting. If the preferences of children often seem odd and peculiar, they appear nevertheless to rest on some structure of human biology. And what also rests on this biology is the predisposition of children to become—at least about toys, clothes, trading cards, hamburgers and television—the most conventional of creatures, finding in a common expression of communal taste a clear certification of their own legitimacy.

I have tried in this chapter to discern an archeology of optimism and to show what its biological origins might be and how the mood optimism may be affected by particular religious and aesthetic practices. My central argument has been that a significant function of the optimistic mood is that it permits individual differences to be, through learning, organized into conventionally accepted social practices by a general response to conventionally accepted symbols. Thus optimism is almost a heightened form of gregariousness—it is, as I earlier suggested, rather like a hormone—in this case a sociohormone—which stimulates disparate parts of the body politic to collective action, just as hormones similarly affect individual bodies.

But, if this is so, how did it come to be? What exactly, and how exactly, do babies and children learn in order to be adults and create and sustain their ideas of their futures? What are the roles of hope, disdain, and fear? What does a fragile animal do with its most fragile members, its infants, to reduce the unequal odds which little children clearly face and adults know they must help them withstand? It is time to turn to the bizarre question of why people have children and what happens then.

Room at the Inn: Room at the Top

When Joseph and Mary, expecting the baby Jesus, were turned away from the inn, they became perhaps our profoundest symbol of the necessary commitment of parents to children and of the questionable commitment of society to families. Their story dramatizes a central moral problem of human organization, and a persistent dilemma of all higher mammals as well: how to reconcile the needs of dependent young with the needs of the community. For, whereas on the one hand society reserves the right to remove a child from a family it regards as irresponsible, on the other it treats children with profound inequality. The children of slaves become slaves while the children of nobles assume titles at birth. Apart from feral children, if any exist, all babies, whether as jewels or as common stones, are embedded in the matrix of society. I want here to explore that embeddedness and what it means and what happens as a result of it.

Let us ignore the question of whether or not there is a God, and if there is, if Jesus was His son, and if He was, if the circumstances of His infancy were as biblically described. The nontheological aspects of the story are powerful enough.

The parents seek nothing more than to attend to the needs of their expected child, yet the corrupt world responds with marked indifference to the demands of the life process. What triumphs in the biblical story is the mammalian sense of responsibility for the young, despite communal indifference symbolized by an un-Godly society's rejection of the God of Love. Subsequently, according to St. Matthew's account, those who see beyond the crass secular concerns of their society perceive the importance of the child and rally to it notwithstanding the humble circumstances of its birth. For, significantly, St. Luke describes the infant as lying in a manger of straw in a stable, like any other newborn infant mammal. (I think, incidentally, that the mixed symbolism here is not accidental and in part accounts for the story's power. The general distaste humans exhibit toward the animal-like aspects of their being is in this case entirely disarmed by the central fact of the account: that Jesus is, although an infant and an animal, the incarnation of God. It is also probably important that he becomes a shepherd.)

The loving and constructive members of the community welcome the birth. Stars of wonder, stars of light and other elaborately imagined signs of general interest attend the event. Their very exoticism betrays the deep importance that is attached to it, to birth. With characteristic élan the central mammalian process becomes the formative religious idea of a massive cultural tradition. The symbols of Christ, his birth, the manger, the animals, the stars, the parents, the unhelping innkeeper—all reflect a generalized adult concern with the birth and protection of infants; this birth, of Jesus, reenacted annually, represents the core of the contract annually renewed which demands protection and love for the needy innocence of children.

I hope in this chapter to elucidate the role of families in the development of species-consciousness and the role of this consciousness in affecting how people deal with futures and the ideas futures produce.

The First Family

Once again it may be useful to begin at the beginning. In one of the most intriguing archeological finds of recent years, Don Johanson of the Cleveland Museum of Natural History and Maurice Taieb of the Centre Nationale des Recherches Scientifiques in Paris discovered in the Omo Valley of Ethiopia the remains of ten probably prehuman individuals who lived some three million years ago. Judging from the disposition of their bones, the individuals lived in close proximity to one another and apparently died instantly and together, perhaps by drowning in a flash flood—Maurice Taieb's explanation (pers. comm.). What is significant for our purposes is that from analysis of their dentition, it can be concluded that these individuals were related.

It is hardly surprising that individuals found close together in an apparent domestic setting should be members of the same family, even one three million years old. But it is surprising that we take what is contemporary so much for granted, as if it were merely ephemeral and not part of an ancient pattern. Similarly it is not surprising that other animals live in families, although initial surprise greeted the data gathered by primatologist Steven Vessey, who first described the groupings of free-ranging rhesus monkeys at night. Using an image intensifier, Vessey noted that "non-human primates spent almost half their time in darkness and complete understanding of their behavior requires night observations. The decreased activity and increased cohesion of most monkey groups at night suggests the opportunity for simpler analysis of social structures." From observing rhesus at the Caribbean Primate Research Center in Puerto Rico, Vessey discovered that 17 percent of sleeping clusters were of unrelated individuals; 21 percent contained at least one nonrelated member (these clusters were more common before the breeding season); 33 percent were of mother and infant pairs; and, remarkably, 63 percent were composed of maternally related monkeys. (Vessey, 1973:615.) As monkeys cannot identify fathers, nor indeed can observers of them, the factor of fatherhood could not be taken into account; otherwise, certainly, the number of individuals who spent nights together with kinfolk would surely be higher than the 63 percent already described.

I do not know of any data of the kind relating to humans. But might not the corresponding figure be higher than 63 percent? My suspicion is that only in a few places—the centers of large cities, for instance—will more than one-third of the population be composed of single individuals or couples living together without offspring. My guess would be that more than two-thirds of human beings sleep in proximity to genetic kin or kin by marriage.

It may be necessary to remind ourselves of the importance and ubiquity of family life. But what of it? At the very least, knowledge of the generality of family experience compels anyone trying to analyze a psychological or social characteristic of a people to ask precisely what implication family life has for this or that psychological or social characteristic. So with optimism. What are the functions of infancy and childhood in producing attitudes toward the future and expectations about it? How do children develop notions of power and size which affect their own development and which later, as adults, may influence how they think about authority and power?

David Hamburg's insight remains fresh and provocative, that an important way of understanding an animal's biology is to discover what it finds "easy to learn." This same principle presumably applies to humans. Indeed, it may be even more relevant to the study of people because we have such an extended period of learning and highly developed apparatus for learning. But immediately this presents a blatant paradox: if humans are so well-equipped to learn, why the hell is our period of learning so long? One reason of course is that there is so much to learn about adult social life that a long time is needed. There may also be built-in safeguards against too-rapid learning. In societies which can economically afford them there is a surprising number of laws and customs against precocity. For example, one must not enter the labor force too young; one may not drive a motorized vehicle when one is too young; one may not marry when one is too young; one may not seek sexual relations with, particularly, females, who are too young; and even if one is to be a king, one must reign only through regents until one is old enough to be a proper full-grown king. And one may not vote, dispose of property, or do a host of other things until one has arrived at an age considered appropriate for the task or status involved.

With these pedagogical limitations may be another more general one, linked directly to the evolution of familial sociability— suggested by primate sleeping patterns on the one hand and the relatedness of fossil prehumans three million years deep in Ethiopian soil on the other. This is that children require a long period of close emotional relationship with protective adult figures in order to be able to function effectively as adults themselves. If they do not have such relationships, whatever technical skills they may acquire, their performance in life will be inhibited or distorted by basic social incompetence.

Certainly this is all very controversial. Arguments have been made for and against the irreplaceability of warm and extensive parental connection for infants and children. Some, such as those of John Bowlby, and DeVore and Konner (1975), maintain that children require nothing less than an extended and searching connection with an adult figure, usually a mother. Others, such as those of David Cooper (1970) and Ronald Laing (1967), claim just the opposite—that it is precisely in family experience that adult neuroses are born. The question is complicated by the addition of historical analyses, such as that of Aries (1962) and Shorter (1975), who describe a variety of attitudes toward childhood and family life held in other cultures and at other times. These appear to call into question any notion of "a normal childhood," which would also presumably be a healthy one. The historical arguments are particularly provocative. (The Laing-Cooper proposition is, I think, hardly sturdy, more of an aperçu about a small number of persons living under special urban circumstances than an analysis of humans in general [see Rakoff, 1978].) Nevertheless, there is considerable evidence about how important to human children is an extended period of protection and instruction; this emerges most painfully but also clearly in orphanages and foster homes. Children who come from these places consistently suffer greater illness, earlier death, less personal stability and poorer socioeconomic achievement than others. While physical nutrition has been shown to be extremely important for the development of bodily tissues, particularly cortical, social nutrition clearly has an impact also (see Ashley Montagu's review essay, "Sociogenic Brain Damage," 1974).

In the following section I will discuss the relationship between what parents and children do and their well-being in both physical and social terms. Then I shall go on to the related matter of how what communities do about parents and children affects families and finally communities.

The Selfish Genitor and the Commune

People have reproductive strategies just as they have economic, political, religious and sexual ones. They must make a variety of determinations about when, why, with whom, and how they will arrange rearing the next generation. One of the basic distinctions which has to be made and has been by Richard Dawkins (1976) is that between ". . . bringing new individuals into the world . . . and caring for existing individuals . . . respectively childbearing and child caring." (1976: 116.) ". . . an individual . . . has to make two quite different sorts of decisions, caring decisions and bearing decisions . . . caring and bearing are bound to compete with each other for an individual's time and other resources: the individual may have to make a choice, 'Shall I care for this child or should I bear a new one?' "

Various animals adopt various strategies for coping both with the problem of whether or not to bear or rear their own offspring and whether or not to assist or inhibit the rearing of the offspring of others. Some of the solutions for the latter problem are dramatically severe. For example, among the langur monkeys of India competition between males for leadership of troops appears to result in the winner of a contest entering the other's troop and killing all the infants in it. "In each of seven cases," Hrdy reported, "infanticide occurred when males entered the troop from outside it. Females whose infants were killed subsequently exhibited estrous behavior and copulated with the new leader." (Hrdy, 1974:19. See also Hrdy, 1977.) Among the Northern elephant seals of California, an important cause of infant death is attacks on the pups by females other than mothers, and also the failure of females to nurse alien pups when they become separated from their mothers—a less virulent version of the male langur tactic. (LeBoeuf, Whiting and Gantt, 1972.)

Dawkins' book provides a general review of reproductive strategies of a large number of species. Among humans infanticide is not uncommon. But it usually does not occur because of parental despair or rage against children. More typically, it results from more or less formal public policy—*i.e.*, who should get born from which sex, social group, or regional area. (Dickeman, 1975.) Her data show, for example, that in classical India upper-class female children were likely subjects for infanticide because of the general practice of females marrying males higher in the status system than they, which obviously created severe marital matching problems in that tightly structured caste system. But it is far more common for communities to deal with the problem of reproduction less drastically and more providently than this. Let us look now at a case of ideological assertiveness about childrearing in which whole communities, not just families with children, are responsible for these children.

It is not ethically possible to conduct large-scale experiments with human societies. In order to learn what effect one thing has on another it is necessary to look to voluntary experiments, which may arise from natural causes or ideology, to try to discern a connection between social plans or structures and social behavior. One widely known and influential experiment, which tried to affect many of the deeply traditional social relationship members had been reared with or were socially heir to, was the Israeli kibbutz movement. Here men and women all worked. All property was communally owned. All food was prepared in communal facilities and eaten communally. All purchasing and laundry and other services were communal. And, most significantly, all children were reared in communal dormitories by professionally trained members of the wider community.

The emphasis for the individual clearly was on "bearing" and for the community on "caring." A radical full-scale effort was made to alter fundamentally the conditions not only of motherhood but of fatherhood as well, and certainly of childhood. Thus the children of the kibbutz would not suffer from, or inflict on their parents, that closeness and constricting intimacy which infected the bourgeois Euro-American family, and which reflected and sustained the non-socialist inequities which the kibbutz system was designed to remove.

To learn what we could from this experiment, I and Dr. Joseph Shepher, Chairman of the Department of Sociology and Anthropology at the University of Haifa, conducted a comprehensive survey of three generations of kibbutz life (Tiger and Shepher, 1975). We interviewed women of all ages and sought to determine through interviews and archives what the founding mothers and fathers of the kibbutz movement wanted to achieve and how they planned to do it. We examined the excellent statistical information the kibbutzim maintain and collected more information ourselves—on the professional, educational, political, military and social activities of men and women. We surveyed people's attitudes toward sex and equality, and we observed two communities for a year. In all, we tried to relate ideological position to actual practice.

And what did we find? Most strikingly, that there was a persistent and vigorous movement toward greater contact between parents—particularly mothers—and their children. The dormitory system, in which children lived from six weeks of age, gradually yielded to a system of family housing. And throughout the period under study, a three-generation span, even matrilineages emerged, suggesting the force and perhaps primacy of precisely the family system that the kibbutz was so radically structured to end.

As an ideal system, the kibbutz has achieved most of its objectives. It remains generally communal. There is little evidence of an emerging class or élite structure. And while there is a marked division of labor between men and women, about which more later, nevertheless all women work in the labor force and all of them take part—again with important differences from the males—intensely in the public life of the community. It seems then that communal ownership of wealth, political equality, and a general commitment to sharing work are possible to achieve in human communities, at least under the circumstances pertaining to the kibbutzim in Israel. What was once said by some to be biologically, ethically or otherwise impossible, has been achieved. Conscientiously applied ideology works.

What then happened about children and about parents of children? Why did this part of the experiment fail? Why do all the indications point to continued ideological failure? Why is it that elements of the family, three generations later, seem to be reassembling themselves in this otherwise still radical social scheme?

Because an ideological failure may be a biological success. To put the matter directly, would one expect something else from a mammal? Particularly one whose period of dependency is as long as ours and in which the demands of children on their parents are so extensive and beguiling? While a number of other explanations for the regrouping of children and parents can be offered (see for example Kanter, 1976), it appeared to us, from the statements of the many women interviewed, that they preferred closeness with their children because they enjoyed it. David Hamburg has asked the important question: "Why are emotional responses so universal in man and so important in behavior if they have not served some adaptive functions in evolution?" His answers: "Natural selection favors those populations whose members, on the whole, are organized effectively to accomplish crucial adaptive tasks. This is where emotion enters." (Hamburg, 1968:39.) Crude though it may sound, being with one's parents or being with one's children is fun. The enjoyment of the connection betrays its importance. I believe that part of the development of an optimistic or benign sense of the future depends on a social setting in which parents and children can conduct their ancient but always immediate negotiations in a manner appropriate to successful evolution.

When a system such as the kibbutz departs so radically from a central biological pattern, then the resulting strain or sense of incompleteness will either be overcome by events, such as occurred in the kibbutz after three generations, or result in persistent personal and social disruption. What is particularly relevant about the kibbutz case is that a return to a traditional pattern of parenting and childhood came not from the founders of the kibbutz, who were born and reared within this pattern, or even from their sons and daughters, but very significantly from their granddaughters, young women reared entirely on the kibbutz and evidently committed enough to its overall practice to remain attached to the system. (Remaining in the kibbutz, incidentally, is purely voluntary; members may have to resist the blandishments and opportunities of Israeli and world society but they are not coerced from within. Significantly, over 80 percent of kibbutz children remain in the system as adults—an unusually high retention rate for communal settlements of such a radical kind.) The fact is that most kibbutz members choose to live where and in the way they do but also argue for social changes if they want them. It is pertinent, therefore, in connection with the role of emotion in the basic mammalian pattern of mothering, that in the kibbutz case it was young women who argued the most strenuously for family housing. They did so against the repeated objections of males who felt that having children at home was a) ideologically in conflict with the kibbutz endeavor; b) expensive, in that it would involve providing rooms for children who presently lived in less expensive dormitories; c) wasteful, in that equipment for child-rearing would have to be provided for each household rather than for just a single dormitory; and d) inequitable, as it would necessarily involve women in more domestic work and thus cause them to withdraw from the labor force—a serious consideration because there is a chronic labor shortage in the kibbutz and even one hour's less work per female would reduce overall productivity. Despite these arguments the females prevailed. In kibbutz after kibbutz the new pattern has been mandated at the General Assembly, which decides all important matters of kibbutz life. In more and more kibbutzim, children now sleep in their parents' homes.

The kibbutz experience suggests forcefully that ideological pressures are unlikely to disrupt permanently the basic mammalian link between mother and child. (The father-child bond is more disruptable, to judge from the kibbutzim we studied.) It also demonstrates the considerable effectiveness children have in guiding their parents' behavior so as to make the parents yield to the childen more time, attention and resources.

The efficacy of children is largely ignored in studies of family systems. The adult-centered assumption is that it is the wider socioeconomic, political, religious, and moral forces in which the family is embedded which cause parents to act in ways useful to the child. This adult-centered perception lacks a proper respect for the firmness and diligence of children in securing their own interests in their families.

Not unusually this assertion of children involves sacrifices by parents or siblings, sacrifices of time and resources. A biology of this interaction is being worked out. (See for example Dawkins, 1976, Chapter 8, and Trivers, 1974.) One of the goals we can be certain children will seek is a "custom-tailored" pattern of childrearing rather than the formal, professional childrearing practiced by trained persons not kin to the children. Certainly this would be the preference of very young children, and it is pertinent to note that the mothers of young children were the most forceful in arguing for change in the kibbutzim. Perhaps this indicates a greater effectiveness of younger children in securing their mother's time and energy in comparison with older kids.

It is also worth noting that younger kibbutz women are now bearing about four children each. This may be related to some extent to the overall military situation in Israel, in which additional people are always useful, and in part to the perception of Israel as a fortress beleaguered on all sides in the Middle East. However, the military and fortress rationales existed even more dramatically in the earlier years of the kibbutz, when many kibbutzim were, as newer ones still are, frontier communities.

Therefore, having a large number of children should have been pursued as vigorously then as now. This was not the case. Thus the present increase in reproduction seems to be owing to the shift to a more intimate pattern of mothering, which provides greater satisfactions to mothers than before. Apparently they increase their satisfactions by increasing the number of children they have. Moreover, not only do they have four children; they also space them so they will be in contact with young children for perhaps fourteen to twenty years.

A long time indeed, were childrearing regarded as unpleasant by them. The contrary seems to be the case, and all the pressures brought to bear by females in the kibbutz system move in the same direction—toward increasing their family involvement and extending their responsibility for their children. It simply will not do to say that these women are oppressed or beleaguered and therefore are unable to govern the way they wish to live their lives. Such a perception of them is pejorative. The more respectful interpretation of their behavior, which happens also to fit reasonably with what is known about mammalian biology, is that these women are persons engaged in living their life cycles in ways which will provide them with personal pleasure and a sense of contributing healthily to their communities in various ways. Inasmuch as they already have the opportunity to contribute economically through their work, the pressure toward childbirth and childrearing indicates that they wish to add a more personal, reproductive contribution.

The kibbutz case is just one of many. But it appeared to Shepher and me to demonstrate the power of the parent-child connection. It illuminated the function of a long period of childhood and the significance of the commitment of children and parents to each other. Obviously children must learn a great many skills in order to survive as adults even in technologically simple communities—it is often these communities in which the margin for error is narrowest and in which the learning of technical skills is most critical. Taking a cue from Montagu's, Bowlby's, Blurton-Jones's, and others' analyses of the importance of a secure parental situation for the well-being of children, we may also conclude that the learning of social skills, emotional responses, and forms of self-inhibition and repression is part of what is required.

Studies of other primates show plainly that a long period of intimate mothering is necessary to produce youngsters able to deal with novel stimuli, to successfully conduct adult emotional transactions, and in general to deal with the social world in a capable way. As shown in the painful experiments of Harlow (1974) and others with infant monkeys deprived of mothering, the whole scheme of such individuals' social lives is severely truncated. (Harlow, 1974; Hinde, 1974; Hinde and Spencer-Booth, 1971; Patterson and Seay, 1975; Seay, Hansen and Harlow, 1962.) They live with considerable fear at all times, even of known stimuli and certainly of novel ones. Only with very considerable remedial training are they able to engage in adult social interaction, particularly in their reproductive phase.

In a suggestive demonstration of this, Mason has shown experimentally that the more unfamiliar a circumstance to a young chimpanzee the greater is its tendency to clutch at the mother or mother surrogate. (Mason, 1965.) Robert Hinde has shown the effect on the morale and social skill of young rhesus monkeys for as long as three months after their mothers were withdrawn from them for a period of just six days. (Hinde, 1971.) I've already noted Hamburg's stress on the ". . . positive adaptive utility of learning about the problems and opportunities of a particular environment during a protected period of prolonged immaturity." (1968:48.) In humans there is a much longer period of immaturity than among the other primates. This must make even more important the early period of social relations, particularly with the mother. It seems a reasonable deduction given the clear evidence of a high correlation existing between the warmth, congeniality, and steadiness of a young primate's mothering and his or her subsequent success in the social group. Confidence, certainty, curiosity, a willingness to withstand the challenges of the environment—all seem to be positively related to a protypically nurturant experience with the mother or mother surrogate. The absence of such pleasing early experience can be remedied by a rich peer environment provided during childhood and adolescence (here the work of

Suomi and Harlow, 1974, is the most relevant). However, this takes considerable and careful effort of a highly sophisticated kind.

Learning Limits; Extensive Learning Limits Extensively

The simple requirement of considerable parental attention common to other mammals may be more significant for us more complex primates than for the others. (Young, Suomi, Harlow and McKinney, 1973.) If for no other reason, the complexity of human transactions and the wide range of available options ensure that where more can go "right" similarly more can go "wrong." A function of the extended period of human maturation must be to reduce the number of things that go "wrong," simply by virtue of repeated instruction, pressure, discipline, punishment, example, precept. Following Llinas's notion of the role of learning, I am implying that the extended time period of human learning serves to reduce the amount of variation in behavior and consciousness which could exist in a species so open to variation. *The unusually great human capacity for adapting to novel circumstances must also produce pressures toward consistency in the absence of such novel circumstances.* Many other animals acquire coordination and predictability through genetic programs with relatively limited bands of variation. Humans acquire coordination and predictability through extensive learning of a narrow band of acceptable behavior chosen by a particular community from the wide spectrum of possible or available ones. In general, children will seek conformity with their communities for a variety of reasons, ranging from imitation through the possibility of reward to the fear of punishment. Whatever the mechanisms employed in the particular cases, the result is a focusing of communal practices on a limited number of possibilities. (Ebling, 1969:xix.) Both Hamburg's "ease of learning" hypothesis and Llinas's notion of the function of learning for producing similarities between members of a species illustrate the importance of superseding the fruitless controversy whether or not learning and nature are opposed in determining behavior. The interdependence of all aspects of the process should be clear. The vital relationship between the history of our species and our choices in the present should also be clear. The fact of the matter is that it is precisely in species, including man, which depend on extensive learning for the development of social competence that a considerable array of "genetically programmed behavioral dispositions" must be available. (Tiger and Fox, 1966.) As Konrad Lorenz has noted, "All learning ability is based on open programs which presuppose the presence, not of less, but of more information in the genome and so-called innate behavior patterns." (Lorenz, 1977:65.)

Now let me sketch out the overall position. Humans have a wired-in propensity to learn rapidly and massively in the early part of the life cycle. There is a corresponding readiness in the adult to teach as well as a concern with the meaning and moral implication of what is taught. There is a biology for both learning and teaching. It appears learning takes place most effectively in a situation of relative protection. Overall, highly stressed and fearful individuals lacking security and some comfort will be less successful in apprehending what their environment is about and how to deal with it. Learning itself is a pleasurable occupation—children gather information about that which interests them with extraordinary enthusiasm and ease. I am not gainsaying here the phenomenon of cruelty to children and the widespread existence of educational systems which appear to be based on punishment and boredom rather than stimulation and delight. Certainly many children in many societies for long periods of time have suffered from educational and associated systems which forced upon them the most charmless conformity, the most arid emotional experience—all in the name of education. Inhumanity to children can occur in various communities, for example, among the Ik described by Turnbull (1973), or in England during the Industrial Revolution; those seeking an ethnography of deprived childhood need go no further than Charles Dickens's *Oliver Twist*. Yet if one compares these patterns of childrearing with, say, the Bushmen's (DeVore and Konner, 1975) or the Russians' (Bronfenbrenner,

1970), one can assess how closely attitudes to children are related to the experience children have during their educational phase.

In all central human patterns there is considerable variation. In how parents treat children we see the gamut from infanticide (again, however, usually committed for reasons of public policy rather than individual passion or hatred; see Dickeman, 1975) to the stereotypical overprotectiveness of parents who become as dependent on their children's immaturity as their children were in infancy dependent upon them. At one end of the spectrum there are countless cases of babies battered by exasperated, desperate, or cruel parents, and at the other, the bewildered reluctance of inexperienced parents to stimulate autonomy in their growing children. But if nothing else, the dramatic success of the human species in populating the world attests to the efficacy of the familial pattern and also to the evidently highly agreeable if also sometimes extremely swift sexual process which initiates the parental decades.

When all is said and done, the activity of being a parent involves a set of radically unselfish and often incomprehensibly inconvenient activities. Two adults who could otherwise employ their time and resources in pleasurable activities of various kinds elect to seek housing and provide food and other facilities for completely dependent organisms whose personal schedules, furthermore, could not be at greater variance with adult ones, and who will involve their parents, literally for decades, in a compromise between a program of work or pleasure and the requirements of their offspring. It is not altogether remarkable that parents may have one child, if only in error or because of confused expectations of bliss. What is truly remarkable is that most parents have more than one child, the overwhelming majority—an index surely of the existence of room at that inn.

Protection is essential to a child's development. It may also be essential to producing and maintaining the tone of hopefulness about his or her life which stimulates the action and zest invested in the accomplishments of children. Trust, as Erik Erikson has described it, or what the psychiatrists call "ego strength," is available to the child who has the unquestionable support of a family.

A recent study suggests the relationship between parental commitment and children's attitudes toward their own lives. Nancy St. John (1972) interviewed 243 black and white mothers of sixth-grade pupils, administered questionnaires to the children, and compared these with their school records. She found a significant correlation between mother's and child's attitudes toward scholastic success. Supportive behavior by mothers appeared to be influential in ensuring success even when the usually potent influences of socioeconomic and I.Q. level were held constant. Surprisingly, "maternal estimations and aspirations are more optimistic than those of their children, but are better predictors of children's attitudes than is family socioeconomic status." (Ibid.:242.)

No one will be surprised that there is a connection between a mother's sense of a child's life and that life. The connections between parents and children are many and elaborate. The contribution which parents make to their offsprings' adult lives can best be measured by contrasting those lives with the lives of persons who as children were deprived of a full range of parental commitment. A number of the outcomes of such deprivation have been outlined by Rohner (1975), who reviews data connecting rejection and deprivation to a variety of characteristics such as unduly aggressive or hostile behavior, excessive dependence, poor self-esteem, emotional withdrawal, and various behavioral disorders and psychopathology. Jacobs et al. (1972) have suggested a statistical relationship between maternal rejection and allergic responses in children. Dealing with more positive matters, Mary Jo Bane has persuasively and incisively described the durability of family patterns even in Pan American societies supposedly experiencing a decline in the importance of family life. She describes, principally on the basis of statistical and demographic information but also with a detailed sense of the significance of this material, how persistently American people of all classes and ethnicities move toward family life. Indeed they insist upon a generous measure of familial and parental experience as part of their lives. She also analyzes in detail the costs and benefits of alternative arrangements for childbearing and -rearing and concludes that while there are plain benefits, particularly for females able to find interesting work, other economic and emotional advantages are not necessarily as extensive as, for example, the proponents of generalized daycare claim. (Bane, 1976:82.) As she notes, "The facts—as opposed to the myths—about marriage, child-rearing and family ties in the United States today provide convincing evidence that family commitments are likely to persist in our society. Family ties, it seems clear, are not archaic remnants of a disappearing traditionalism, but persisting manifestations of human needs for stability, continuity, and nonconditional affection." (*Ibid.:* 141.) She goes on to indicate that there appear to be important conflicts between public ethics of equality, meritocracy and impartiality in the conduct of social life and family ties, which are non-meritocratic and are based on private needs and wishes and may well be at odds with declared public ethics.

This problem persists in any structure larger than a family. The web of familial affections must somehow be penetrated by a clear force of public objectivity. Rules against nepotism are the most obvious. What is confusing about this general problem, at least in North America in the 70's, is that the anti-familial ethic has achieved almost unchallengeable stature in much liberal, ideological discourse. As Bane concludes her argument: "The historical trend has long been toward greater equality and it is unlikely to come to a halt now. On the other hand the strong commitment to family institutions and values which is such a persistent theme in American society is no more likely to go away. It is time to accept the persistent tension between family and public values and to design creative ways of living with both." (*Ibid.:* 143.)

In the Family/State

Societies with strong attachments to public equality may try to realize equality by stressing the importance of public over private life. In the kibbutz, as we have seen, the emphasis in the early years—until recently—was on public responsibility of parents to the commune rather than on private responsibility to their offspring; in the first generation couples were even expected to seat themselves apart during meals and assemblies. (Tiger and Shepher, 1975:37.) Similar tensions between family and polity existed in the early days of the post-1949 Chinese revolution. There was particular drama in the confrontation between the deeply traditional and highly structured familial pattern of traditional China with the radical, apparent anti-familialism of Mao and his followers.

Many radical or revolutionary movements try to restructure the family system, presumably in order to acquire an additional lever of influence over citizens who might otherwise respond unduly to the blandishments of the familiar rather than the lure of the possible. For example, early Christian procedure involved such a renunciation of familial ties. It is interesting that this renunciation usually emphasizes the paternal far more than the maternal force—the hostility appears to be encouraged against the father rather than the mother. For well-known psychological reasons this may be quite strategic for boys, who may turn against their paternal figure even when no revolutionary or radical ardor fires them. And whereas in terms of conventional psychiatric wisdom it would be expected that females would find their major enemies among maternal figures, interestingly most female radicals in feminist programs have directed their primary animus against the male group or groups.

So for both sexes the males are the sources of antagonism, an ethologically or primatologically understandable situation, even if it is also unduly baffling for the males themselves, whose capacities to understand antipathy and respond to it may be considerably more limited than their capacity to stimulate it. But let us not expend much energy on sympathizing with them. Since males have more or less consistently and universally maintained control of political systems it is scarcely unexpected or inappropriate that they should be the major target for those who wish to change these systems.

Religious organizations try to bridge the discontinuity between family structure and general public belief—for example, by using family terminology in religious life. The most obvious case is that of the Catholic church, in which religious functionaries are given familial names—Father, Sister, Brother, Mother. The concept of Catholic social structure itself derives from a familial expectation. The relationship of the devout to spiritual forces is also mediated by familial terms—God the Father, the Son of God, the Holy Mother, the Holy Father. Whether or not this identification of family with religion serves the family is another matter. Does religious organization buttress the authority systems within the family by surrounding the family with an external force of apparent potency? So it would seem. On the other hand, perhaps only because there is an original system of authority within the family can a relationship exist between family and church. Most likely the connection between these small family units and large religious ones is symbiotic. In any case, the connection clearly is a complex one.

The relation of family to church bears directly on our central theme, because the control of the future through religious organization and the effort to envisage and expect a benign future are evidently related to individuals' familial experience in the present and past. Certainly the connection between religious organization and important family experiences—such as birth, baptism, initiation, marriage and death—is widespread. While it is scarcely surprising that organizations claiming power over life and death should confront people during the various critical events of their lives, it is surprising that organizations which are familial and those which claim to deal with the future are so nearly identical.

The relationship between families and other structures is always an artifact of many influences. The relationship between political revolution and hostility to the family is not one-to-one; nor is the opposite the case—that established organizations such as major churches are necessarily pro-familial. Examples run the gamut from the fierce anti-familialism of Maoist China and early Christianity to the strong affirmative connectedness between individual families and the larger family of the Catholic church. One trend seems clear, however, and that is that no particular family pattern necessarily holds a patent on producing offspring of either a radical or conservative political bent. Indeed, if one defines political action in terms not of the ideological positions of the wider community but of the emotional patterns of the particular family, then the words "revolutionary" and "conservative" come to have quite different meanings. For example, Peter Marris, in his sensitive analysis of sadness, social change and revolution, has argued that particularly in revolutionary times will a conservative focus, such as the family, provide people with that amount of consistency Marris regards as finally necessary for a coherent social life. (Marris, 1974:170.) My uses here of the words "conservative" and "radical" or "revolutionary" refer more to emotional modalities than to specific positions on the right-left political spectrum. As we know, social movements which are radical with respect to, for example, the ownership of property, the control of public resources, and the ideology within which social behavior takes place, such as in Russia under Stalin, may nonetheless be extremely conservative emotionally and constitute for members of the population involved a highly stable, for many too stable, force in the society. Alternatively one can see that some upper-class groups committed to very traditional notions of the political sanctity of rules about private property— privileged elites, etc.—may comport themselves emotionally, psychologically, sexually, and familially in ways that seem quite radical to their communities. My point is that, because of the vital connection between the development of a sense of the future as either benign or ominous and the natural conservatism of the family, managers of either radical or conservative political movements must possess an attitude to the family. They must determine whether they will use its structure cooperatively or seek to create a new energy by denying the family's validity and thus presumably developing greater psychological mobility among its political adherents.

A series of questions seems to arise here and, though I do not intend to discuss them in detail, they should be noted. For example, what is the connection between persons deprived by their families of personal optimism and future benignness and

claims made on the state or similar structure for wonderful outcomes? Does the fascist expectation that the superordinate state
will provide both order and glory, if one obeys it, arise from a
particular kind of childhood which was rather less than more
affected by parental warmth and assurance? Does the authoritarian personality emerge from families which demand obedience as the cost of avoiding punishment or from those in which
equality is the norm?

I am not saying that lovingly reared and hopeful people will
necessarily be politically quiescent or conservative. On the contrary, a person brought up in the "ideal" congenial fashion to
which I have alluded may well be a personality committed to
extending equity in the social structure and thus he or she may
be urgently committed to seeking social justice. Though this
may lead to radical political activity, it does not mean that the
individual will be experiencing behavior radical to his or her
own person; indeed there will likely be a consistency of commitment and purpose throughout this person's life. There will
be no discontinuity between family equity and affection and its
political projection in the larger social sphere. (For an effort to
relate the process of youthful outrage and cortical procedures,
see Davies [1976], and my own comments, largely critical, on
this [1976].) I think Peter Marris is correct in perceiving that
what he calls "the conservative impulse" is a constant feature
of human societies and that this impulse results from familiar
social arrangements which provide an agreeable or at least tolerable sense of the future. This, I argue, has clear origins in the
family system, that system described as so sturdy by Bane
(1976), Rohner, and others.

This benign process is conservative in another quite critical
way. It provides the basis for its recapitulation in succeeding
generations. While a correlation apparently exists between
being beaten as a child and being a child beater as a parent,
individuals given affection and the promise of its continuity
will have reason enough to maintain this pattern during their
own parenthood. Unhealthy traits, of course, do emerge from
healthy families. Children reared in the agreeable way I've described may emerge as complacent and insensitive members of

grievously unfair societies. They may also confuse their own rote and thoughtless behavior as parents with strongly felt traditional warmth.

And, on the other hand, some increment of personal competence and energy may result from precisely the challenge of parental inattention or absence. An intriguing suggestion of this appears in research underway in the laboratory of Dr. Herman Roiphe of the Department of Psychiatry at Mt. Sinai Hospital in New York. Roiphe and his associates have been studying the behavior of children between nine months and two years of age. They find that when infants at this early stage are separated from their principal caretaker (though they are minded by capable and responsible people), in as few as five days they will yield an increase in verbalization, in various assertive motor patterns and, with striking frequency some days later, in a physical illness. In other words, when the child is separated from its source of security it seeks more urgently than ever to expand its skills. There is an increase in smiling, too, suggesting that the infant is seeking to assert its power over the environment more effectively.

These findings about speech and pre-speech are fascinating. If the infant is still at the stage of making relatively undifferentiated sounds before the separation, he will make more of these, and make them more rapidly, after the separation. Similarly, if the child has a vocabulary of ten words, say, before the separation, he will increase it to twenty or thirty words after the separation. If the child is able to produce syntax, he will create forms more complex and involved, using more syntax, after the separation—again with a disproportionate and sudden increment. The fact that both illness and increased achievement alike result from these separations may suggest how ambiguous precocity may be. For some reason, as I consider these matters, the image keeps recurring to me of the gangs of Roman children five or six years old who foraged for survival in Rome after the Second World War. For them, precocity was essential; but it would be interesting to know what long-range effects, if any, were visited on the survivors' lives. (Meierhoffer, 1972.)

This is an utterly perplexing puzzle, at least to me. On the one hand, it appears that children learn best in circumstances of security, after they have been given reason to trust their environment and to attend to what adults and/or peers teach them about it. At the same time, stress may stimulate learning just as trust does. Is what is learned in trust the same as what is learned in stress? And is it learned in the same way? Are certain skills, attitudes or beliefs learned more readily under certain stimuli? Can we begin even to speculate about significant differences in school and other performances of middle-class and working-class kids in the context of different styles of learning which may exist in different social classes?

That this would be a useful area of research is suggested by the work of Basil Bernstein and others in London, who discovered a marked difference in coding patterns, use patterns and forms of meaning between the language of working-class English children and that of middle-class ones. (Bernstein, 1971.) Have these differences to do with patterns of mothering and fathering, or are they more tightly linked to the enriched environments available to wealthier children? What are we to make of the unduly ignored finding of the Coleman Report (1968), which indicated that the best predictor of success in the school system was not whether one was white or black, rich or poor, but whether one was from a small as opposed to a large family. Children of small families do better in school than children of large families. Has this to do with the amount of parental attention available to each child as he or she struggles to find a path between the comfort of routine—and hence non-achievement—and the excitement of achievement?

Further, do boarding schools, and particularly those which take children from their families in primary grades, create a likelihood that the products of these schools will be less concerned than other children with personal contentment and more committed, even if from necessity, to successful careers? (This argument has been made, at least, about the relationship between the British Colonial Service and the boarding school system in England. [Wilkinson, 1963.]) Marris also portrays the typical member of the British Colonial Services as a middle-class, university-educated individual with no personal ambiguity about self or community, able to sustain a pattern of life and work in situations of almost complete isolation from the society which produced him. Marris's point is that the colonial system depended upon individuals raised to be ignorant of, insensitive to, or undeterred by what might be the psychological needs and vulnerabilities of people very different from themselves. [Marris, 1974:13.])

So some element of stress may be, on balance, useful to a child. It may help him prepare for environments more challenging than the family. The most dismal symbol of the extreme of this, of course, was provided by Harlow and his associates, who showed that mothers deprived of mothering were themselves incapable mothers—they would either forcefully reject their offspring or betray consternation about what to do with them. We have seen that some rehabilitation of the wounded victims of such experience is possible, though careful and rather demanding arrangements must be made. Surely it is also true that children will respond enthusiastically to the improved and agreeable circumstances of outside care and social life, and subsequently they may display significantly less psychological evidence of rejection. (For a review of this, see Rohner, 1975:59 *et seq.*) This possibility reinforces the view that interventions in the lives of disadvantaged children may have permanently ameliorating effects on their capability and their enjoyment of life. Undoubtedly, early experience is extremely influential in children's lives. But subsequent experience is not without influence either; therefore, particularly for those already deprived, any remedial benefits are useful. So even government programs, such as the "Head Start" venture, may provide extremely useful opportunities. It appears that at least by the (questionable) standards of politician-bureaucrats such programs frequently fail; however, this may be more a comment on the programs of these very politician-bureaucrats than on the purposes they are supposed to serve.

The harsh controversy about I.Q., early environment, and subsequent performance is frequently cast in racial terms. Much of the discussion focuses on the futility of seeking remedy for individuals who are allegedly genetically inadequate—

a clearly political judgment. In my view the function of I.Q. tests has been magnified out of all proportion and the tests and scores become metaphors for another discussion. I do not believe that they are adequately free of those cultural influences which would almost ensure performance differences between different groups. I do not believe they are at all attentive to the implication of sex differences, since questions which distinguish between the sexes are usually removed from the tests. Finally, that they predict performance in the educational system is scarcely surprising since the educational system is itself a reflection of a set of cultural values enshrined in pedagogical procedures. In effect, the dismal discussion *has* been political, and *is* racist.

At the same time it has had one redeeming feature—its contrast to discussions of race in the past. Once the discussions revolved about such massive phenomena as master races or biologically depraved races or classes. But now the entire controversy focuses pettily on a few percentage points of difference in performance on arbitrary tests of questionable value and relevance. While it is small comfort that death camps are unlikely to result from I.Q. tests, nevertheless the effect of expanded human compassion about race since the Second World War and the wide understanding of the biological truth that race is a very trivial biological fact have contributed to a fortunate trend away from racist diagnostics.

The attention paid to I.Q. statistics rather than to the obvious social and economic circumstances underlying the performance of children creating the statistics is an index of a larger problem—the effort to escape social reality by retreat into mock technical numerology. Rather than observing children carefully and evaluating their performance within a long period of time within the context of some well-understood standards of educational activity, it is more attractive to create assessments on the basis of an almost surgical encounter of child with test in a brief, finite and teacher-controlled situation. The general trend toward machine-graded tests is another version of the process of technologizing a life process, the educational one, which should by definition be extremely personal and socially mediated. When decisions about how to treat people are made by the numbers supposed to represent these people rather than by means of encounter with the people themselves, then there is a failure to use precisely those social skills and resources which are the patrimony of the species. It is certainly easier to push the "on" button of a grading machine than to conduct a searching conversation, but that this is done in the name of biological equity—or, worse, meritocracy—is laughable.

We know that children can improve their I.Q. scores after they have been immersed in a benign and helping environment. We also know that children who are poor students can improve their performance when they are put in classes with bright children. While there obviously are differences between people and some of these differences have to do with what is called intelligence, the differences are not permanent and they may also depend for their emergence on a social system. For example, in order for bright children to act as the intellectual leaders they will presumably become, should they not be in classes with less bright individuals, if only to learn the skills they have? Should they not also learn to share their own skills? Why should schools have elite classes whose programs are accelerated to make the race to maturity more rapid? Even in a mobile society which values speed there is presumably no reason for speed and efficiency to be as important for children as for vehicles. After all, in practical terms, how can the fast be defined as such without the slow, and the slow without the fast? I think variety is not the spice, but the protein, of nature's systems.

I have so far been discussing the matter of family life from the perspective of children—what they need, and what they get. My emphasis has been on the functions of families for children. In a moment I will go on to discuss the functions of reproductive and family life for parents and the wider community and how these functions are related to a sense of and control of the future. I want to conclude this part of the chapter by recalling the principle described earlier: that the work of the learning system, particularly in complicated animals and certainly in man, is to turn individual variation into communally acceptable similarities. We can expect families to try to maximize their children's advantages and opportunities. In this respect the function of a school system, along with the other agencies outside the family, is to create and maintain a structure within which additional socially agreeable ways of living are learned. This presumably applies equally to the desperate over-achiever balancing on a high wire erected by ambitious parents and the lethargic, probably hungry child engaged by little in his school and urged to little by his family. The family is the first and primary means through which children learn about themselves and their futures and how to deal with these. What goes on outside the family, in school and play, must usefully translate these often wordless understandings into soluble problems and plans for a useful life.

The advantages families can bestow or withhold from children are clear and they may persist despite rigorous, hearty, and committed efforts to exclude familial influence from educational ranking. For example, in a study of some 14,250 children in a sector of Warsaw in which the Polish government had established school attendance without regard to social class, the mental performance remained clearly and strongly linked to parental occupation and education: ". . . an egalitarian, social policy executed over a generation failed to override the association of social and family factors with cognitive development that is characteristic of more traditional industrial societies." (Firtowska et al., 1978:1358.) But this and similar reports should be less a counsel of despair than a stimulus for continued and more formidable efforts to achieve equity.

Consenting Parents

Why have children? Why become a parent? Why do parents do what they do? What happens when many people have no children? What happens when there are few children? What happens to grown-ups because of children? These are all questions which are implicit in the theme of this chapter and which also are rarely asked, if only because the answers to them seem so obvious—or, at any rate, so grand. However, a biological perspective on human social behavior must perforce look directly at what reproduction or its absence means for the lives of individuals, if only because the relationships between the genetic past, present and future of people are so close to our reproductive patterns. Perhaps we are the spitting images of our parents or oddly evocative hints of our great-grandparents. Perhaps our children are temperamentally like us or furiously different and opposed. Nevertheless our flesh and bones and the behavior that animates them are irretrievably linked through our genes. I've already tried to show, in the story of Jesus, how even elaborate human symbols may be linked with this most elemental process, the reproductive. Now I want to try to describe aspects of this process which are related to the principal theme, the forms and functions of optimism. In doing so I will focus on what adults do and why and what its effects are on children, also the consequences of childlessness. Of necessity, I shall examine both technically complicated matters and matters relating to social policy—issues such as contraception, abortion, family limitation and population decline. But I think no serious discussion of how people think of and deal with the future can avoid careful attention to those who might populate such a future—born and unborn children—and the circumstances within which these children will themselves come to reproductive age. If our knowledge of mortality makes us aware of death our understanding of reproduction may provide an intimation of transcendence.

Sexual intercourse is highly pleasurable. It has been estimated that for each time intercourse is intended for procreation it is enjoyed for its own pleasurable sake 2,000 times. (Ackerman, 1972:132.) Given human zest for copulation, it is remarkable that there are so few children in the world rather than so many. People appear to seek sexual congress relentlessly, imaginatively, often at great expense of spirit and resources, and it is rarely a wholly casual matter. Before, during and after the advent of the *Kama Sutra*, aids to lovers have offered advice and instruction ranging from elegant variation through better marriages to the improvement of communal relations by means of group sexual activity. Only extremely self-confident communities, such as Roman Catholic ones in the past, are able to control the reproductive consequences of sexual intercourse by simply instructing people not to have intercourse unless they are in a suitable married situation or, as the Chinese did after the Revolution, by markedly reducing the importance of sexual stimuli by decreeing antisexual costuming and by restricting early marriage and promoting neo-Victorian morals. (Djerassi, 1974.) The persistent and extremely explosive growth of human population in modern times suggests that enthusiasm for sexual activity persists even among people who, according to one report, would like to have far fewer children than they do have. In a sample of people in ten countries, including India, Jamaica, Korea, Malaysia, Philippines, Puerto Rico, Thailand, Turkey, Hungary and Japan (Udry, Bauman and Chase, 1973:366), it was discovered that actual birthrates were more than three times wanted birthrates. In some societies—India, Jamaica, Korea, Puerto Rico, Thailand—and in the two more developed countries, Hungary and Japan, actual rates were half again as large as wanted rates. The annual rate of national increase, even in those two countries, was at least twice the desired one—a major improvement over, for example, Jamaica, where the actual rate of national increase was six times the desired rate, or Korea, where it was thirteen.

The rapid growth in human population is indication enough of the commitment people have at least to sexual intercourse if not also, as is likely, to children. It is also pertinent that the affair of sexual encounter is not solely an erotic, physical one, but typically involves a more or less greater component of symbolic and social ambience. Even the crudest form of encounter, sex purchased with money from a stranger, is not without a mise en scène which in the case of, for example, the classic bordello may mean very sumptuous and elegant appointments indeed. From the one extreme of the prostitute for hire—male and female—to the other of almost totally symbolic love, as among the troubadours, for example, there is an inevitable and critical component of cognitive activity. Humans have quite successfully managed to employ vividly the large brain in the service of even a process as ancient as reproduction. Characteristically, we also managed to generate a staggering series of cognitive accompaniments to the basic process. Not only do we enjoy the physical sensations involved in sexual contact, but we are endlessly interested too in the social and symbolic aspects of it.

In the context of David Hamburg's comment that the function of emotions is to induce states of feeling in us important for our evolution and contemporary survival, let us consider love affairs. While particular love affairs or particular phases of them, particularly their endings, may be painful to the lovers, the real and fictional energy and commitment which are mobilized during love affairs suggest how very effectively the evolutionary process has assured our faithful and persistent attention to the reproductive needs of the species. Never mind that now, and indeed for most love affairs at most times, reproduction is not the paramount intention. In many cases it may be the least desirable of goals insofar as lovers can articulate goals. For example, homosexual love affairs may involve much the same set of forces and valences as heterosexual ones do, even though no possibility of reproduction exists. So loving evokes emotions which were important and successful in our evolution. When we love now we hark back to what we did so usefully then. With the homosexual love affair the heterosexual one shares the characteristic that the particular relationship is held by the partners to promise unusual, important, and in any event necessary benefits to both parties. I suppose that in general, particular lovers usually cease being the particular lovers of each other, thus mocking one aspect of the turmoil of the encounter—that it is total and forever. Love affairs begin on the road to a happy ending.

The ingredient of expectation or even certainty of this happy ending distinguishes the love affair from the more prosaic encounter, for example, arranged marriages, coerced by kinship systems. This tempestuous quality—of the promise of sudden improvement, glory, glamour—presumably underlies the danger love affairs pose to established systems of kinship. Yet this stormy and attractive quality undoubtedly accounts for the reappearance of love affairs in life cycle after life cycle.

While there is a difference betwen love affairs conducted by people who are married and by those who are unmarried, the one quality they all share is direness. In the case of the unmarried, a love affair can be a preliminary step to a potentially radical change in life with sudden alterations in dwelling patterns, personal economy, amounts of loneliness, and certainties about self-worth. For married persons, an affair outside of marriage can provide a cognate but different set of possible and hopeful outcomes—the restoration of an earlier reproductive tonus, greater pleasure, the possibility for social and sexual experience of a different kind. In the statistical scheme of things, most affairs are doomed to a conclusion without issue. Yet they are part of the system of sexual selection and may have, if children do result, implications for ethnic or class homogeneity and heterogeneity, or genetic variability. But these concerns are not normally the concerns of individuals. What may be at stake for them is more likely energy, time, funds, self-respect, sense of confidence, and even, should an affair end drastically, the ability to face one's socio-sexual future with some benign sense of capacity.

The costs may be high, but many of the attendant benefits of the affair, apart from the physical ones, are considerable. For people who do not enjoy living alone the simple avoidance of solitude or loneliness is an important advantage. It is scarcely surprising that loneliness (which so adversely affects children deprived of early social experience) induces adults to enter into perhaps difficult relationships, often with people with whom under other circumstances they might not become so involved—but who, in the context of solitude, become tolerable and sometimes even necessary in a dire way. When love affairs do end to the satisfaction of both parties, either when they separate or do not, then the clear hazard of putting one's private and public person at risk has been worthwhile. In the case of older males and females who succeed in regenerating their own socio-sexual vitality by associating with a younger partner (this seems to apply to both heterosexual and homosexual persons), then a biological coup has been made. These individuals have gained a disproportionate amount of the potential reproductive opportunities of their communities. At the same time, the risk in these cases of appearing or feeling ridiculous or manipulated is not absent either; the gainer of a temporary advantage in this contest for the ardor, time and bodies of other people may lose disproportionately should the pairing end badly.

I have used the love affair as a way of showing how forceful connections are in the reproductive system. No family or kinship system can or does ignore the urgency of the valence between males and females. All make more or less elaborate rules about what may happen, with whom, and what are the privileges, penalties, and implications of particular matings. Perhaps the lyrical happiness of lovers is too troubling or depressing to those unfavored by the bliss. Apart from the brief stage of post-coital *tristesse*, which may simply be fatigue and oxygen deficiency, lovers are usually seen as happy. Possibly in compensation, lovers may be somewhat punitively required to subject themselves to a series of disciplines ranging from formally happy bourgeois marriages on the one hand to the dreadful fate of Romeo and Juliet, who too ardently loved against a too formidable structure of human antipathy.

The sexual scenario may not involve even the prospect of the birth of children for the individuals involved. Proof of that is, as I've noted, that homosexuals can be as stirred by a love affair despite its infertility as someone heterosexual and fertile. The energy and pleasure in preparing for reproduction are easily divorcable from the end product to which the overall process is biologically attuned. This is also obvious from the fact that the increased availability of contraception quickly results in at least some decline in birthrates, revealing plainly that people are happy to enjoy sexual congress without bearing children. (Westoff, 1976:40.) Though there are some complications in this proposition, which I will discuss shortly, sexual relations nevertheless can be readily enjoyed entirely for their own sake. Moreover, that they are so enjoyed world wide demonstrates that they must make people feel good. And they make people feel good because an ancient, deeply programmed biological process is enacted in sexual activity—that process which maintains the size of the population, causes it to grow or decline, and connects the passionate present to the social future.

Strategies of Loving

The fact that children in certain cases cannot be born from intercourse does not mean that the emotional processes evolved to produce erotic connection are absent from it. Endless songs, stories, films, ballets, plays, and totemic pinup men and women are all features of a process of symbolizing, reminding and maintaining tonus for and skill in an old and influential system of biology. With greater or lesser success and avidity, both men and women seek to keep themselves as youthful as possible, often lying about or withholding their ages. If they undergo plastic surgery, exercise themselves, cosmetize themselves, or otherwise confect themselves, this is presumably not unrelated to the stern and coercive fact that younger bodies are better child-producers and that aging implies not only a lessening of one's period of life ahead but a decrease in the likelihood that that period will be reproductively effective. It is superficial to attribute only to "vanity" a female's concern with wrinkled facial skin or a male's with the loosening muscles of the belly. These are signs of age and thus of declining fecundity. The increase in congenital abnormalities in babies produced by older as opposed to younger women—thirty-five appears to be the statistically crucial age—is one practical index, but only one, of the general preference of men for younger rather than older partners. The problem of aging falls unequally on males and females. Added to the other structural inequalities which females suffer in most communities, as far as work, money and power are concerned, even in the sexual connection inequality is harbored by the very tissues. In discussing the politics of pregnancy and the different strategies which males and females employ in their sexual lives, Kristin Luker notes ". . . for women, unlike men, there is an advantage of striking a bargain as soon as possible because they largely bargain with ascribed characteristics (beauty, youthfulness, 'sexiness') while men bargain with achieved characteristics (power, income, prestige). Thus women's potential depreciates over time; they get older, less beautiful, and less sexually attractive with the passage of years. Men, on the other hand, get richer, more powerful, and have more status with the passage of time—or it is assumed that they might. As a consequence the time variables structuring the bargaining of the two sexes run in opposite directions." (Luker, 1975:121.) The most drastic reflection of this—a situation known at least anecdotally to most people— is the pattern in which a male proceeds through one phase of family life perhaps having several children with one woman and then at a point in their lives when she is, in Luker's terms, less "attractive" and he more efficacious, possibly wealthy, and hence more attractive, a divorce will be created with the husband becoming linked to another, usually younger, female. He may or may not restart the reproductive cycle, but this form of serial polygamy graphically illustrates the manner in which sexual inequity can be maintained in a non-polygamous society. Insofar as it appears women, at least in the U.S., are entering marriage later than the women of several decades ago—those presumably in the situation I've just described—the disparity between the ages of wives and of potential second wives may become less marked and hence less distracting to males. (The U.S. Bureau of the Census, Current Population Report: "Population Characteristics, 1975.")

I have tried to begin to describe connections between optimism and the family. My reasons for doing so are quite clear, and not the least of them is that it appears unlikely that any human phenomenon as important as I believe optimism to be should have no relationship to something as important as we know families to be, so there is at least a programmatic reason for reviewing the connection. But there may be other reasons as well. So many certainties surrounding human sexuality and its reproductive implications have been questioned or shattered since the Second World War that it becomes a matter of some public urgency to inquire about the consequences of socio-sexual and reproductive patterns for communities' generalized attitudes to the present and the future. I am *not* invoking the cliché of the decadent community whose passage into moral and political decline is accompanied by a decay of familial stability and sexual probity. Indeed there is no reason why major changes in socio-sexual behavior should not produce citizens with a generous attitude to themselves and to their futures. And there is also no reason to assume that children born to communities which organize their reproductive lives differently from those in the past will necessarily be damaged, or be markedly different from children raised under other circumstances. Nevertheless some of the changes are in themselves interesting, and they become more so when inspected in the context of the proposition about optimism at the heart of this book.

In discussing the social changes which affect family life, I will be dealing with aggregates of people, large groups, people in classifications, and not individuals. Obviously individuals or small groups of people will act in ways quite different from the patterns described here. Yet it is important to survey the behavior of communities in the aggregate.

What do we see? There is a decrease in the age difference between males and females in first marriages. In the United States, males born in 1900 were about four years older than their wives, whereas those born forty-five years later were only two years older. (The U.S. Bureau of the Census, 1975.) There have been major changes in employment opportunities for women and corresponding attitudinal changes as well, so that both women and men can, if they choose, live their personal and economic lives with greater freedom than their parents did, and with concepts of behavior much less stereotyped. Marked increases in divorce and remarriage rates as well as a general decline in birthrates all reflect considerable change in how people choose and maintain intimate relationships and whether they will undertake the lengthy and demanding steps of child-rearing in the context of these relationships.

Various other changes in reproductive behavior suggest on the one hand the reproductive zest of young people and on the other the social and psychological mayhem which can occur when such reproduction takes place outside a structure suited to raising offspring. There were indications in 1977 that the behavior of young women was relatively "traditional." Young women of fifteen to twenty conceived children outside of marriage in proportions described as epidemic. In other words, despite the widespread availability of relatively inexpensive and effective contraception, young women and men conduct themselves in a way widely defined by their communities as reckless and irresponsible. Whatever the causes of their behavior and the long-term consequences of it, for their own lives and that of the community, it is clear that these young women and men have responded in an unexpected way to what had been hailed as pronounced and fundamental shifts in socio-sexual roles. I noted earlier that young people were the most effective reproducers in the population and I think it is reasonable to predict that, other things being equal, they will try to reproduce; I believe that is what is involved in this sudden rise in pregnancy among very young women. Even though there are ample reasons to believe that postponing parenthood offers increased opportunity for educational and financial betterment and even to improve marital adjustment and lower the probability of divorce, a large group of young people in the population appear not to respond to these obvious possibilities but rather to impulsive enthusiasms. This is not at all unusual in the larger perspective; evidence suggests that conception of offspring before marriage has been a frequent occurrence and occasionally even an inducement to marriage. (Whelan, 1972 a,b.)

These findings make all the more remarkable the recent U.S. Supreme Court decision holding that federal funds cannot be used to provide abortions on demand, except to women subjected to rape or incestuous intercourse. If it is the mark of a civilized community to be magnanimous toward the frailties of its members, then it is curious that a community is willing to spend money on reformatories but unwilling to spend money on medical care for unwed expectant mothers. Human beings who are youthful and healthy, who engage in sexual intercourse and also conceive children, are acting in biologically the

most healthy way. Yet they are plainly unable to deal providently with the babies they produce and there is no question
but that the consequence of their compulsory parenthood will
be children highly likely to suffer drastically from their parents'
or mother's poverty in experience, maturity, and social advantage. I do not want to become involved in a discussion directly
of the ethics of abortion, which is an exceedingly complex and
profound matter. But since the issue has been raised at the
public level, it must be discussed not only in the context of its
profundity but also in the context of the conventional public
consequences which follow from liberal or nonexistent abortion
policies. It is also necessary to recognize that for many people
abortion is a gruesome fact, and it is well known that medical
practitioners rarely like working where abortions occur. I've
been told (by Evelyne Sullerot, pers. comm.) that in Eastern
European countries medical practitioners who are political dis-
sidents may be assigned as a lingering, long-range punishment
to abortion wards, and in North America it appears to be not
unknown that unpopular or unwanted hospital personnel are
likewise assigned to this area of hospital care, the sooner to
urge them to leave the institution. However, since medical personnel are also expected to be sophisticated about their own
feelings toward patients and professional about these, abortion
is presumably not an impossible act to ask them to perform.

There appears to lurk in the Court ruling and the popular
constituency it represents the assumption that because people
can choose whether or not to have intercourse—and if they do,
to use contraception—the results of their behavior should be at
their own risk and expense. The same policy position could be
taken toward persons who receive public monies for treatment
of lung cancer brought on by smoking or youths who go on
drugs. Presumably because a particularly elaborate kind of
pleasure is involved in intercourse the community, speaking
through its courts, felt it must limit its support.

But turn the matter around. If it is true, as I think it is, that
young women are "designed" keenly to want to make love,
become pregnant, and then mother—and many do—then are
not those women who present themselves for the depressing,

often painful and deeply dispiriting abortion process among the most responsible and provident of all? For example, a study of women in Hawaii, which had the first nonrestrictive abortion legislation in the U.S., revealed that the reasons most frequently cited by abortion patients were "I am not married" (36 percent); "I cannot afford to have a child at this time" (26 percent); "a child would interfere with my education" (16 percent); "a child would interfere with my job or other activity" (12 percent); and "I think I'm too young to have a child" (9 percent). These are very prudent, sensible reasons and the most often cited one ("I am not married") may have a strong moral overtone as well as a considerable amount of economic and practical sense. So while the act of seeking an abortion as described in this study (Steinhoff, Smith and Diamond, 1972; see also Watters, 1976) can be seen as a measure of responsibility, the public has announced through its judiciary that it is not responsible to help. I will go on to discuss why it is the very availability of female-controlled contraception which makes abortion so much more important to women, and hence communities, than it was before. But for the moment it seems appropriate to acknowledge that individuals engaged in a process of the deepest hopefulness, however impractical and thoughtless they may be, and who are willy-nilly the people on whom the community will partly depend for its own replenishment, are rejected by their community at a time when they are the most patently vulnerable. The consequences of this rejection, the birth of a child without what may be an adequate network of time, resources and people around it, is the result.

But why does the vexed problem of legal abortion exist? Let us use North American society as the basis for a discussion, a continent where various effective contraceptives are quite readily available to men and women. While it is true that younger women in particular may not fully understand the technology or implication of various means of contraception, they cannot be entirely without understanding of the contraceptive process and without resources for handling it. One need merely recall that at the same time they are held to be unsophisticated about a matter requiring one or two or at most three components, they are nevertheless extremely skilled at dealing with cosmetics. The answer must lie not in incompetence or fecklessness, as the Supreme Court's decision would seem to suggest, but in a deeper and more complex level of psychobiological reality. In her remarkable and controversial analysis, Kristin Luker suggests that it is the very availability of contraceptives, easily used and obtained, which causes women to accept the risk of non-contraception in order to achieve other ends (Luker, 1975:123). Now we must recall two important pieces of background. The first is that a substantial number of conceptions, and presumably more before oral contraceptives, occurred before marriage and in many cases formed a prelude to marriage itself (Whelan, 1972 a,b). Secondly, as Luker pointed out in 1975, it is extraordinary but correct to recall that ". . . only slightly over a decade ago the most common contraceptive in the United States was the condom." (Luker, *ibid.:*124.) The condom is a male contraceptive (as Luker notes, "The demand that someone should invent a male contraceptive shows how total the attitudinal and technological changes have been"). But recently contraception has become associated with being female: "The technological and social change concomitant with widespread pill use has produced a generation of men and women socialized into the notion that only women have contraceptive responsibility. . . . Women have now internalized the idea that getting pregnant is their fault, even when it occurs in the context of male collusion with the risk-taking." (Luker, *ibid.:*128–129.)

The situation is, of course, quite involved. Because many women are contracepted, therefore it is possible for males to avoid inquiring of any particular female whether she is—there is a good possibility that she is. As well, since abortion is available in the event of conception, then the "costs" of pregnancy to the male even if he pays for the operation are relatively low, certainly in comparison with what have been traditional pressures on the male to "do the honorable thing" or otherwise involve himself in a serious way with the woman in question. Then where does this leave the female? According to Luker, she appears willing to take the risk of not taking contraceptives in order to capitalize on whatever effect a pregnancy might end up having on her personal circumstances. That is, she might become married, she might have an abortion or cement her relationship. But in any event she will be able to estimate the extent of the commitment of the male with whom she has been involved. (Luker, 1975:123.)

Here we approach a speculation. One of the remarkable changes in the medical-moral practices in many countries of the world has been the rapid increase in pro-abortion or permissive abortion legislation. The trend seems to exceed what we know about the rapidity with which people's moral values change, particularly on such a central issues as abortion. Thus it seems doubtful that social changes have been solely the result of value changes. My speculation is that the pressure for liberalized abortion laws is directly correlated with the shift from contraceptive technology used by males to that used by females so that males are no longer responsible for the consequences of intercourse and pregnancy but females are. And for the reasons I have just discussed the very existence of contraception almost assures that a certain number of women will risk pregnancy and a certain number become pregnant and some of those in turn require abortion. Married women also wish to control their childbearing, another important source of pressure for liberalized access to abortion. It is worth recalling that the principal proponents of abortion reform have been women (its principal opponents as well). A clear demand confronted legislators who were formerly remarkably recalcitrant in this area. Surprisingly, given the history of the matter, they liberalized or permitted abortion in countries where it would have been unthinkable several decades ago, even in communities formally committed to Roman Catholicism.

Much of the discussion of issues surrounding contraception, abortion and changing patterns of sexual encounter has focused on questions of morality, alienation, or the decline or renewal of communal standards. But any discussion of the functions of childbearing and rearing for men and women must take place in the context of the overall set of energies and strategies involved in organic survival and the cognate process to this, organic reproduction.

Any child and parent must know that rearing children involves an immense expenditure of time, energy, attention, affection and concern. One would therefore expect that, by that standard economic calculus which economists find suitably realistic for their management of the world, persons with children would experience various deficits of health, joie de vivre, etc. However, as is quite widely known, this is not the case; an overwhelming preponderance of women plan to have children. "In 1975 less than 5% of wives who were interviewed about family plans expected to remain childless." (Bane, 1976:9.) The low level of birthrates in the early 70's may obscure the fact that, while women are having smaller families, as many or more than before are having families. Westoff has suggested that a substantial part of the reduction in birthrates arises from a decline of unplanned births. The implication is that those births which do occur are typically the more wanted and reflect individual parents' estimates of how they wish to apply their time and resources. (Westoff, 1976.) In terms of the principle that "nature makes people do what it is good for the species to have done" we see here a reasonable fit between the real cost of having children and the biological benefits—to the gene pool—of so doing.

A case for the importance of parenthood to individuals would be strong even were it supported by no other fact than that an overwhelming percentage of people have, are planning to have, or try to adopt children if they are unable or unwilling to have them themselves. Even though there are some pressures in communities against having many children the effects of absolute childlessness are hardly trivial. Childlessness remains problematic for most childless people despite apparent shifts in attitudes toward population. (Bierkens, 1975.) Indeed there is evidence of a relationship between adequate income to spend and children on which to spend it; furthermore the popular myth that "the poor have children while the rich get richer" is questionable. It appears that lower-income persons are more likely to be childless than higher. There is a very consistent correlation between increasing income and the absence of childlessness (Kunz, Brinkerhoff, and Hundley, 1973); money is converted into children.

Beautiful Is Small. Small Babies?

If a population is to replace itself every woman on average has to have two children. This is a considerable requirement for the population of a society seen overall. A number of women and men will be unable to produce children, a number will not marry—though as we have seen this is a rather small number—and despite improvements in medical care some small percentage of women, particularly in poorer countries or among poor people in richer countries, will die during pregnancy or, more likely, childbirth itself. This implies that some women at least will have to have three or more children and presumably many will, particularly in societies with conditions favoring large families. However, what if the rate of two per female is not sustained and women and men elect to deploy their lives in a different way than replacing the existing members of their societies? What, for example, would result from a widespread disaffection among potential childbearers from the state of the social world into which their possible children would have to be introduced—a form of the hesitancy which appears to inhibit reproduction during depressions and wars? Social scientists are aware of the consequences of rapidly expanding populations and the increased demand for resources, natural and social, which such expansion creates. But what about a declining or stationary population? Is it clear what the results of such a phenomenon would be? After all, it has become the conventional formula of government and much commercial planning to assume constant increase in production, income and available resources. The notion that decline not growth might mark the style of the future may not have been adequately explored in biosocial terms despite the beginning of an economic analysis based on the "no growth" possibility.

In Chapter Five I will deal directly with the relationship between money and optimism and try to show how interconnected are the notions of economic productivity, skill, and return with the basic optimizing in terms of which many humans conduct their lives. But for the present I would like to withhold discussion about the relationship of population growth or decline and the ways in which people view the future and their personal future, and explore further the more intimate interactions and decisions which surround the turbulence of eroticism, commitment, love and self-perpetuation.

A fundamental principle of reproductive biology is that organisms are propelled by various socio-sexual mechanisms to reproduce themselves. This reproductive process is broadly "satisfying" to the individual organisms. It is implicit that a failure to reproduce deprives the animal in question of a variety of "satisfactions" which are fundamental to its overall welfare.

In the human case the rendition of these principles is always extremely complex and therefore it may be useful to scan some evidence about how the resources available to potential parents and how they perceive these resources affect their behavior and in turn affect the behavior of others. I should note that the resources in question are not solely economic but may well involve health, psychological stability, amounts of compassion, loyalty, and similar valuable components of human lives.

There is a tradeoff and accordingly evidence suggests that there are higher rates of childlessness among couples in which husbands have lower incomes than the norm for their occupational category. There is also a ". . . very high rate of childlessness among wives of college educated husbands in the lowest income category." (Kunz, Brinkerhoff and Hundley, 1973:142.) To the extent that pregnant females and those caring for very small children may still require some assistance from a male or other family member, it is likely that they will be more hesitant to subject themselves to the strains and stresses of childrearing with a male who cannot provide adequate support. This may also be related to the trend I've already noted toward a narrowing of the gap in age between males and females. As male income, except that for manual workers, is strongly correlated with age, the fact that women marry younger men today will often mean that they marry poorer ones. I take this to be not only an economic problem but also a social and psychological one. We know that females mature more quickly than males and are in general sooner able to deal with their adult lives. It can be argued that apart from the economic factor—certainly an extremely important one—another reason for the longstanding age differential between males and females is that it "evens out" the maturational differences between the sexes.

The preliminary results of a fascinating study by Heather Fowler on the processes of mate selection by females suggests the importance of potential male parental effectiveness. Fowler's comparison of the ideal men females have in mind at the beginning of their mating-reproductive life with the men they actually marry suggests a discontinuity between the glamorous and romantic courtier they desire and the dependable, provident if relatively pedestrian mate they choose. Thus the birthrate of a community may be affected by the assessments made by women of the potential roles which particular men will play in their own reproductive lives. If the available males are unpromising, or seem unwilling or unable to commit themselves to effective pre-fatherly actions, and are furthermore less psychologically and economically mature than females find acceptable, then women will be less inclined to mate and have children with them.

The decisions of individual men and women add up to general social trends, which in turn affect economic, social and governmental planning. Since the human species has always persisted by replacing or increasing its population, there is now the real possibility that in certain communities population levels will not even be maintained but may decline. My estimate would be that when population decline begins, governments will take direct action—by making abortion more difficult, as has happened on some occasions in eastern Europe, or by introducing directly affirmative measures. When Western Germany was faced with a low birthrate it altered its tax program to provide increased benefits for families with children. (*The Wall Street Journal*, July 18, 1977.) Along with East Germany and

Hungary, West Germany showed the lowest birthrate in the world among nations with more than 10 million people. (Berelson, 1974:7.) It is interesting that both East and West Germany share the same birthrate when they possess such different economic and political systems. The common trauma of the Second World War may continue to affect both parts of the former Reich, irrespective of the experience of the most thriving of capitalisms on the one hand, and state-controlled Communist structure on the other. For all their country's vaunted concern with the cosmetic and other rigamaroles of love, or perhaps because of it, the French have had only a small amount of natural increase, and the government has recently sought to promote considerably more. It has been seeking ways to convince women not only to have two children, which many do, but also to have a third and a fourth. Theirs is a fully pro-natal policy. (Evelyne Sullerot, pers. comm., 1976.) Not that radical anti-natal policies are necessarily more successful than, for example, the French pro-natal one. The macabre and portentous career of relatively stringently enforced sterilization in India under Indira Gandhi's regime—apparently an important factor in the downfall of that regime—is presumably a cautionary tale for governments seeking to forcefully interfere with their subjects' reproduction.

If it is true, as Pierre Trudeau has said, that "The state has no place in the bedrooms of the nation," when it intrudes, through population policy, it must expect at times such unexpected responses as the Indians' to the political party which had been their ruler since the British raj. As Bernard Berelson, the President of the Population Council, has noted, "Coercion as to fertility is morally repugnant and politically unacceptable, and virtually impossible of administration anyway." However, Berelson is guardedly optimistic about the possibilities for some fertility control: "Once more we cannot know for sure, but it is not at all unlikely that in today's world governmental policies to reduce fertility rates are proving more effective than governmental policies to increase fertility rates." (Berelson, 1974:11.) The considerations involved in establishing government policies or in forming attitudes to population levels are legion. For example, one problem to be faced is whether or not the number of people being born who will enter the labor force twenty or thirty years hence will be adequate to produce sufficient wealth to pay for pensions or other social security benefits to those adults who will be retirees by then. This was evidently one of the considerations which led to the decision by the Rumanian government to curtail sharply the availability of legal abortion. Needless to say, illegal abortion quickly increased in consequence. (Berelson, 1974.)

Perhaps contemporary interest in the relationship of changing birthrates to social policies reflects little more than the availability of more exact data, so that concerned individuals and institutions can attend to the ramifications of changes and how people conduct their reproductive lives. Whether or not this is the case, it is possible to try to relate some important social processes to changes in birthrates, particularly to their sudden rise and fall. For example, a period of low birth followed by a period of high—precisely what happened during the Second World War followed by the baby boom—will have a considerable effect on mate selection and very likely on overall patterns of sex roles. I've already noted that women tend to marry men older than they; this can occur smoothly when a constant number of childen are born in any period of a year or two. However, as we can see from the World War II baby boom, sharp changes in birthrates make this pattern difficult to follow. For example, between 1942 and 1945 relatively few children were born—that means relatively few males. From 1946 to 1948 relatively many children were born—that means relatively many females. Since females normally marry males between three and six years older than they, a large number of females would find males of the traditionally appropriate age simply unavailable.

We have already seen one result of this unavailability—that women are marrying men closer in age to themselves. Some women are marrying men the same age as they and a few, men younger. Alternatively, in order to find mates, women may join with formerly married, recycled men who may be considerably older than they. Or, they may not mate at all. Whatever their decision, they cannot accept the traditional definition of what they are supposed to do maritally because there are simply not the candidates available for them even if they want to marry, which in some subgroups of industrial societies seems increasingly questionable. Since this central and traditional pattern of mate selection has changed for demographic reasons, one can readily understand why thoughtful and energetic women would simply not accept stasis in other central and traditional patterns, particularly of work and politics. They have in effect said that since the traditional package—mating with an appropriately aged male—was unavailable, they would insist on another package which involved expanded opportunities for work, politics, and similar fulfilling activities.

Along with changes in contraceptive technology and ideology, this seems to be an important factor in the shift in attitudes and practices about sex roles which came into effect from about 1969 onward—precisely the period in which women would be clearly experiencing the effects of the disjunction between available males and available females resulting from the period of World War II. Furthermore, the earlier perturbation creates others over the longer period too. If men are marrying women in their own birth cohort, then they will be unavailable to marry females in the one younger than theirs; accordingly the pattern of male advantage in age becomes more difficult to sustain. The upshot is that females must have to interact with males who are socially and economically less mature than they might wish, and this must affect in an important way women's attitudes to men and their efficacy; accordingly it may make more attractive the autonomy of females. This effect of demographic change on how people evaluate their own reproductive future is difficult to describe and analyze precisely. Nevertheless there have been in the past patterns of feminist assertion which followed such demographic changes as have just occurred in Euro-America. This evidence roots such feminism firmly in the basic stuff of social life and provides it with a force and legitimacy in addition to that stimulated by moral, egalitarian and compassionate concerns.

If demographic downturns of a major kind may have a depressing effect on individuals as they approach the reproductive, adult phases of their lives, they may also have an exhilarating and potent effect on particular groups of individuals (and their surrounding community) when they are younger, full of questions and possibility. For example, an unusually large birth cohort came through the social system of Europe and America at once. The baby-boomers of the post-Second World War period came to adolescence and then maturity in the mid-1960's and early 70's. Particularly in England, an otherwise stable and neat society, this large and energetic group seemingly burst on the scene. Cogently and elaborately it defined the music, cosmetics, dress and tone of the period. It was the first generation in English working-class history of young reared under the National Health Service, which furnished their pregnant mothers with orange juice and themselves with such services as dentistry, lunches at school, and a health service defined by the needs of patients. So an unusually strong, lusty and healthy generation entered the community of discourse of that settled and unsuspecting country and defined much of its hope for almost a decade. With youth and numbers, it overcame patterns of social discrimination and private privilege which had dominated English society for centuries.

In America a similar group of young arrived on the scene, its optimism forged in grim opposition to a disastrous war waged by a lucklessly misdirected and deluded government. The force of a huge generation of draftable youths skilled in the arguments of progress met the "immovable object," a military war machine, and won. A President resigned and the country withdrew from its role of world policeman.

The critical artistic figure was Bob Dylan, who most signally changed popular youth music from ritual songs of frustrated love sung in passionless bars and cabarets to clear, lyrical statements of philosophies, knowledge and conviction. Dylan and his peers changed the notion of mass culture as a prevaricated and false commodity into the promise of an impeccably important, true communication. He and his elite corps of anti-warriors led and were led by a generation moved equally by dreams of widespread equity and cynicism about power. The consequence was a symbiotic, long, Anglo-American party, an epidemic of connection born of youth fares, the minute effusions of transistors, and the relative wealth of still hard-working parents. For a while, perhaps demography was the generator of optimism. United by a generous vision of a possible world, the postwar generation swept away shibboleths about stability, propriety and scarcity which had existed for decades. Even the proud parents of this birth cohort, born in the Depression and scarred by the War, appeared to lose their certainty about life's sometimes chilling finiteness and they donned the denim, sang the songs, and shared the hopes of their children.

For a while the guests at this party seemed immune to the antibodies of so-called "maturity." Yet eventually the clumsy realities of jobs, mates, children, and other personal exigencies slowly muted the colors of the costumes of the protagonists of hope. There followed a dreary progression of aging, recession, pollution, and nagging vexation about the price of housing, the grimness of cities, and the obvious vulnerability of even excellent progressive schemes. This group may yet emerge as a fertile client of the very right wing which despised it and it despised. It may even recall how alarming, if charming, its young legions were when they thrilled and baffled their elders with their youthful visions. I am merely suggesting that the demographic numbers are not mute records of simple events, but also rather like elements of chemical formulae which may sometimes yield explosions and sometimes nothing at all.

If at least reasonably wealthy communities can respond with a sense of prosperity to a large population increase, what happens to the optimism factor when their populations stop growing? There are contradictory views, ranging from a belief that the psycho-social effects of population stasis or decline will not be depressing (Richards, 1974) to the skepticism of Nathan Keyfitz of the Department of Sociology at Harvard, who regards a stationary population as a strong inhibitor of personal mobility: "An increasing population facilitates individual mobility. One of the consequences of moving toward the inevitable stationary population is that mobility will become more difficult. . . The effect will turn out to be numerically substantial—change from the annual 2 percent in the U.S. a few years ago to its prospective stationary condition implies a delay in reaching the middle position of the average factory or office of four and one half years." (Keyfitz, 1973:335.)

Keyfitz assumes that organizations will then tend to take a hierarchical form. More senior and competent persons will have the responsibility for the work and behavior of others. There will likely be more inequitable levels of remuneration too, though this is not central to his argument. Given Keyfitz's assumption, it is intriguing to note how changes in population size will affect individual careers and presumably people's notions of their own well-being. "It suffices to say that a person born in a cohort that is small in relation to those before and after him will be advantaged by many people retiring ahead of him, leaving places to which he can be promoted. Even when he is young, effects will reach him through retirements that have to be filled by people older than himself for whose places he will in turn be a candidate. At the same time he will be followed by many new entrants, and these will require instruction and supervision so that he will be quickly pushed up." (Keyfitz, 1973:346.)

As a member of a relatively small cohort, I quite understand the disproportionate advantages I have had in an occupation, education, which expanded very rapidly to deal with the many members of the exceptionally large "baby-boom cohort" which followed mine. Moreover, it is now clear that in North America as well as much of Europe, those born in the large cohort face serious difficulties in securing employment in the educational world, particularly because of the declining demand for education after its expansion to service the baby boom. Furthermore, following Keyfitz's argument, there is an additional inhospitality to the young in the system because of the fact that positions to which newcomers may aspire are already occupied by persons such as myself, who can be expected to try to retain their positions for literally decades—in my case, two and a half. (The escalated intensity of the discussion about the propriety of academic tenure certainly has to do with this demographically based rigidity in the system.) Indeed, the demographic effect on the morale of individuals is nowhere clearer than in the educational field. The efforts of the existing system to expand its range of functions by moving toward educating adults, retired persons, or people already in jobs, is one response to the demographic problem. But I think it will fail to deal adequately with the large disproportion between positions wanted and positions available. In effect, the imbalance began in the early 1970's, when large numbers of men and women came through the educational system to find they were being prepared to fill jobs which no longer existed because those whom the jobs were supposed to serve did not themselves exist. To complicate the matter, unless these children of the baby boom produce large numbers of children of their own to service as parents, educators, doctors, plumbers, etc., it is forseeable that their opportunities will be more limited than either they or their leaders would wish. Not only they but their parents, in their old age, will have to adjust to downward mobility. The offspring of upper-middle-class engineers, executives, professors and the like, may well have to find employment in less prestigious fields, or avoid the problem altogether by establishing small enterprises of their own, which however may have the merit of a clearer social function. One thinks here of the array of artisan's shops, health-food shops and restaurants, and other vaguely countercultural endeavors which have become the small businesses of the expensively educated children of well-off parents.

Keyfitz proposes three possibilities for "mitigating the depressing effects on personal mobility of a slowdown in population growth. A) Increase the markers of social status—the differentiation of Foreman Grade One, of Foreman Grade Two, provides opportunities for promotion . . . for this to happen people would have to become more sensitive to subtle nuances of status . . . B) Make social status and mobility less important, the opposite of A. People may be opting out of the mobility rate, partly in response to the greater difficulty of ascent as population growth slows." His third suggestion involves changing the structure of work altogether. He proposes we ". . . apply technical advance to change the structures . . . in the preceding discussion . . . " and thus ". . . real income can

. . . be made to increase. People may become more concerned with pay and the goods they can buy than with rank and title. Our increasing command over goods may compensate for diminishing command over people." (Keyfitz, 1973:348.)

He proposes that several or all of these remedies be tried. The central point is that some remedies may be necessary if people are not to be—using Keyfitz's word—"depressed." While Richards (1974) does not regard a replacement birthrate as necessarily depressing, as Keyfitz does, he does note that "a stable population and economy probably involved much more stability in the overall society. This might produce a much less positive attitude toward change and toward achievement." (Richards, 1974:7.)

There is of course nothing intrinsically wrong with this. It accords well with the "small is beautiful" tenor of ecological arguments which are in good measure the stimulus for concern about population increase itself. However, humans are a kind of animal committed to some sense of a desirable future. My own fear is that it will be difficult for governments to accept replacement population policies or even declining population policies, if only because of already existing economic practices—I will describe these later—which presume economic growth as a means of mollifying populations suffering from inequality in the present.

More! More Oliver Twists?

Population growth and economic expansion provide a clear prospect of prosperity. It remains to be seen if governments can reconcile the problem of world population stasis or decline with their own desires for continued political power. One ready solution to the problem of a declining native population is to permit immigration, both to accomplish work which natives are reluctant to do because of its menial, unpleasant, or dangerous quality and also to create a castelike group which forms the new base of the economic structure, thus permitting members of ethnic groups which arrived earlier to experience an increase in their relative prosperity and status. A comprehensive study of how such stratification occurs in an industrial society is contained in John Porter's *The Vertical Mosaic*, which describes clearly how Canadian society is formed of ethnic groups ranged in a linear hierarchy. (Porter, 1965.) The same principle of immigration-generated prosperity has frequently been noted in the United States. Another version of the same process of placating populations revolves around inflation, induced or permitted, which provides citizens the illusion that their incomes are increasing. Clearly the phenomena of population trends and inflation are not unrelated and I will return to this subject in Chapter Five.

Heretofore I have discussed how elaborate are the personal inducements to reproduce and how they go far beyond even the pleasure of the act, yielding reproduction itself. They raise the gravest of issues. One of the most galvanizing news stories I have ever read appeared in the *Toronto Star* in June 1977. It was about an eight-year-old boy, killed by a hit-and-run driver. The boy was struck in front of his home; his father rushed out to discover his son on the road. The father said that the last thing his child told him was, "Daddy, I think I am dying." It is difficult to imagine a final communication by a small child to his parent more questing, more troubled, more direly childlike. My empathy was total, but my overriding concern was about my own child, at that time 400 miles away. My next response, one of disorganized oceanic belligerence about frailty, was to want to become parent to another child. It appears there is a ruthless calculus to parenthood: how many, how many survived, how many grandchildren, how many great-grandchildren? What is one's place in the future?

In any species reproduction is a psycho-biological matter of deep moment; each generation has to come to terms with private urgencies in the context of public opportunities. Thus, with almost ludicrous devotion the salmon fights its way through miles of water and then upstream to a particular spot where caught in the scheme of things it reproduces and dies. Male dogs and cats endure the rigors of being selected by a female in heat. In turn she will provide, often without urging, much contented maternal care to her young. In the human case it appears that more than vanity and more than delightful lubricity encourage the reproductive act; parents perform for their children an immense number of often difficult, costly, and inconvenient services, yet remain suffused with a warmth and certainty about these services which they may experience under no other circumstances. I have already alluded to one recently developed theory of genetics which focuses on the principle of altruism—really a principle of familial selfishness, however—a theory which describes how individuals allocate their resources and enthusiasms in close proportion to the lines of kinship. (Again, for the best general review of this material, see Dawkins, 1976.) This remains a controversial theory and it may not, at least for some scholars of the subject, satisfactorily explain the variation and diversity of human kinship systems. (Sahlins, 1976; see also Alexander, 1977.) I happen to think that the theory is substantially useful if still imperfect, and that it alerts us to some underlying features of human social activity, particularly those directly related to reproduction.

The suggestion has been made that a fair amount of exchange of mates and prostitution-like behavior may reduce birthrates. For example, it has been reported that there is a reduction in fertility of women or even sterility as a consequence of prostitution and sexual promiscuity. (Ackerman, 1972:132.) This is reminiscent of the so-called Bruce Effect among experimental rodents—pregnant females of which will spontaneously abort when brought into the presence or even close to the smell of other males than the one who fathered the fetus they were carrying. (Bruce, 1970.) One is tempted, perhaps unduly imaginatively, to wonder what effect promiscuity has in the human case. We know that as many as 20 to 35 percent of human conceptions spontaneously miscarry, arguably because some deficiency has been noted by the "genetic testing devices" which routinely monitor the normality of the processes *in utero*. However, it is also possible that a sociogenic cause, like the Bruce Effect, may have an additional influence on what have often been thought to be purely physiological processes. Of course other factors which may be linked to sexual contacts with more than one partner, such as stress, uncertainty, fatigue, unconscious guilt responses, may also be involved in spontaneous abortion. It is exceedingly difficult to consider this matter with any confidence and certainty. But since there is an emerging body of knowledge about the social and psychological causes of infertility, for example among couples experiencing difficulty in achieving pregnancy, it may be merely prudent to bear this extrapolation from animal data in mind.

I will conclude this chapter shortly with a discussion of relationships between contraception and reproductive optimism. But I want to turn briefly to two phenomena which may have some bearing on this matter. The first is the effect of employment on women's reproduction, and the second is the effect of bottle-feeding as opposed to breastfeeding on birthrates.

One of the clearest indications that reproductive genetics is not an implacable force and that the satisfactions of working and similar contribution to the community may compensate for reproduction is the reasonably close connection between the level of female employment in a population and the birthrate. Women who have an opportunity to work at rates of pay they regard as reasonable are less likely to have children than women who don't. As Hoffman has noted, "If women are employed they will have satisfactions such that their enthusiasm for motherhood will be decreased: they will want fewer children and their motivation to practice effective birth control will be increased." (Hoffman, 1974:99.) This is not by any means the universal pattern in industrialized countries, while it is even less so in non-industrial or industrializing ones. But there is some general support for the notion that when women have satisfying and remunerative employment and the reproductive role per se is not the only significant one available to them their reproductive rates will be lower than otherwise. In the past, Hoffman notes that this pattern may have reflected an incompatability of maternal and occupational roles. Her suggestion is that should the organization of work become more flexibly attuned to the organization of mothering, then it is quite possible there will be no reduction in the birthrate of working women. *Indeed there may even be some increase insofar as additional*

household income may be translated into additional children—
we have already seen that there is some correlation between
higher income and birthrates.

Two subsidiary aspects of female employment are worth noting briefly. The first is that women with employment or in a
process of education leading to desirable employment are likely
to postpone their reproductive activity for a few years at least.
They may do so by marrying later (at the very least they will not
need the income which a marriage might provide) or they may
want to establish themselves professionally in a relatively unassailable way before subjecting themselves to the additional
burdens which motherhood may bring. And insofar as simply
extending the length of time between generations is a very
significant factor in birthrates, then even delays of several years
may have considerable consequences for population in the long
run.

This same factor, length of time between generations, comes
into play in the second of the two situations I want to refer to
here—namely a relatively sudden and widespread shift from
breastfeeding to bottle-feeding in the world. For example, in
the United States the percentage of infants who were breastfed
by the time they were discharged from the hospital fell from 65
percent in 1946 to 37 percent in 1956 to 27 percent in 1966.
(Knoedel, 1977:1111.) To some extent this may reflect the declining period of days spent in the hospital, but the trend is
unmistakable. As Knoedel has observed, the changes are more
recent and perhaps even more drastic in urban and suburban
areas of the developing world. He refers to "dramatic decreases
in the proportion of urban women who breastfeed their infants
for prolonged periods . . . in Chile, Mexico, the Philippines,
and Singapore." Several things go on here. First of all not only
are fewer numbers of infants nursed at all, but those who are
solely breastfed are breastfed for a shorter period of time. While
this may in part reflect employment of females outside the
home, which makes breastfeeding inconvenient, it appears as
well to be a consequence of a widespread belief abetted powerfully if perhaps cynically for their profit by companies selling
artificial milk that bottle-feeding is a more modern, progres-

sive, and generally desirable form of mothering. Breastfeeding on the other hand is seen as traditional, retrogressive, primitive. The incompatibility between work and breastfeeding need not be as severe as Knoedel suggests; Robin Fox has told me of his own recollections as a child being raised in the mining district of England. He recalls mothers coming from the mines and plants where they worked at noon and having their infants thrust over the walls within which they worked by relatives so that the mothers could nurse the infants and have them returned home. While there have been a few cases of facilities provided for this under more sophisticated circumstances, the difficulty of breastfeeding while working remains.

There are a number of extremely important consequences of this shift from natural to artificial feeding. The first is that particularly among the poor and in poor countries facilities for sterilization and refrigeration are very few, and bottle-feeding may yield a very high increase in child mortality because of infection. Knoedel cites a study by Wray, who "has estimated indirectly from data for four areas in different countries included in a Pan-American Health Organization study that mortality risks during the second six months of life are from 6 to 14 times higher for children breastfed less than six months than for those breastfed longer. Quite in the contrary direction, however, is the fact that it appears that breastfeeding interferes with the resumption of regular menstrual cycles and hence acts as a 'natural contraceptive' for a period of up to eighteen months to two years. So on the one hand population growth is reduced by an increased hiatus between the birth of children, which can have a considerable effect. On the other hand the increased mortality resulting from bottle-feeding may counteract this trend. It even appears possible that a shift away from breastfeeding could lead to a decrease rather than an increase in the number of infants who survive to their first birthday." (Knoedel, 1977:1114.)

I'm concerned here with the overall impact of these changes on the notions people and particularly mothers have of what is happening to them in changing circumstances. We can understand why women might be impressed by the lure of modernization and the blandishments of the skilled advertisements by milk companies. On the other hand one can also know with immediate sympathy how dreadful are the consequences of the deaths of young infants. So the movement to modernity for these women would be marked by tragedy and loss all the more dreadful because their causes may elude the relatively unsophisticated users of this allegedly modern technology. It is likely that physically able parents will seek to replace their infants who die and, given the still potent danger of childbirth in poor countries, one can readily imagine the human costs of this effort to replace babies in effect killed by a misplaced technology. It would appear to me utterly more sensible for the clamorous proponents of "Right to Life" to focus at least some of their attention, now reserved wholly for the issue of abortion, on the subtle carnage, particularly in the poorest countries of the world, which the adoption of an unnatural form of infant feeding has created.

Pills, Scalpels, and the Great Chain of Being

I have tried to approach from various directions the question of how people see mortality and their future, examining it in the context of both reproduction and wide social patterns—demographic, occupational and political. In the next chapter I will deal extensively with the chemical bases of some of the moods related to our subject, but for the moment I want to look at the consequence of using a particular drug, the contraceptive pill.

What effect does long-term use of the contraceptive pill have on the women taking it, and on the men with whom the women are presumably involved? For years it has seemed to me that the information available to scientists about the behavioral effects of the pill is altogether inadequate given the physiological implications of the drug, perhaps the most powerful one prescribed on a daily basis to healthy people. As early as 1969 I commented that there could well be behavioral consequences of the physiological interruption induced by the pill. (Tiger, 1969.) I remarked in particular that, inasmuch as the pill caused

females to become chemically pregnant and so unable to conceive, it might also cause them to behave in ways similar to
those observed in pregnant females. Of particular interest was
the possibility that the pill caused females to cease sending
signals of a chemical or other behavioral kind which might
attract males. At the time, the phenomenon observed in other
primates had only recently been identified, particularly by Michael and his associates, who showed that female rhesus monkeys taking the contraceptive did not attempt to entice or cop-
ulate with the males by whom they were surrounded. (Michael,
1968.) I also remarked on reports that women employing the
pill showed significant amounts of depression, which suggested that other physical and psychological effects might have
resulted from pill use as well.

Thereafter I was commissioned by a highbrow American
magazine to survey the material. My basic conclusion was that
there existed almost no evidence of consequence about the behavioral effects of the pill and that this was a scandalous avoidance of responsibility by manufacturers, government regula-
tory agencies, and doctors, who cavalierly prescribed it without
anticipating even the physiological dangers which subsequently proved to be real—embolism, high blood pressure, etc.
I said as much in the article, which was rejected on the ground
that I had discovered no significant evidence about the behavioral effects of the pill! Subsequently the content of the pill itself
was changed to reduce the hormonal material. The formula now
used is the same as that used in the People's Republic of China,
where there were ". . . exceptionally low daily doses of proges-
tin and estrogen in pills (a possible partial explanation for the
reported absence of thromboembolism) . . ." (Djerassi, 1974:1.)

It is likely that the reduced dosage of hormonal material has
reduced accordingly the effects on users' moods, social responses and enthusiasms. Nevertheless, as with Valium and
Librium, the most extensively used mood-altering drugs in the
world, which have recently themselves come under criticism
for their possible side effects, reliable information about the
long-range social/behavioral consequences of the use of the pill
is still inadequate. As Luker has suggested, there are major

social implications arising from the pill. There may be major private ones as well. Are the corresponding micro-social ones— ones on the intimate scale that affect what women feel and how men feel about them—adequately understood? This is not to mention the grosser and more macabre uses to which the pill is put by some young women, who evidently take the pill throughout the entire month in order to avoid menstruation and thus interruption of their sexual lives. The consequences of this, given disruption of menstrual removal of materials which can cause gynecological infection, are also inadequately addressed.

But the broad social questions may be the pill's ultimate test. What is the effect on a population of having its most thoughtful and sexually active young women in a chronic state of technical pregnancy? How does this affect younger women and older women? Their senses of well-being? Their own reproductive vitality? How does it affect men? I'm not implying that use of the pill or other contraceptives is morally wrong, untoward, or irresponsible. But I do believe that patients and doctors should understand better what may be involved in the pill, that there should be a more sensitive overall appreciation of possible consequences arising from its extensive, quasi-official use.

One interesting piece of evidence about the effect of the pill on the behavior of women with other women derives from a study by Martha McClintock of patterns of menstrual synchronization among women living in a college dormitory. The majority did not use the pill. McClintock found that these women, who lived together and were close friends, began the academic year experiencing menstrual periods unrelated to one another but ended it markedly tending toward synchronization. Thus some kind of pheromonal or other form of communication appeared to determine physiological response. (McClintock, 1971; Tiger, 1975.)

This is an extremely interesting finding. My own view is that the pattern of menstrual synchrony, if indeed it is a pervasive one, makes evolutionary sense. It implies that sexual selection and impregnation depend not on chance factors—who is ovulating—but rather exclusively on the factors of social selection which determine the patterns of bonding of males and females. In other words, the processes of social and sexual choice which are presumably being exercised by males and females take place on neutral ground—that is, primarily unaffected by which females happen to be ovulating and therefore possibly more desirous of sexual intercourse. Such a pattern would be particularly important in small, isolated communities, those in which the number of males and females is limited and opportunities for contacts with outsiders rare, because it would reduce the factor of chance. The dictates of natural selection imply that sexual selection should take place freely on grounds of individual choice.

In any case, McClintock found that women using the pill did not display such menstrual synchrony, which suggests that chemical pregnancy precludes response not only to men but also to other women.

Perhaps one indication of increasing suspicion of the short- and long-range effects of the contraceptive pill is the extraordinary increase in sterilization for contraceptive purposes. A recent survey based on a sample of 34,030 persons interviewed in 1975 by Westoff and Jones of the Office of Population Research at Princeton University suggests that approximately 6.8 million married couples in the childbearing ages had elected contraceptive sterilization as against 7.1 million using the contraceptive pill. (Brody, 1978.) "The increase in the proportion of sterilized couples was found to be greatest among those married ten or more years. But even among couples married five to nine years, 22 had chosen sterilization by 1975 compared with only 8% in 1970. . . . The percentage of married couples in which either the husband or wife was sterilized for contraceptive reasons increased from 8.8% in 1965 to 16 in 1970 to 31.3 in 1975." This is a striking increase, particularly in view of the fact that sterilization operations have been available for many years. It would appear that the increase must reflect not technology but social and personal values.

Sterilization is an exceptionally important positive factor in population control. However, its widespread use likewise raises serious questions about its effect on peoples' attitudes toward themselves and toward their futures. When one or both married partners elects to undergo sterilization both presumably expect that their marriage will last, that they will not want children with each other, that they will not divorce or be bereaved and then want to reproduce with another partner. Yet at the very time when the stability of married pairs decreases precipitately—between 1953 and 1974 in the United States the number of divorces increased two and a half times—irreversible operations of fundamental consequence, presumably based on a naïve view of marital permanence, are sought and given. This problem particularly affects couples married five to nine years, as there is an inordinate likelihood of divorce for these pairs.

What is to be made of this unprecedented development? On the one hand it is a positive step toward limiting population. On the other it may prevent those people who have elected to make themselves non-reproductive from adapting to changes in their social circumstances, such as bereavement, divorce, marriage and remarriage. Moreover, it may change their attitudes toward children. The evidence is not at all clear; what are the psychological effects of sterilization? We know that men and women who are infertile or lose their fertility are very frequently deeply concerned by their state. Is voluntary loss of fertility, sterilization, worth the psychobiological price?

One may fear that medical practitioners offering sterilization to patients will offer them no better in this respect than the women had who were given the old contraceptive pills. In any case, I foresee that the voluntary sterilization of people on a large scale will have significant, if subtle, effects on general attitudes toward educational systems, pension plans, rights of children, and attitudes toward them, and on the inter-generational process in general. Will bitterness replace fecundity? Will hostility toward children come to mask despair at one's own folly? Is it not likely that those who have interfered, however voluntarily, with their fertility in an irreversible way will somehow be seriously affected in as yet unpredictable ways? These ways may be restricted to their private and familial roles or may embrace, through their influence on the political system, long-range planning, school systems, daycare facilities, and tax advantages to parents, etc. There may also be complex, almost cosmological effects, particularly among persons sterilized at a young age or before they have become parents themselves.

These remarks apply, it should be noted, to irreversible sterilizations, not less final procedures which may be developed in the future—these presumably being the optimal means for contraception should they ever be satisfactorily developed (see Brody, 1978).

My emphasis on the relationship between fertility and social behavior has so far been directed toward females and the consequences of the major shift in control of contraception from male to female; I've argued that the availability of contraception controlled by females has been fundamentally and unprecedentedly important in permitting females a more careful choice of progenitors for their children. Women may occasionally have exercised this choice in the past but only within comparatively narrow social limits, and with less reliable means of contraception. It seems reasonable to suppose that the declines in birthrates which have followed the introduction of female-controlled contraception in many countries reflect an increasing selectivity by females in their choice of males. The declines may reflect as well the determination of women with children not to have more.

In addition, the rising divorce rates in countries as structurally dissimilar as the United States and the Soviet Union (where the divorce rate reportedly has tripled since 1960; according to Reuters, there were 332 divorces for every 1,000 marriages in the Soviet Union in 1976) may reflect a greater selectivity in choosing marriage partners owing to decreased necessity occasioned by unplanned childbirth.

If the new fact that females can carefully choose with whom and when they wish to reproduce affects birthrates, so also must the new, or changed, circumstances of males. When females control conception, males must feel increased uncertainty about whose child a woman bears. The confidence of males in their part in the reproductive process must be diminished in an unusual, perhaps decisive way.

This new social phenomenon is connected with an important development in biological theory—the hypothesis that the dynamics of biological selection entail a requirement that fathers of whatever species must have some reasonable means of convincing themselves that it was their own copulation which produced the young that they rear. I have already referred to the case of the langur monkeys described by Sarah Hrdy. Among these animals, when a new male enters the harem one of his first acts is to kill the offspring of the previous incumbent of his role. Not only does this assure that the resources of the community will not go to "stranger" genes, but also that the bereft mothers, no longer breastfeeding offspring, will become receptive to copulation to produce future young. In the human case, of course, the matter is handled in far less draconian ways, although infanticide by conquering soldiers or even stepparents is not unknown.

The consequences of increased male reproductive uncertainty are hard to overestimate, particularly when one considers why males are so generally willing to devote nearly all of their earnings to a domestic system involving primarily a female and offspring. Mere sentiment? Social pressure? Habit? Relative ease? Of course all of these and similar reasons apply. Yet there may well exist a different reason directly connected with the reproductive urgency, particularly of an animal as symbolically constrained as the human: the route to male genetic immortality leads through the female line. While I recognize that to express this reality is to invite a certain antagonism, nevertheless it seems indisputable that the situation confronting contemporary males is quite unprecedented. Moreover, it may be important to investigate the extent to which male behavior involves ensuring confidence of paternity or, failing that, responding, perhaps with preposterous bravado and cruelty.

The best study of the problem is that of Mildred Dickeman (1977), in my view a major accomplishment both in uniting biological theory and social science and in postulating the possible ramifications of this union for social policy. Dickeman's analytical tour de force presents a picture of human males accustomed to controlling paternity and building their confidence—their reproductive optimism, if you will—by a variety of measures, such as evaluating virginity highly, applying the double standard, employing the legendary chastity belt, and endorsing the generally sterner moral code governing females' sexuality which pervades most of human society.

Writer after writer has commented on the ubiquity of inhibition of female sexuality to serve male reproductive ends. The means are often brutal, especially in Moslem societies, in which women suspected of adultery may be murdered at will by their husbands. Such cases are the pinnacle of a process by which males seek to protect their genetic futures through control over females. And when men fail, the fragility of their control is plainly displayed. Now that technology has removed from males any semblance of authority over this central reproductive episode, we may expect to see, may already be seeing, social and private consequences of an unexpectedly ramified kind.

In this chapter I've tried to show what might be the effect of families on children, of children on families, and the absence of children and of families on communities in general. I've tried to relate some obvious social processes to some less obvious biosocial ones. While it is a truism that any concern about the future must in large measure focus on the population of that future, i.e., today's children—nevertheless the number and ornateness of the links between parents and children may warrant our making a fresh inspection under the lens of biology. The biological act of reproduction creates the most social fact of all, an entirely new social unit. Thus an integrated view requires that the functions of genes and the functions of communities be considered together. Bodies are not only containers; they are also citizens.

Nevertheless, there is a strictly physiological realm to be explored and I want to turn to that now, to take an inward look at what goes on inside the container when we feel good, bad, in despair, and hopeful.

Hope Springs
Internal

At a 1973 conference sponsored by the Harry Frank Guggenheim Foundation in New York City, Jane Goodall projected a
sequence of slides which she had recently received from her
associates in the field station at the Gombe Stream Game Re-
serve in Tanzania. The sequence concerned the death of one of
the important senior females in the community, Flo, a chimpanzee. Chimpanzees do not treat the death of one of their
number casually (Teleki, 1973): they appear to have a rather
characteristic, apparently almost ritual and considered response
to the event. This death particularly hurt Flo's son, Flint, who
had always been unusually attached to her and had spent even
more time with his mother than other young chimps do.

Flint became extremely subdued. He was clearly morose. He
ate hardly at all. His social interaction all but stopped. He was
an animal dejected and in deep psychological pain. The sequence of slides showed the wretched chimpanzee in various
stages of grief. The final slide showed Flint leaving the group
and the camp toward the place where he had last seen his
mother's body before it had been taken by the scientists for

autopsy. His shoulders, his posture, the general slackness of his body, even from the rear, even from a distance, clearly betrayed his misery.

It was the last photo taken of him because several days later he was found dead near where his mother had died. An autopsy was performed on him too; his death had been caused by a common virus infection, normally benign. Apparently Flint, a young, healthy animal, had died of grief.

Ideas may be trivial or important, but they always have to do with substances and vice versa. There is always a physiological, neurochemical basis for the ideas we have about the world, and for the plans we make to respond to the world. Ideas have the capacity to make us sad or happy. They can change our bodies. The loss of a relative or beloved cellist thousands of miles away, disclosure of personal adversity or of a moral disgrace, a natural tragedy or reported cruelty—all can cause varying amounts of distress in different people. How can words taken into the skull through the eyes from a newspaper cause a person's body to sicken? Alternatively, how can good news, about a friend, a political party, a scientific venture cause a person to feel physically better? While I do not pretend to know the answer to these questions I know that there is an answer and that ideas have effects on bodies because ideas are real things inside bodies. And if we also understand that social circumstances—my mother has died, my job was abolished, I have been drafted into the army—can affect the ideas people have about themselves and their world and if these ideas in turn can influence their bodily states we begin to see the connection between social process and medical fact. Indeed, this has been one of the important advances of scientific understanding. We now appreciate that there is a connection between the body and social behavior as exemplified by the practice of so-called psychosomatic medicine. There also has been some progress in understanding the relationship between ideas people have about both themselves and their social circumstances, and their individual states of health.

I began this chapter with the story of Flint to try to establish a case for a physiological basis for optimism by describing some consequences of its absence. In this chapter I want to deal with physiological states themselves, to assess what is known about the relationship of physiology and moods—and to consider the connection, if any, between bodies and symbols. This discussion will have to be very general; volumes have been written about depression alone, and I am neither a psychiatrist nor a physiologist. Nevertheless, even though the sophistication of neuropharmacological, neurochemical, physiobiological and associated science is now immense, I believe it is possible to come to terms with the broader implications of the detailed materials without doing violence to scientific fact.

A body of knowledge exists and its details fit into a larger and describable pattern. Because this knowledge is directly associated with therapeutic medical practices, one can feel some assurance that the data are sound, despite our incomplete understanding—for example, of how drugs taken over a long period of time may affect behavior, moods and perceptions. For certain chemical substances, however, there exists a reasonable assessment of the drug/behavior connection and means of testing and refining the assessment.

Garden Variety Depression

Depression is generally regarded as an illness and it occurs widely. In fact it is so common that it has been described as the "common cold" of mental illness. The National Institute of Mental Health in the U.S. estimates that as many as eight million Americans should, each year, visit a doctor because of depression. In the U.S. about a quarter of a million people were recently hospitalized in one year for depression. As a feature of day-to-day life, depression is an important factor in what people do about themselves and to others. To combat it they use a variety of weapons—blood tonics, huge doses of vitamins, alcohol, sessions with interior decorators, vacations, shopping sprees, movies. It is generally agreed that cheering up depressed friends, relatives and associates is a fitting intervention; it does not violate their privacy or dignity. Frequently the intervention is successful from everyone's point of view. However, the medical case books reveal that many such lay efforts are unsuccessful. More complex and often strenuous treatment may be necessary—such as regimens of drugs, intensive therapy or, most perplexing of all, electric shock treatments, which appear to help some depressed people through some mechanism not well understood.

Is there a common cause of this common ailment? The usual answers to this question range from "depression is caused by unpleasant, chaotic, heartless environments, including parents" to "depression is caused by genetically inherited or predisposed states of biochemical imbalance or deficit" or "depressions are the result of the effect of both the physiological condition of a person and the nature of his environment." My own preference is for the third answer, since it seems most consistent with the evidence. Any illness with a social component must result at least partly from some social action. Even if, for example, the direct cause of the depression is a deficit of a particular substance circulating in an individual's brain tissue, it is entirely possible that the early or adolescent social experience of the individual was partly responsible for the biochemical shifts predisposing that individual to adult depression. (To be sure, innate biochemistry must make some people more sensitive than others to social rebuff or personal adversity, thus triggering occasional episodes of depression.) So it seems most reasonable to view depression as the outcome of a set of forces operating with varying intensity but combining to reduce a person's enjoyment of life, vivacity of response, and sense of pleasure about his future.

Alternatively, we can make parallel comments about the psychological mood which is generally seen as antidotal or opposite to depression: the optimistic mood. Optimism, as I defined it at the outset, is not generally treated as an illness. But, whereas certain kinds of collective optimism are socially acceptable, their private counterparts are often seen as pathological. Thus a group of people in Geneva or Albi or Utah or Jerusalem may decide on various theological grounds that they are the children of God and act accordingly, weaving a fabric of social life on this belief. But if an individual in another community were to take the same position, he or she would likely be regarded as aberrant. It is the individual who on his own adopts an exotic point of view about himself who is the psychiatric risk, although that particular point of view may be no more odd in logical terms than another point of view widely and acceptably shared by a large group of people. The significant feature of the deviant's position is not what the position is but the deviance itself.

I've already recalled Freud's prediction that eventually central understanding of human social process would depend on a knowledge of the chemical transactions occurring in the brain and the rest of the body. Certainly the remarkable understandings of modern neurochemistry and pharmacology show the value of Freud's prediction and the shortsightedness of its critics. Some recent discoveries about the brain have gripped both public and scientific imagination, and also relate directly to my optimism hypothesis: there are processes in the body which produce morphine-like substances which operate on specific receptor sites in the brain and spinal cord. These appear to reduce the experience of pain and may also in part cause the organism to "feel better." The literature on this subject, while relatively recent, is already considerable and the scientific field is in a state of rapid growth and explanatory quest. (See among others, Goldstein, 1976; Marx, 1976; Snyder, 1976, 1977; Stein, 1974.) Indeed the field of neurochemistry is undergoing a convulsive upheaval because of this new work. From the point of view of the argument here, *these findings are directly relevant to the possibility that there is a location in the brain for good feelings about the present and the future. For the first time we may be on the way to finding a specific source for notions of personal well-being and for the sense of optimism in one's life.*

My program in this chapter will be first to glance at the problem of depression, because of the amount of scientific material available about it, which helps clarify its origin and forms, and second to contrast optimism to it. After considering depression, I will discuss euphoria and its related states and then concern myself with the overall problem of mood-altering substances—

controlled, such as alcohol, cocaine, marijuana, etc.; and un-
controlled, such as caffeine, sugar and common nicotine. I will
approach the general problem of how people manage their use
of such substances to affect their experience of life and themselves. This will be followed by some comments on "little optimisms"—those personal and communal activities which are
closely related to states of private well-being, such as diets,
exercise plans, regimens of vitamins. Also considered will be
some self-induced physiological changes to suggest the effect
of the body on the mind. Finally, I will try to evaluate the
functions of placebos and comment on possible justifications or
lack of them for legislation restricting their sale.

Let us begin by discussing the relationship between aspects
of social process and the internal secretion of opiates. We know
that there is a connection between stress and hormonal secretion and that the connection involves personal status and patterns of dominance. Insofar as this dynamic relates to breeding
systems in other animals and possibly to reproduction among
humans, the subject of the last chapter, it must recapitulate the
social-sexual systems involved in evolution and help explain
what kind of animal we are now.

In his chapter on the "sick soul," William James discusses
"thresholds"—the points at which certain states of mind pass
into others: "The sanguine and healthy-minded live habitually
on the sunny side of their misery-line, the depressed and melancholy live beyond it in darkness and apprehension. There are
men who seem to have started in life with a bottle or two of
champagne inscribed to their credit; whilst others seem to have
been born close to the pain-threshold, which the slightest ir-
ritants fatally send them over." (James, 1958:117.) He goes
on to describe some consequences of this melancholy: "A chain
is no stronger than its weakest link, and life is after all a chain.
In the healthiest and most prosperous existence how many
links of illness, danger, and disaster are always interposed?
Unsuspectedly from the bottom of every fountain of pleasure,
as the old poet said, something bitter rises up: a touch of nausea, a falling dead of the delight, a whiff of melancholy, things
that sound a knell, for fugitive as they may be they bring a

feeling of coming from a deeper region and often have an appalling convincingness. The buzz of life ceases at their touch as a piano-string stops sounding when the damper falls upon it. Of course the music can commence again—and again and again—at intervals. But with this the healthy-minded consciousness is left with an irremediable sense of precariousness. It is a bell with a crack; it draws its breath on sufferance and by an accident." (*Ibid.:*118.)

The state William James describes so poetically has also been described, at least in part, neurochemically. For example, as early as 1956 Board, Persky, and Hamburg discovered that among acutely depressed, newly admitted psychiatric patients there were high corticosteroid levels. In another group of thirty-three patients they studied, ". . . those suffering most intensely had the highest elevations of plasma corticosteroids . . ." and later on Gibbons and McHugh reported a "positive correlation between weekly plasma corticosteroid levels and depression ratings . . ." (Cited in Hamburg, Hamburg and Barchas, 1974:29.) Another interesting study showed a change in internal secretions of substances, in this case MHPG (three-methoxy-four-hydro xyphenylglycol) in the body of a patient with manic-depressive cycles *before* the switch in behavior. This is striking; it implies that the changes in the physiology associated with changes in behavior may occur before behavioral change, an argument for a biologically based theory of the origin of psychological disease and by implication psychological normality (Jones *et al.*, 1973).

Another study of the relationship between drugs and behavior was of six adult macaque monkeys living in free-ranging colonies on Guayacán Island, Puerto Rico. As the behavior and social position of these animals was known from research before the experimental manipulation, it was regarded as very significant that after they were injected intraventricularly with a substance which depleted norepinephrine in the brain, they exhibited far less social grooming and self-grooming, engaged in generally fewer social interactions, initiated fewer threats or attacks, and in general lost status in the social system from which they had come. The animals which had been treated in a sham manner, that is in which actual substances were not injected into their bodies, did not change their social positions—all of which suggested that a depressive reaction in social terms could follow a chemical intervention of a relatively precise kind. (Redmond, Hinrichs, Maas and Kling, 1973.)

A study of a quite different kind likewise bears out the interaction of body chemistry and behavior. In it, autopsies were performed on the brain, particularly the hind-brain tissue, of three groups of deceased people: one which had committed suicide after depression, another which had committed suicide without depression, and a third which had died of other causes unrelated to depression. There were significant differences in relevant brain substance in all three groups. (Bourne *et al.*, 1968.) A variety of other studies of endocrine status of depressed patients similarly has shown significant relationships, and these also indicate that there are meaningful subgroups in the chemistry-depression relationships. (Hamburg, *et al.*, 1974: 31.) Furthermore, this relationship may depend not only on increased or decreased amounts of endocrine products but also on the extent of a person's variation in normal values: "within an optimal range [adrenal cortical steroids] probably enhance a person's ability to cope with stress. In excess, deficiency, or distortion, they probably impair one's ability to cope." (*Ibid.:*33.)

Because we know that forms of depression are linked to parts of the brain and other physiological systems, such as the endocrine ones, we disserve ourselves worrying about metaphysical concepts in trying to understand the problem. The romantic angst of Goethe's Werther, the grief of the bereaved parent or disappointed lover, the personal trauma of the unemployed— those experiencing each of the above are not only involved in obvious social processes; they are the hosts of biochemical ones which affect the body and how it responds to and interprets their behavior. To be sure, we do not know precisely what many of the relationships between the body and its behavior are. It is unclear why certain drug treatments of psychological states are successful and how they work. (Winson, pers. comm.) How the various substances which have been isolated and described actually function, where they come from, what their relationship to genetics is, and how modifiable all this is, are questions which have yet to be answered fully and precisely. Nevertheless, at least the outlines of the problem and the opportunity are now clear; Freud's prediction about chemical processes as basic factors in behavior is true.

In a moment we will turn to some speculation about the genetic cause of these processes and the extent to which they may be independent of strong genetic programming. Whatever the gene/brain relationship is, however, it remains very significant that the brain actions and the drugs which affect them involve the evolutionarily early parts of the brain. The chemicals—the amines—which are principally involved are to be found throughout the brain, but their greatest concentration is in the limbic system—the phylogenetically old section of the cerebrum. As we have already seen in referring to Paul MacLean's research, this system is elaborately involved with sexual activity, emotional states, hunger and depressive behavior. In this context depression seems to be associated with those paleopsychic processes to which MacLean referred. This suggests that depression as a phenomenon is not simply a creature of industrial societies in the form of alienation (Marx) or of particular kinds of family life (the double-bind process described by R. D. Laing) or even of a failure to "express one's self" (classical and modern lumpen/psychoanalytic/psychological rhetoric). The problem is much older and much less circumstantial and probably affects animals even as simple as lizards and other reptiles, though, as usual, the human rendition is probably the most elaborate and elegant.

However, given the venerableness of the neurochemistry involved, I think it is reasonable to see depression as a fundamental response to the circumstances of life of any gregarious animal. Because of this relationship between depression (and I will obviously go on to argue in a moment, optimism) and the substances found in the oldest parts of the brain, in trying to understand the problem it seems reasonable to look first at phylogenetically old behaviors associated with these old parts of the brain—hunting/gathering, reproducing, striving for place, seeking equity. This is why I discussed in the last chapter how reproduction was related to psychological tonus and perhaps to the overall sense of efficacy and pleasure which people and communities have about themselves and their futures. In the next chapter I will approach from the same perspective the question of earning a living and spending one's resources. For the moment suffice it to say that what are involved here are ancient processes—artifacts of our past. They are now known to be elaborately involved with the oldest parts of the brain. How they are involved has begun to become clear only in the past fifteen or twenty years. The relationship between behavior and neurophysiology is a ramified one. And while it is often extremely subtle, hardly ever is it trivial.

That there is an almost discernible location of the wellspring of grief and other emotions seems to me not only interesting but reassuring. Rather than being a matter of indulgence or frailty or neurosis or intransigence, grief becomes a predictable and healthy response to losses of sociobiological consequence, rooted in the body, expressed through it, and relevant to its eventual health. For example, Hofer has shown that the excretions from the bodies of parents grieving for their children who have died are chemically different from those of unafflicted parents. (Hofer, 1972.) Perhaps this and related chemical findings help explain the widespread existence of ceremonies for grieving and rituals for its passage. (Rosenblatt *et al.*, 1975.) If humans have much the same bodies and metabolic processes over the world, then it is scarcely surprising that they have contrived similar ways of responding to and mitigating the bodily perturbations caused by calamity. There is a chemistry of the rage against mortality and it dignifies the value of philosophical concerns. To be or not to be, how to be and how not to be, the questions of Job, are all finally questions about matter. They represent the connection between symbolic capacity and real bodily states. I think William James would have been pleased by the specificity of the connections we have now made.

Likewise, one can imagine how pleased he would be by another major new index of the physiological component of depression—the drug treatments for depressive illness. As is now well known, regimes of various medications, such as monoamine inhibitors or tricyclic antidepressants, have been repeatedly successful in reducing the severity of depressive episodes. A general if perhaps unduly assertive discussion of the usefulness of recently developed drug therapies is Fieve's (Fieve, 1975 a; see also Fieve, 1975 b). The fact that some of the particular drugs used and some effects of treatment may remain controversial should not obscure the central point, which is that an unexpectedly large number of chemical solutions have been found to alleviate problems of personal performance—problems which some doctors once believed could be alleviated only by extensive psychoanalysis.

In fairness, much of the causation of psychological ills appears to lie in precisely those sociopsychological circumstances with which traditional psychotherapy is concerned. Even if drugs can solve the problems created by these circumstances, the circumstances are not necessarily less important or more ephemeral than psychotherapists have thought in the past. We know, for example, that changes in status or bereavements can markedly affect physical states; some individuals may simply be unable to recover rapidly or enough from these behaviorally induced physiological afflictions. Presumably such people are constitutionally less likely to be able to respond well to traumatic circumstances, about which more later. This makes it important that a rapprochement has been achieved between physiological and psychotherapeutic sciences so that doctors treat physiologically what are at least partly sociogenic problems. People with physiologically rooted difficulties may require psychotherapy in order to come to terms with them; perhaps the most common case is that of people suffering from a physical stigma and who are sufficiently traumatized by their appearance to require psychotherapy. (Goffman, 1963.)

There are several other brief comments to be made about the phenomenon of depression. The first is that the diagnosis of depression itself may be an artifact of a particular cultural attitude. For example, it has been argued by Fieve that North American psychiatrists are far more likely than British ones to define a particular set of symptoms as schizophrenic; the same set of circumstances will tend to lead English psychiatrists to the diagnosis of depression. I am not able to evaluate this argument, though some evidence contradicting it is from Mendelewicz (1974), who also suggests that there are relationships between blood groups and diseases—*i.e.*, manic-depressives are more likely to have blood type A than O, while the reverse is true among schizophrenics. If culturally determined biases affect how ill people are diagnosed psychiatrically, so do technical difficulties arising from the diagnostic measures used—a factor which must also be taken into account. (Luria and McHugh, 1974; Luria, 1975.) But whatever the specific instruments used to diagnose it and whatever the particular enthusiasm or skepticism with which psychiatrists do so, depression does appear widely and regularly enough in the human population so that it becomes important to explore what genetic bases or factors may be involved in its ubiquity and persistence.

We will begin with the possibility that any widespread behavior or phenomenon in the human population must have served a useful survival function at some time and has not been sufficiently crippling or debilitating to be completely selected out of the human gene pool. First let us glance at some of the evidence pertaining to the question of the genetic origin of depression and its counterfoil, optimism. There are now interesting experimental data suggesting that in simpler animals, such as the rat, strains bred with certain genetic susceptibilities consistently exhibit these under conditions of stress. For example, two strains of rats were selectively bred to respond differently to salt ingestion, which has a marked effect on blood pressure and hypertension. Under controlled circumstances rats were fed either under conditions of diabolical stress or of open access to their food. Even though the two strains appeared to behave rather similarly they showed "dramatically different . . . blood pressure responses . . . [and] psychic stress . . . appeared to be selectively efficacious depending on genetic predisposition. This may help explain why the role of stress in hypertension has been such an enigma." (Friedman and Iwai, 1976.)

Of course it is awkward to extrapolate from rats to humans

(even though this was customarily acceptable in research when stimulus-response theories of behavior were still regnant). But the existence of these data in other species at least provides a basis in comparative theory for studies conducted on humans. They tend to support the view that, other things being equal, it is possible to inherit some predisposition toward specific behavioral deficiencies such as depression or schizophrenia. For example, Winokur has provided a detailed analysis of genetic factors which may affect two types of depression—the bipolar or manic-depressive kind; and the unipolar, which is depression as a consistent state. As a general fact in affective disorder, Winokur notes, identical twins are more frequently sufferers than fraternal twins and there is also an "increase of affective disorder in family members over what one would expect in the general population . . ." (Winokur, 1973.)

I've cited a number of human genetic factors which affect substance levels in the body and brain and in particular inhibit or stimulate certain behaviors, some of them disorders. Hamburg *et al.* (1974) suggest that particular genetic factors, such as levels of brain amines and metabolism, "may make it more difficult for some persons to sustain an affective response to prolonged stress, more likely to explode in anger or slide into despondency." They also cite the work of Goodwin and Bunney: " 'Let us imagine that an individual with a very strong family history of affective illness has a genetically transmitted defect in one of the systems subserving the increase in neurotransmitter amines which normally occur in response to stress. In such an individual under chronic or recurrent stress the stores of the critical neuro-transmitter amines could eventually become depleted, which according to the amine hypothesis would lead to a clinical state of retarded repression.' " (*Ibid.*: 50.) Their overall assessment is that "genetically determined variation involving the biogenic amines and their physiological regulation may provide a basis for significant individual differences in emotional and endocrine responses to stressful situations. . . . We consider it likely that some severe emotional disorders involving intense anger or depression may be partly based upon genetically determined alterations in normal biochemical processes. These biochemical predispositions must interact in complex ways with environmental factors such as separation, loss, or other jeopardy to crucial human relationships." (*Ibid.*)

Mood Evolution

If there is a partly physiological basis and/or consequence of depression and also presumably of optimism, how did these "get into the system"? As far as depression is concerned, why did humans and other animals evolve or tolerate the existence, on a relatively widespread basis, of genes for a relatively unpleasant and seemingly unproductive state of mind? I find attractive the general hypothesis offered by Price and Slater, who suggest that some of the psychological states now defined as illness or pathology may once have had adaptive usefulness during human evolution. In this case then depression—after all, an extremely common ailment—may have served and may still serve some advantageous functions for both sufferer and community. Perhaps depressed persons slow down or otherwise inhibit social action. They may constitute a conservative force, particularly in communities undergoing rapid change and disruption—we know that such rapid social change may be accompanied by depression. They may serve, thus, both as an "early warning system" and a countervailing force. I'm not suggesting that people suffering from depression should not be treated or helped because they are allegedly serving some communally useful natural function. Quite the contrary. Perhaps these people are responding not only to their own personal situations and frailties, but as unusually sensitive or vulnerable members of the community responding "for the community" in certain trying circumstances. If that is so, one may hope there will be less emphasis on the personal frailty of the sufferers and more on alleviating the destructive circumstances in the community as a whole to which depressed persons may be disproportionately and the more sensitively reacting.

An analogue to illuminate the proposition comes from aller-

gies. These plainly result from a large measure of genetic inheritance of physiological characteristics. Environmental
changes speed up, slow down, or exaggerate the range of intensity of allergic response. Nevertheless certain individuals seem
to be "programmed" to be less tolerant of certain elements in
the physical environment than most other people. Heretofore
this has been widely regarded as a form of personal weakness
or a failing; it is certainly true that people suffering from various allergies do indeed suffer reduced energy, often competence, certainly pleasure, and usually peace of mind. Here I
want to turn Hamburg's "ease of learning" hypothesis about
behavior on its head—perhaps the allergies are physiological
indices of what is "difficult to tolerate." One needn't be a gas-
tronomic enthusiast to conclude that there is a fairly close relationship between foods tolerable to the human system and our
patterns of taste—what we enjoy or reject for eating and drinking. Now this is not a wholly perfect guide to desirable nutrition, if only because (as I will argue later) a genetically uncon-
trolled enthusiasm for sugar has been satisfiable in the last
hundred and fifty years with unprecedented regularity and largesse. To a lesser extent the same holds true for carbohydrates,
as most carbohydrates now routinely eaten perhaps would not
have been safely digested until the development of fire. (Leopold and Ardrey, 1972.) Fire also may have been necessary before we could find adequately palatable the animal fats we now
eat—perhaps too much of, if warnings about the relationship
of animal fat and coronary disease mean what they imply. Perhaps an animal with a relatively fragile coronary system was
not evolved to eat cracklings, or corn-fed beefsteak—the juicier
the better, but the fattier. In any case the range of foods required by the ideal patterns of meals in various cultures with
resources and wealth enough to enjoy a choice usually reflects
a nutritionally justifiable balance. That is, the traditional
Chinese meal, the French one, the Indonesian rijsttafel, the
Italian, Spanish or Indian—all with their range of fruits, pro-
teins, carbohydrates, etc.—suggest that ritual expectations
about food have come to reflect nutritional requirements. In a
contrary way, the allergies reflect the reverse of what is healthy

and appropriate for people. For example, the recent alarming rise in allergies involving air is surely a sign of the physiological not to mention aesthetic consequences of air pollution and possibly wider pollution as well. And it cannot be ignored that there is probably a synergetic or cumulative effect of even minor changes in the environment which will suddenly or disproportionately produce allergic-like responses.

Even if depression may serve some provident function for the group at large, what could be the function of its extreme opposite, mania? I find it useful to comment to students that "in dealing with natural systems the shortest analytical distance between two points is a normal curve." If one of the functions of depression under troubling circumstances is to inhibit or slow down or even halt certain kinds of action because of the relative recklessness of members of the group, then perhaps the strident exuberance of the manic phase is an energizing and unsettling stimulus to communities otherwise too complacent and unchanging. Certainly there are indications of this, as we shall see, in the religious field, where certain individuals with improbably grandiose ideas coupled with very imperious attitudes toward other people may produce charismatic religions or political groups which often have extraordinary effects on formerly settled social systems. It may illustrate this principle to recall a particular form of diabetes, albeit a relatively rare form of the disease, in which the diabetic may eat no sugar, no flour, and only meat and vegetables. The patient typically suffers from great fluctuations of mood from the manic to the depressed. When requiring meat the patient is "high"—supremely confident, untroubled by discordant circumstances and in general prone to decisive and grand action. Understandably enough, such people carrying such genes would be inclined to stimulate hunting or gathering for the particular foods they can tolerate. As such, they would be, in terms of their wider community, advantageous stimulants to useful action.

The assumption here is that the gene or genes associated with this diabetic state and other allergic forms are selectable in themselves and are not carried along with some other, perhaps unrelated, characteristic, such as red hair, height or foot size. If it is carried on its own, how would the process work by which the allergic or diabetic pattern became part of the group in question and eventually of the wider human community? Since throughout the formative period of human history and evolution we appear to have lived in small groups, there would necessarily have been a considerable amount of genetic relatedness in any group. Accordingly, if an individual with the particular form of diabetes described above was in such a group and did energize it to seek the meat or vegetable the individual needed, then the whole group would benefit, including the genes which the individual shared with his family members. While an individual prone to depression might respond to a hazardous new environment or circumstance with the customary withdrawal or lassitude, the manic diabetic would have an opposite reaction; the group as a whole would stand to benefit from one response under some circumstances and the other under others—precisely the function of variation in natural systems and precisely the basis upon which the Darwinian theory of natural selection is based. As I mentioned earlier, variety is the protein, not just the spice, of natural systems; particularly when it relates to the gathering of protein it becomes critical, as it surely was to early populations. The fact that these adaptations are no longer as useful as they once were is a different question—this is really a reflection of the relative conservatism of the gene pool.

I recognize I am open to the charge of being a biological Pollyanna because I've tried to offer or suggest a useful function even for such unpleasant conditions as diabetes and depression. Nevertheless it seems prudent to claim a little space for this idea inasmuch as there are now known genetic components to some mental diseases. Under the radically different circumstances of our earlier formative lives these may have had some of the uses I have suggested. Furthermore, viewing mental illness in the phylogenetic perspective may permit not only a shrewder understanding of how modern social circumstances may stimulate these afflictions but also of how they may be alleviated or cured.

The genetic linkages yielding mental disease are probably

complex rather than simple. They are not likely to be the result of what Theissen has called "genetic junk." (Theissen, 1972.) Let me explain. Genetic junk refers to those genes affecting relatively unimportant aspects of the animal's behavioral and physical systems, for example, blue eyes as opposed to brown eyes, blond hair as opposed to red, slender fingers as opposed to stubby. Even I.Q. is a highly labile, changeable characteristic in the short run, and thus not terribly important to the overall survival and reproduction of an animal. For example, if individual A has an I.Q. of 130 and B of 70 they may both have equal numbers of offspring, so that the factor of I.Q. is to the overall system as junk is to the basic properties of an economy. Moreover, as Heather Fowler has pointed out (pers. comm., 1977), intelligence may not be reflected in I.Q. test results. Nevertheless, in a situation of difficulty, resource shortage or other challenge, it is surely arguable that more skilled individuals will be more likely to survive than less. Therefore, while intelligence may not directly be related to reproduction of offspring, it may be related to their ultimate survival.

We have been discussing diseases with elaborate implication for individuals and for communities. So it seems acceptable to claim that mental illness is not the effect of "genetic junk" but rather of general and pervasive patterns of genetic constitution with important links to the reproductive efficacy of individuals bearing these diseases. Several kinds of evidence support this view. The most obvious has to do with the perceived relationship between physical and psychiatric deficits. Not only may psychiatric difficulties be genetically linked but also they may not be solely carried environmentally—they may depend on an interaction between the individual and the environment in the same way that, for example, resistance or nonresistance to diseases depends both on the individual and the existence of the disease outside the individual. (Eastwood and Trevelyan, 1972.) There are also several suggestions that the existence of mental illness itself is relatively stable and has been over time and cross-culturally. For example, in an examination of rates of admission for serious psychoses in mental hospitals over a period of more than a hundred years, Goldhamer and Marshall

(1953) found no significant change throughout this period despite major shifts in the effectiveness and precision of psychiatric skill and diagnosis. As well, in a controversial but elaborate review of material, Jane Murphy suggested that at least several forms of mental disturbance and how people respond to them are fairly common patterns in even disparate cultures. Among the Eskimos, for example, shamanlike behavior has consequences for leadership of general social life. Nevertheless Eskimos make a distinction between the illness of "insane people" and the performance of shamanism. Murphy notes that the extent of "insanity" among Eskimos was 4.4 persons per thousand, and among the Yoruba of Nigeria 6.8 per thousand—rates not unlike the percentage of diagnosed schizophrenics in Euro-American cultures. Do we see here another version of the idea that there is indeed a genetic regularity underlying psychological states, including the pathologies? (Murphy, 1976.)

Of course these will remain controversial matters. All I have tried to do here is suggest the possible relationship of depression to the genetic system. A virtue of the biological perspective on behavior is that it permits specific investigations of the physical components of even complicated behaviors. So depression, which is composed of a variety of rather elaborate behavioral factors, can be and has been related to specific events of a chemical kind in the brain and the rest of the body.

Friendly Opiates

Now I want to return to the question of the opposite of depression, optimism. I will inspect briefly one possible component of this which has been newly researched, the so-called internal opiates secreted and used by the brain. The discovery of these substances may be the beginning of a breakthrough to understanding benign feelings. It seems appropriate to focus on them now.

Certain substances cause people to feel less pain if they are experiencing it. They may feel better about themselves simply because of substances they have taken. This is both a medical boon, in anesthesia, and a social problem, in addiction. Presumably the substances help people "screen out" ambiguous or unpleasant stimuli. Opium has been widely used, at least since classical Greek days and probably before (Malcolm, 1971). Other substances such as alcohol, cocaine, and the more recently synthesized artificial substances such as morphine and LSD have had effects on the experience of large numbers of people. It almost appears that the specific opiate does not matter—the body will crave it, and the person will often turn to extreme means to acquire it. Drugs supposed to cure addiction to drugs have frequently turned out to be addictive themselves. Thus heroin was produced in an effort to cure addicts to opium. In some communities efforts to reduce heroin addiction by the substitution of methadone have resulted in a new group of addicts, this time to methadone.

Why? It appears that the body "wants" addiction to narcotic substances or at least is at great risk of this. Again, why? One reason for scientific excitement about the discovery of the internal opiates is that they are associated with receptor sites in the brain and spinal column, and while there are no non-addictive substances yet available which act on these receptor sites, at least the location of them and knowledge of what they're like means that pharmacological efforts to find a non-addictive pain-killing drug can be more specific and prudent.

In terms of general scientific interest these discoveries relate to two important questions, one which affects all animals and the other principally the concern of humans. The first is, why should animals evolve a system that suppresses pain, their own analgesic system; and second, why should there be in the body a mechanism which can so readily produce feelings suggestive of euphoria, at least in the short run? In general, why should animals have developed or retained receptor sites in their brains and spines which respond so effectively in reducing pain?

In a talk to the Department of Psychiatry at the Albert Einstein Medical School in 1976, Larry Stein of the Wyeth Laboratories approached these questions through an interesting if diabolical experiment on rats. The animals were required to apply their tails to a hot source and the time taken for them to flick these tails was gauged under two conditions: the first was the normal one and the second was after the rats had been injected with the substance enkephalin, one of the bodily-produced pain suppressors. It turned out that enkephalin has a profound analgesic pain-killing effect, for about eight minutes.

This again raises the "why" question. What advantage would there be to animals of a species in being able to withhold response to painful stimulus for as long as eight minutes? The answer is presumably a subform of the general proposition being made here about optimism itself—that the ability to withhold unpleasant sensations from one's self may permit the individual to take steps to overcome the unpleasant stimuli—either by avoidance in the case of temporary pain, or by outright conquest as in fighting or defense or in escaping dangerous circumstances such as fire or smoke. Insofar as pain is itself a warning system to organisms that something is wrong, then the secretion of substances which overcome the warning system is an intriguing check of one evolved process by another. It suggests an interesting way in which natural living systems are able to maximize their opportunities to deal effectively with their environments.

There is some question about the relative effectiveness of the natural opiates and man-made morphine. The earliest studies concluded that man-made substances were considerably more potent than the naturally occurring ones, but it now appears that this finding may have reflected the fact that the naturally occurring substances are broken down chemically by protein enzymes much more rapidly than morphine and hence, after being injected into the experimental animals, their effectiveness was artificially reduced. It appears now that the potency of the natural substances is, in fact, greater than that of the synthetic.

In any case, the broadly physiological approach of researchers in this area may miss the point of the function of the endorphins if it is assumed that these substances principally serve to restrict pain messages in the organism. They may not serve principally to reduce pain, though that is one of their effects.

Their major function may be to anesthetize the organism against responding too directly and forcefully to negative cognitive stimuli in the environment. They permit the animal to obscure the understanding that its situation is dire when it is in a bad fight or in a fire or already wounded and allow it to continue to function as if it were not operating under such adverse circumstances. That is, in effect, the *naturally occurring opiates need not be very powerful; their function is not to significantly shift the body's capacity to perceive pain but to produce small changes with large consequences in the organism's cognitive assessment of its survival situation.* For the organism to be able to sustain a social rebuke or threat or ambiguity and uncertainty without cringing or fleeing, not much "mind change" may be necessary.

What is involved here is far more subtle and elusive a process than permitting that same organism to sustain injury to its tail for a long time. Once again those studying the effects of substances on behavior, in this experiment for example, are not testing behavior but rather physiology. How much pain? How long? What dosage? These are questions appropriate to understanding the physiology but not to understanding the social behavior of the individual. Once again those testing drugs are far less interested in the effect of the drug on the social intercourse of individuals than on the relationship between chemicals and bodily tissues. The body of the rodent is being treated as if it were mainly a shield in a fire station rather than as a center of the most vivacious and subtle of socio-cultural enterprises.

Unfriendly Opiates

I think this principle applies also to experiments on people. One can get a sense of this from the addictions. People become addicted to drugs not because the drugs reduce pain, as most addicts are not under medical treatment, but rather because the drugs affect the addict's social sense and sense of himself in society. My basic point about the possible functions of naturally occurring opiates is that they are not principally involved with avoiding physical pain. Rather they stimulate a social and psychological state which augments the animal's survival chances under circumstances in which a cold and correct assessment might be sufficiently demoralizing to mean the difference between life and death. What nature has provided—apparently to all the vertebrates from rodents to man—addicts seek more powerful versions of. So *addiction is based on a natural process, not an unnatural one.* This is reason enough for the difficulty of coping with it and a clue to how centrally it roots itself in the living system. Thus, as machines are to human muscle, man-made opiates are to natural ones. Like the lever, the morphines, LSD, amphetamines, etc., magnify what is already there. That is why they are so effective and that is why people who take them find them so desirable.

A well-known clinical phenomenon appears to underscore the importance of the social aspect of the use of addictive substances. It is apparently rare that patients who are suffering severe pain and who are given morphine as an analgesic become so addicted to the substance that they crave it when they leave the hospital or their treatment abates. If they are unaware of the nature of the substance they are being given or if they are understandably enough preoccupied with the pain they are suffering then it seems as if substances which lay harsh claim to the loyalty of the bodies receiving them lose this effect in a marked way. Peculiarly enough, even such a drastically tangible physical phenomenon as the craving of addicts may depend upon a socially mediated and stimulated factor. In any case it is hardly surprising that substances with strong effects produce different responses in people who know they're receiving these substances as opposed to those who do not. The morphine-drugged patient in the hospital who knows only of pain and its relief and not of a drug and the states of consciousness it can produce is plainly a different kind of candidate for addiction than the person seeking definitive changes of personal state because of dismay with his present one or an experimental sense of a possible one. And of course the old adage of folk psychology, that it is more damaging and dangerous to drink alone than in the company of convivial others, underscores a recognition of the principle that even the supposedly wholly private matter of how the inside of a body deals with the substances it receives has a directly social aspect.

Commentators from Marx to Chaplin have claimed that man's technology has outrun his ability to encompass and respond to it. Perhaps the technology of substances also operates without built-in natural controls. We do not yet know if the naturally occurring opiates rise and fall in dosage level according to various social-physiological circumstances. (My suspicion is that they would not vary very much and that if an animal is physiologically "permitted" by its internal secretions to optimistically evaluate its situation, it will do so with a more or less constant intensity; that is, without very much variation.) There may be considerable variation between individuals but much less variation within individuals' own routines.

However, when man-made substances are administered, the body evidently quickly becomes accustomed to the low levels of intake and, in order to achieve a significant effect from the drug, demands larger and larger doses. As Mandell has commented, there may be limits to the experience of euphoria because the bodily system quickly adapts to a particular dose of the euphoria-producing drug, for example, LSD, so that "a daily dose of 50 micrograms would be euphorigenic on Monday, mildly stimulating on Tuesday and almost without effect on Wednesday." (Mandell, 1973:572.) It appears that the brain adapts quickly to regulate its own intake; this may be an impediment to the long-term use of euphorigenic drugs for the relief of patients suffering from, for example, terminal multiple sclerosis or cancer. There may be a major discontinuity between the technology of drugs and our human ability to respond to them. Mandell's concluding paragraph in the essay I've cited reads: "It may be philosophically important that human beings are so quickly habituated to drug-induced pleasure. I recall a statement Heinz E. Lehmann made recently after hearing some of this work: 'It seems to me that the puritanical attitudes towards pleasure must have as part of their substantive grounds these neuro-biological mechanisms of adaptation.' Perhaps pleasure must (*sic*) be transient and can only be experienced against the background of its absence!" (*Ibid.:572.*)

Perhaps now the puzzle of why optimism exists becomes clearer. Is it because each individual secretes a substance or series of them which affects in the optimistic manner the tissues of the brain and other centers of response and social evaluation? If it is a natural system then because of what we know about individual differences we will expect important variation from one extreme to the other. This could explain on the one hand the crazily manic or hopelessly euphoric individual who is beyond any connection with reality and on the other the profoundly depressed person remote to all stimuli and responsive only to those generated by chemical distortions of normal experience. These extremes are somewhat caricatured and yet we do know that communities may be as concerned about over-optimistic, completely euphoric, millennarian-minded people of thorough impracticality as about those unfortunate depressed persons we've already discussed.

But this is not the place to try to come to terms with the way in which communities respond to dreamers and cosmic optimists. Instead I want to continue along the chemical road to see what more we can learn about how the brain responds to opiate substances and how we compare with other vertebrates who share these substances with us. The central message of Mandell (1973), along with others such as Hamburg *et al.*, (1974) is that there is a system to moods. This system is related to the body. The interaction of moods with the body is complex but knowable. My extrapolation is that there are also social structures and cultural patterns which reflect these systems. These are as real and knowable by a comparative approach as the chemical states themselves.

Let's begin with some examples. The amine compounds are to be found throughout the brain. They are most concentrated in the limbic system, that phylogenetically old section of the cerebrum. When we referred to MacLean's research we saw that that system is elaborately involved with sexual activity, emotional states, hunger and aggressive behavior. Because of the association of depression/optimism with these old parts of the brain—because they are paleopsychic processes—it may be revealing to glance at what happens among other animals. As I've indicated, all vertebrates appear to possess the internal opiates, and there seems to be no pattern of phylogenetic evolution of the quantity of receptor sites for them in the brain of various animals. For example, the swine hog has the most receptor sites, rats about 70 percent more than mice, while the primates average about the norm for the vertebrates. So the efficiency of the receptor sites has not simply to do with density or mass, unlike for example the cerebral cortex in the human, which is large compared with that of other animals.

But there is obviously some more arcane or subtle relationship between how many receptor sites there are and what they do in the wider context of the whole brain system. One fascinating aspect of the location of the receptor sites is that in the monkey, at any rate, the anterior amygdala has by far the most receptor sites by a ratio of 65 to 1 as compared with the next most receptive area, the posterior amygdala, with a 34 to 1 ratio. Other parts of the brain are far less receptive. The information about humans is not yet available; however, these findings are most intriguing because the amygdala seems to substantially affect monkeys' aggressive and fearful behavior.

The important work here is by Kling (1975, and Kling and Steklis, 1976), who has conducted a series of experiments involving monkeys with removed amygdalas. Kling has shown that when these animals are kept alone in cages they are aggressive and fail to respond to normally fear-provoking stimuli, are angry, and become hyperactive. However, when they are returned to their fellow monkeys under natural circumstances they become fearful and extremely withdrawn. Their physical survival is literally in question. Is this an extreme form of depression? Is the absence of receptor sites for internally occurring opiates as well as the better-known neuro-transmitters causing these animals to constantly and grimly evaluate their circumstances pessimistically—and, finally, ineffectively? Of course we cannot know nor can we, for many excellent reasons, extrapolate from amygdalectomized monkeys to normal humans. However, among the few things known about the amygdala is that it is an important organ for the regulation of anger and rage. *It may well turn out that the "taming of the amygdala" by internal opiates is a salient feature of cooperative, non-aggressive, benign behavior.*

I have already noted the ways in which humans share with other animals a characteristic pattern of "stop" and "go" systems, the two most obviously distinguishable categories of organic behavior. Do we also share with them, in the "go" category, a fundamental, organically related optimism about the next moment, the next meal, the next day, the next breeding episode? There is no reason to believe that the great chain of being does not include this as one of its links. And if we accept, even as an irony, William James's comment I've already recalled—that humans, being more complicated animals, must have more instincts than others—then we are presented this possibility: *our brains are higher brains, more efficient at diagnosing and ferreting out possible hazards, impediments, problems (moral and factual), and demons and shades with which we can be harassed. It becomes all the more important then that we possess an overriding internal censor of all these mean and depressing thoughts so that we are not immobilized and disconsolate forever.* Once again William James effectively has described the basic problem faced by an animal as skillfully analytical as we: "Life and its negation are beaten up inextricably together . . . The two are equally essential facts of existence and all natural happiness thus seems infected with a contradiction. The breath of the sepulchre surrounds it . . . and so with most of us: a little cooling down of animal excitability and instinct, a little loss of animal toughness, a little irritable weakness and the scent of the pain threshold will bring the worm at the core of all our usual springs of delight into full view and turn us into melancholy metaphysicians. The pride of life and glory of the world will shrivel. It is after all but the standing whorl of hot youth and hoary old. Old age has the last word: the purely naturalistic look at life, however enthusiastically it may begin, is sure to end in sadness. This sadness lies at the heart of every merely positivistic, agonistic, or naturalistic scheme of philosophy. Let sanguine healthy-mindedness do its best with its strange power of living in the moment and ignoring and forgetting, still the evil background is really there to be thought of, and the skull will grin in at the banquet. In the practical life of the individual, we know how his whole gloom or glee about any present fact depends on the remoter schemes and hopes with which it stands related. . . . Let it be known to lead nowhere, and however agreeable it may be in its immediacy, its glow and gilding vanish." (James, 1958: 120–121.) Yes indeed, it *is* almost simple and trivial. The framework *should* be gilded, but how? Build a cathedral? Shoot up? Go on a diet? Pray and wield one's immortal soul? Buy lottery tickets at three different shops for better luck? Have hair styled or salon-painted? Is what's in Pandora's box a simple trick, chemical in this instance?

Which takes us back to our first question. How do nice ideas make people feel better, evidently even in their bodies, and how do bad ideas, and threats of bad things to come, cause them to feel bad, apparently even in their bodies? Are the promises of Marx, Mohammed, Jefferson and Jesus engraved not on stone but in chemistry, and would it be frightening were it so?

I do not want to overestimate the implication of all this chemistry because we are talking here about clues, not proofs. Yet I believe we should not underestimate the possibility that laws of experience may be understood through the tools of chemistry, even experiences held to be of the very highest moral, spiritual or political order. Intellectual workers are generally trained to skepticism about appearance and are finely honed for the description and diagnosis of pathology—social and medical. Even so, maintaining some amount of focus on benign and delightful elements of social and private worlds may not only be essential but certainly desirable. It is at the very least useful to know what the elements might be of these pleasing chemical phenomena if in fact they are important, just as we know fairly precisely at just what point the most nutritious and well-prepared food eaten by a healthy person becomes excessive and causes illness.

Before concluding this chapter I want to investigate two other sets of clues which may bear on the question of how ideas and social situations affect bodies and the reverse. First, I want to look at how placebos work and don't work and why they appear to be widely used. Second, I want to examine the relationship between two extreme social circumstances—incarceration in concentration camps, despite which prisoners competently survive, and reaction to drastic failure ending in the dolorous matter of suicide.

Sometimes it is possible to see a connection between a social event and a bodily one even though the precise interaction is not known. A quiet but alarming report some years ago suggested that there was a rise in infant mortality in the vicinity of London's Heathrow Airport, to a rate which was "greater than the average for stillbirths in the Greater London area generally." (*The Times* of London, July 3, 1973.) While no positive evidence linked the adverse trend near the airport to its noise, similar reports from elsewhere tended to bear out the connection. I happen to be writing this in the countryside of Tuscany, near Siena, a beautiful and reassuring environment, timeless in its suspension in grape, fig and olive growing. However, nearby, near the city of Pisa, is a NATO Air Force base, and from time to time extremely noisy fighter planes scream overhead, presumably on those days devoted to the exercise called "Flying Fast and Low." The noise is breathtakingly loud, and I can readily understand how a newborn baby or even a fetus of a startled mother might be so alarmed as to distort a vital system and either die or be mortally damaged. Perhaps the shock of sound waves is as real to the body as crashing into metal or ingesting poison.

Noise is real. So are sugar pills—and yet they are not supposed to have a real medical effect. Nonetheless, they apparently do. The "placebo effect" may be defined as what happens when there is a change in the status of an illness or pathology which cannot be attributed to the operation of chemically active substances upon the organism. Beecher has estimated that there is a more or less standard rate of cures by placebo-type treatments of roughly 35 percent. (Beecher, 1968.) Obviously much of the effectiveness of treatment must be owing to the fact that any such treatment involves social interaction and thus implies participation in a group. At the very least, in a gregarious animal the mere reiteration of social bonds would have a benign effect on its state of being. If we assess the importance of "mere" social connection, keeping in mind the circumstances of the patient, who may feel frail and unwell, frightened by the direness of solitary confinement, and tormented by loneliness, then we can understand why the donation of even a useless so-called drug will be revivifying if it cements a social tie. The placebo is not the drug; the dose is of social encounter.

A corollary to this is the so-called "Hawthorne Effect," named after a series of tests done at the branch of the Western Electric Company at Hawthorne, New York. The tests, involving women working at wiring banks of electronic instruments, were controlled to show the effects of different conditions of work. Thus, when lighting was increased production went up. When a rest period was added production rose further. More lighting, additional rest periods, a longer lunch break—all yielded the same result. It seemed in that golden age of industrial management that a brilliant discovery, and useful economic tool, was at hand.

However, a management skeptic then reduced levels of illumination, shortened the rest periods, cut the lunch break—and still production rose. It became clear that what was involved was involvement itself—showing management's concern for employees, by any means, improved their effectiveness. Ever since then the one-to-one relationship of cause and effect in controlled studies has had to take account of the Hawthorne Effect (Roethlisberger and Dickson, 1961)—an effect I feel confident is fully implicated in the placebo effect. For in many of the major assessments of new pharmaceutical products circa 1960 a principal and constant aspect of a wide range of drug reactions clearly was the effect of human involvement.

Placebo is the Latin word for "I shall please." *The Random House Dictionary of the English Language* offers this definition: "A substance having no pharmacological effect but given merely to satisfy a patient who supposes it to be medicine." As Jerome Frank notes, the word "merely" in this definition presupposes that any physical benefit is purely coincidental. He

points out that placebo techniques may produce direct physiological effects, for example, through their ability to induce healing of certain tissues: "The placebo treatment of warts . . . by
painting them with a brightly colored but inert dye and telling
the patient that the wart will be gone when the color wears off,
is as effective as any other form of treatment, including surgical
excision, and works just as well on patients who have been
unsuccessfully treated by other means as on untreated ones.
Apparently the emotional reaction to a placebo can change the
physiology of the skin so that the virus which causes warts can
no longer thrive." (Frank, *Persuasion* . . . 1974:140.) Even
bleeding peptic ulcers were improved among 70 percent of patients who received injections of distilled water which their
doctor had told them was a new medicine. A control group,
given the same injection but told that it was only an experimental medicine whose effectiveness was uncertain showed a cure
rate of only 25 percent. (*Ibid.*) Shapiro has argued that this classic placebo effect, combined with the basic fact that many ailments cure themselves, helps explain the more or less consistent reliance upon placebos by physicians in western Europe
for the past several thousand years; this principle should apply
to other cultural traditions as well. (A.K. Shapiro, 1959:298–
304.) Lewis Thomas has also noted the frequency of self-limi-
tation of illness and the extensive catalogue of largely useless
drugs, confidently maintained in the pharmacopoeia for decades. (J. Bernstein, "Profile," *The New Yorker*, December,
1976.)

It has been assumed, certainly in the Western European tradition of medicine, that much of the efficacy of placebos resulted from a patient's belief that the useless substance administered to him was in reality an active one. However, Park and
Covi found that even when subjects were informed that they
were being prescribed an inert drug the placebo response
among them remained constant. (Park and Covi, 1965.) Obviously a number of factors are implicated in the success of
placebos. For example, the enthusiasm doctors and patients
may share for a new course of treatment, even when the doctor
knows it is based on inert substances; the ritualistic or drama-

turgical structure within which drugs are given and taken; the association between the unpleasant taste or attributes of medicine and their potency; and the fact I've already mentioned that the association of drug-taking with a caring community is reflected by or personified in the medical practitioner.

There have been several attempts to locate the dominant cause of the success of placebos in a personality type, the so-called "placebo-reactor" type. (Madison *et al.*, 1973; Honigfield, 1964a,b.) However, countervailing evidence suggests that success depends on the milieu and situation in which the placebo is administered. The general conclusion of such writers on the subject as Shapiro, Rickels and Honigfield is that what works or is usefully manipulated is "expectancy," a psychological construct or condition. The possibility surely exists that "expectancy" has or will be shown to have definite neuroanatomical and behavioral correlates. The internally secreted benign opiates may play a role in the placebo reaction. But we can only derive partial certainties from the range of evidence about the placebos; as Frank notes, ". . . the major conclusion to be drawn from studies of the placebo effect is that its simplicity is only apparent." (Frank, 1974:151.)

Not only are responses to placebos themselves physiologically complicated but there are a variety of social and ethical issues which must be confronted. For example, Bok (1974) has discussed the overall ethical framework within which placebos may be given, ranging from the obvious questionableness of giving placebo birth control pills to women who wish to avoid pregnancy to the general problem that student physicians receive surprisingly little discussion and analysis of placebo treatment. In a sample of nineteen popular recent textbooks in medicine, pediatrics, surgery, anesthesia, obstetrics and gynecology, only three even mention placebos; none deals with either the medical or ethical dilemmas which placebos present. On the other hand, Benson and Epstein argue that placebos are an overly neglected medical asset. They say physicians' reluctance to employ placebos may result in prescription of expensive drugs with possibly deleterious side effects. (Benson and Epstein, 1975.) On one hand, Bok argues that the use of placebos contributes to the corruption of the patient-physician relationship, if only because it violates norms of non-deception in human relations. On the other hand, Benson and Epstein suggest that "patient and physician attitudes that create a sound doctor-patient relationship contribute to the production of the placebo effect. The placebo effect in most instances enhances the well-being of the patient, and thus is an essential aspect of medicine." (*Ibid.*, 1226.)

Bok clearly shows that powerful drugs are often prescribed which broadly function as placebos since their real function is unclear. This may be medically as well as financially costly, since frequent use of antibiotics may reduce their impact for particular patients over time. Prescriptions of antibiotics for minor virus diseases serve primarily as placebos, and the cost to the public of these drugs in the U.S. has increased from 350 million dollars in 1962 to about 657 million in 1972. Available unnecessary drugs may encourage patients to rely on these drugs rather than on natural means of overcoming medical difficulties. For example, one study of childbirth pain suggests that training before birth and a positive attitude to involvement in childbirth are likely to make childbirth more bearable or at least less painful than otherwise; subsequent performance as a mother may also be affected positively. (Davenport-Slack and Boylan, 1974.)

Illness is often a means of coming to terms with various difficulties and problems in social life. Too rapid prescription of placebo or any other type of medicine may deprive patients of a period of respite from obligations and responsibilities which the "sick role" can offer. (Shuval, Antonovsky and Davies, 1973.) Placebos may have positive effects on individuals otherwise regarded as sophisticated and skilled. This is suggested by a study performed at the Mayo Clinic which revealed that 39 percent of patients suffering from cancer (112 of 288 patients examined) reported that placebos relieved 50 percent or more of their pain. ". . . those who responded most to placebos were the highly educated farmers, professional workers, women working outside the home, and patients who were widowed, separated or divorced. Those who had a low response were the poorly educated, unskilled workers, housewives, smokers, and married women without children." (*The New York Times*, March 13, 1977.) This suggests one reason for the peculiar intensity of the advocacy of Laetrile as a cancer-curing drug, despite the fact that all good scientific evidence denies its efficacy.

It is by no means clear how placebo-type reactions affect particular people with particular backgrounds and under a variety of circumstances. There is an immense literature on the processes which are involved in pain (Casey, 1973; Melzack and Chapman, 1973), on the effects of placebos on perception of pain if not on its actual experience (Feather, Chapman and Fisher, 1972), and even on the relationship between aspects of mysticism and meditation on the control of experience and forms of physiological pain. (Gellhorn and Kiely, 1972.) The matter has been made even more complex by the finding that in rodents, at least, administration of sugar, often found in placebo drugs, appears to stimulate the secretion of benign endorphins!

The upshot of all this is that whatever generates the power of suggestion, the power is real. The relationship between a social bond and a medical response is firmly established even if the precise mechanism underlying the relationship is not clear. It is not surprising that a gregarious creature who craves social experience in infancy should in illness respond within the web of society rather than alone. In the Eastern philosophical tradition, with its relatively undeveloped scientific component, the effect of mysticism on medicine is direct and considerable, and this is surely understandable. Why, then, if one assumes that there are few differences between world cultural groups as far as the tenacity of the grip on life is concerned and the urgency of steps taken to preserve it, should we be surprised if in scientifically based communities of Euro-America there remains a considerable if perplexing component of quasi-mysticism—for example, with placebos—in medical practice? This too should not be surprising; one must assume the generous amount of mystical behavior in our species is unlikely to stop at the borders of scientific cultures.

This may present a problem to people such as myself raised within the austere, angular skepticism of scientific and secular cultures. We will no doubt continue to insist that there is a knowable pattern to all this strange stuff, as indeed there must be. We will try to protect as firmly as possible gullible and unskeptical people from those clever enough or ruthless enough or needy enough to exploit their gullibility. This group of exploiters may contain as many neurophysiologists employed by drug companies as it contains cardinals of the Catholic church or swamis who are profitably self-employed. Not only may there be some reassurance in the direct connection between the cunning snake of the Garden of Eden and the snake oil elegantly purveyed by specialists in these industries. There may also be another aspect to gullibility which may reveal our human capacity to draw on unusual reserves of energy and skill. Perhaps there are sources of energy and experience not easily located by heretofore conventional understanding. These may affect directly even life and death itself, and it is provocative to explore this a little further. So I want to turn now to the problem of why some people refuse to be destroyed while others destroy themselves.

The Most Drastic Contortion

When I told him about my study of optimism, the University of Western Ontario anthropologist Lee Guemple, an expert on Eskimo hunters, wrote me the following remarks, which I quote with his permission. "There is evidence to show that after two or three days of continuing starvation there is a complete lack of appetite, *i.e.*, symptoms of starvation . . . disappear. Presumably this would sustain the optimism of the organism by maintaining a feeling of well-being and of an ability to 'cope' in the face of a serious problem. . . . Eskimo accomplish much the same thing through symbols. As long as they have tea and coffee—before the trading period it was doubtless something else—there is no feeling of deprivation and no loss of confidence in their ability to cope. When these things are with-drawn, however, they fall into a profound kind of depression from which it is difficult to stir them. Note that neither tea nor tobacco has anything to do with nutrition."

An intense interest exists in how people survive adversity, what mechanisms they use, and what, even, might be the internal physiological causes and effects of survival. A fairly substantial literature on survivors has been recently and usefully summarized by DesPres (1976), and a number of quite incontrovertible conclusions have been drawn from studies of persons exposed to the dreadful experiences of concentration and other kinds of prison camps. Eitinger has studied the effects of imprisonment on the health of an unselected total prisoner population and in so doing throws light on the effect of excessive stress on the organism. (Eitinger, 1973.) The persons studied were Norwegians who spent an average of twenty-three months in German camps and prisons for non-Jewish prisoners during World War II. By comparing the imprisoned population who survived incarceration with the Norwegian population as a whole, Eitinger showed that there was a significantly greater vulnerability of the ex-prisoners to various diseases, in particular tuberculosis, cancer, and even accidents. Eitinger also discovered that ex-prisoners were much less stable personally: "Nearly 98% of the controls had one residence only while the ex-prisoners moved much more, either because of their restlessness or in order to find new jobs. . . . One out of four is characterized by an obvious professional decline while this can be seen in the controls in only one out of 25." (Ibid:204.) As far as physical symptoms were concerned, ex-prisoners again were more at risk—for example, they had three times as much absenteeism from work because of gastric and duodenal ulcers as the controls did. "This difference is only outnumbered by the differences in psychiatric disorders. . . . They represent a group which is more sick, more often sick, has lower working capacity and stability and thus lower income; a group with pathological changes also in areas where we are not used to looking for such changes. On the whole a group which, in spite of the relatively ample pension they are receiving in Norway, seem to have fared much worse than their matched controls." Elmer Luchter-hand also has studied prisoners, those transported in particu-larly punishing carriages called "gondola cars," and comes to similar conclusions about the profound effects of even a rela-tively brief but intense period of incarceration on survivors' health and social disposition. (Luchterhand, 1966–67.) Clearly there is an interesting connection between a person's ability to overcome adverse physical circumstances and the particular means by which he manages to survive.

But for the present I am more interested in the opposite case, of those who finally yield to death coerced by social circum-stances such as concentration camps, or to illness or, in the most drastic case, suicide. A poignant intermediate case was revealed in a particularly grim experiment with children dying of leukemia Spinetta and Maloney, 1975. The hospitalized chil-dren were given toy hospital rooms with which to play, and asked to place dolls representing themselves and others how-ever they wished. In each case as the child's illness progressed a regular pattern was observed—the closer the child to death the farther away from the doll representing him were placed the figures of the doctors, nurses, and most pathetically, the parents. With unfailing regularity a few days before a child died all the figures were placed outside the toy room represent-ing the real hospital room. The implication of course was that the child knew he was dying and rendered in all-too-dramatic play the real drama of his increasing distance from the forces of social life.

But how did he know? How are internal bodily processes perceived, symbolized, and rendered in behavior? How possi-bly could a small child understand enough about his failing health to spare the living from poignant contact with the soon-to-die? Of course "understanding" may be the wrong word and "knowledge" may describe better what the child perceives.

Apparently a connection exists between an idea about life and the physical living of life. In the extreme case, suicide, an individual translates an idea about life into the fact of personal death. It is the precise and devastating reverse of the survivor's optimism.

Let me explain. One tragic case I know involved a young woman who'd had a turbulent adolescence and was then unfortunate enough to require a gynecological operation which either caused or revealed sterility. Despite protests by her relatives, her doctor felt compelled by medical ethics to tell the young woman of her condition. Thus was added to her general depression the information about this profound curtailment of her life's force. Perhaps this stimulated her to curtail this force altogether by the drastic act of suicide. Those around her felt that had she not been told of her sudden biological incapacity she would never have done what she did. Was it a sense of foreclosure and choicelessness which was a paramount consideration here, the complete loss of an opportunity to "live on a chance," as William James put it?

"Voodoo death" likewise suggests the importance of a sense of hopelessness—in this case in causing not only humans but other animals to die apparently spontaneously. In a classic article on "voodoo death" the physiologist Walter B. Cannon sought to establish that in a variety of unsophisticated peoples around the world death did in fact result from a psychosomatically initiated reaction to various "hexing" practices. Witchcraft itself killed. Death did not result from clandestine administration of poisons—as was thought to be the case by ethnographers acquainted with the problem. (Cannon, 1942.)

In an effort to test some hypotheses about sudden death, Richter (1957) used a control group of laboratory rats who had all been exposed to various kinds of "fight or flight conditions" throughout the course of their lives. When these and wild rats were subjected to extreme stresses, the wild rats perceived their circumstances as novel—as presenting problems they could not solve. For example, in one experiment Richter immersed rats in large glass jars of water and played jets on them to force them to swim actively in order to breathe. The average laboratory rat swam for sixty to eighty hours before drowning. However a large proportion of the wild rats lasted not more than two or three minutes; they took "suicide dives" to the bottom of the tank and displayed electrocardiogram readings that reflected shock rather than hyperactivity of the adrenalin system.

Richter interpreted this to mean that these rats had perceived their situation not as a standard "fight or flight" one—for which rats have an adaptation—but as an entirely novel problem and as a consequence had "despaired." In order to test this theory, he immersed additional wild rats for two or three brief periods and then rescued them; afterward, he subjected them to the primary test. Having learned about the option, and the expectation of possible relief, the wild rats, like the lab animals, swam for up to eighty hours under the experimental conditions I've described.

In his discussion of Cannon's article, Richter suggested that a similar phenomenon was involved in "voodoo death" after hexing. Inasmuch as indigenous belief systems precluded any hope of escape from death, fainting and a gradual "withering away" of the body occurred, accompanied by hyperactivity of the parasympathetic system. (The parasympathetic system in part is responsible for coping with shock.) Furthermore, all social treatment of the hexed individual as a living person ceased. As he was treated as "already dead," all avenues of expectation or hopefulness were closed off. The complete lack of optimistic possibility was in these cases apparently as effective as a bullet or chemical pill in ending life. However, in cases in which the hexed person was told that a mistake had been made, and that the hex was lifted, this information produced rapid recovery and even some form of "immunity" to the particular kind of hexing the sufferer had overcome.

Just as a sense of option and possibility can be taught in several trials to wild rats, so can a sense of despair be taught to humans and other animals by convincing them that their circumstances are hopeless. What Martin Seligman has called "submissive death," or "learned helplessness," is clearly a feature of the process of demoralization which occurs among victims of voodoo and witchcraft. (Seligman, 1975; see also Wintrob, 1973.) It also affects those in prisons, both real and imagined. What happens under these circumstances? Let us assume that a feeling of efficacy involves some neurochemical balance of internal opiates or something like them with other substances of the brain. If so, does submissive death or suicide itself involve interruption of such internal opiate secretion? Of course, there are numerous socially explicit stimuli for suicide—these are vividly described by Alvarez (1972)—yet inasmuch as the general social and aesthetic conditions which may accompany suicide apply to vastly more non-suicides than suicides, it appears only sensible to look for internal as well as general causes for acts of suicide. An additional inducement to explore this chemistry is the frequently repeated observation that persons undertaking suicide may have—before the act itself—endured self-administration of various substances such as alcohol, addictive or non-addictive drugs and stimulants. (There is also an implicit kind of suicide, marked by immensely hectic inadvertence—for example, the improbably dangerous driving by [principally] young males under the influence of alcohol [Zylman, 1972.])

The issue of suicidal intention is very clouded. Unquestionably a great number of suicides were intended as attempts and social warnings. Human incompetence and misjudgment must at least be as critical in such attempts as in other dire actions, and one must assume that some proportion of those who succeed in killing themselves ardently wished to fail. The numbers of attempted suicides are not trivial. Weissman, Fox and Klerman have noted the incidence of suicide attempts in the New Haven area and showed the relationship between attempted suicide and depression. (Weissman, Fox and Klerman, 1973; see also Weissman et al., 1977.) There are differences between people simply suffering from depression and those who attempt suicide, but there is enough of a connection to suggest that the movement from depression to attempted suicide to suicide itself is relative and gradual, not stark and categorical. And this implies in turn that the principle of the normal curve continues to hold and that there is biological continuity in death-seeking as in other events of great biological consequence.

Weissman also reports that in the New Haven area 88 percent of attempted suicides involved ingestion of pills, in many cases sleeping pills. Does it not seem scandalous then that so many doctors prescribe sleeping pills to so many people, even though it is well known how short-lived is the efficacy of sleeping pills and how both in the short and long run they interfere seriously not only with those night-dreams which make day life organized and tolerable but also with the physiological processes of reparation which sleep permits? It is also relevant that people who kill themselves with sleeping pills (or attempt to do so) live with sleeping pills. Chemically induced disturbances of their natural systems appear to augment their feeling of shabby experience, depressed futures, and miserable present. Indeed the general phenomenon that the bodies of attempted and successful suicides are afflicted by some ingested substance or substances—amphetamines, sleeping pills, alcohol—is one gloomy but strong indication of the physiological aspect of self-destructive behavior.

In this context the willingness of medical practitioners to add to the possibility of self-destructive behavior among people already displaying personal trouble by being unable to sleep is scarcely encouraging. Ivan Illich's notion of "iatrogenic" disease—disease caused by the very cures which medical science propounds—is particularly relevant here, even if the overall statement Illich makes may be unduly sweeping. (Illich, 1976.) Any individual wanting to commit suicide can secure sleeping pills through one means or another. The fact that these pills are issued by persons in authority and are readily seen as benign may generally facilitate the suicide process among people who—as the percentages reveal—are willing in only one out of five cases to commit their own deaths to the violence of a bullet, a screaming leap from a high level, occupancy of a crashing car, or the even slow daze of poison gas.

There is relatively poor information about possible constitutional and physiological determinants of suicide. In a review of 378 papers on the subject of suicide, DeVries (1968) failed to find a single study of constitutional and physiological determinants of suicide. In a survey of some 500 publications, Struve (quoted in DeVries, 1968) found a comparable situation. But this may be changing. Struve, Klein and Saraf (1972) recently reported results of a study of possible relationship among abnormal brain electrochemistry, suicidal ideas, suicidal ideas in addition to suicide attempts, and aggressive-destructive behavior without a suicidal component. For both males and females a positive and significant association was found between the syndrome of suicidal behavior and a particular pattern of brain performance. How this occurs or why the authors are not certain, though they speculate on the possibility that "the EEG patterns reflect a patho-physiology that predisposes to the development of depressive affect, of which suicide is a secondary expression."

In an investigation which took into account more psychological issues, Thomas and Greenstreet (1973) were able to predict occurrence of suicide and four other disease states—mental illness, hypertension, coronary heart disease, and tumor—among 1,130 medical students participating in a longitudinal study which was begun in 1948 at Johns Hopkins University School of Medicine. Some of the factors in their prediction were clearly sociological, such as closeness to parents, employment of alcohol, etc., but other determinants, such as resting diastolic blood pressure and cholesterol level, appear more physiological. A great difficulty in understanding the physiology of suicide is that suicide is rare; in order to detect what may be predisposing circumstances an enormous number of people must be studied, relatively fruitlessly and usually at considerable cost.

There is too much to say about suicide for it to fairly occupy much more of my essay here. But let me try to put it into a perspective which may illuminate its source and importance in the human system. We began with survivors of extraordinary adversity, nearly all of whom appeared to suffer some permanent damage to their bodies and their psyches no matter how resolute they had been during their period of trial and however cordially they were welcomed on their return to civil society. At least they survived; the least successful survivors were those who died. Inasmuch as there is a natural system involved, some survived a little, some a lot, and some until in fact they overcame the adversity altogether; somehow the most poignant stories of concentration camps are those about inmates who died in the days immediately before the camps were liberated. Had they been a notch up on the normal curve of survival or had the liberating troops been a little faster they, too, would have been survivors and not victims. Like suicides, these people in a sense arranged their own deaths by yielding to disillusionment, depression or bereavement. Perhaps suicide is a more energetic and certainly more aggressive version of this process, albeit suicide is far less poignant. On the contrary, it is vicious, distorted, unbearably painful to family and friends, and a gross violation of the tentative truce with mortality which all humans must make. Nevertheless, suicides, apart from those induced by either real or spurious heroisms, such as Mishima's, make a major statement about the value of life and thus call into question the very source of optimistic gregariousness which sustains us all. When I was working at the University of British Columbia, I became involved in a project with an extraordinarily talented, charming, seductive and psychologically dramatic professor. With him and three other members of the faculty, I spent about a year evaluating the university's educational program. Together we wrote a series of recommendations which stimulated a rather successful set of innovations, although the radical nature of some of these caused much bitterness and disturbance among the university's more conservative centers of power; the report, in fact, was awaited with considerable and violent tension. One day, shortly before the report was to be issued, a swastika was scratched on the door of this professor—the first Jew appointed to a major post at that university. Although the incident was quieted, it clearly revealed the continuing issue of his appointment and what he was proposing to do.

The pressures were great and the professor suffered enormous anguish. At length he requested a leave of absence and was admitted by a psychiatrist to a local hospital for at least a weekend of quiet rest. A decision had to be made whether the patient should be put in a room with bars on the window or an ordinary room; it was decided that given his powerful intellect and unusual grip on life, an ordinary room would be less dangerous in the long run than a room with bars, with all that implied. But there was no long run. The patient, who had studied hospitals professionally and understood the nurses' routines, seized a brief opportunity available to him and plunged thirteen floors to his death.

I cannot begin to describe the profoundly demoralizing effect his suicide had on those of us around him. He had seemed such a trove of life, such a proponent of the complexity and joy of thought. Yet this was what he had done. Perhaps I was the last of his colleagues to see him alive, because the night before he went into the hospital I was working late in my office and looked across the quad to see his light on. I was worried about the reason why, so I went to his office and we talked. Unexpectedly he wept and with weird and passionate naïveté exclaimed that his colleagues had lied to him systematically, cynically lied, even about matters he could check. We talked some more, a telephone call came from the president of the university wishing him well, and he calmed down and expressed hope that this respite would solve his problem, that we would all overcome the difficulty of the task which lay ahead—a difficulty we certainly overestimated.

The next morning he was dead. Monday morning, when the members of his department returned to work, the atmosphere was unbearable. Some of the senior members, who had known him a long time, simply stayed away in stunned disbelief or abhorrence. I recall being strangely and extravagantly grateful when one of those who didn't came into my office, seated himself, and said without ceremony, "The only way to deal with this is to realize that——was a bastard." Plainly, he meant to deny the positive impact this man had had on all of us, to make a tolerable equation between the aggressive act of suicide and the life it had ended.

Later that morning the university was embroiled in activity. Rumors spread about the fate of our imminent report and our opponents declared that it would never be released. The four remaining members of the report staff met that very morning and resolved to proceed. The responsibility for presenting the material to the faculty fortunately devolved on a man who because of his seniority, compassion and provident religious conviction succeeded in retrieving victory from the disaster.

As I write this, I realize that these events, which occurred a dozen years ago, are as vivid as those of yesterday. I can't escape them. I was a junior member of a faculty of which this professor was a major symbol of achievement, of brilliance, and I admired him greatly. But the complex, life-giving forces which he had generated he snatched away. Years later I was told by the then chairman of my department that he had recommended I be given a year's leave because, he said, I was gravely depressed and needed to escape the blight of what had happened. Was his diagnosis correct? I think so, although I wasn't aware of the degree of my despondency then.

There is nothing so demanding of the optimistic system as a suicide. When my best childhood friend, whom I had not seen for twenty years, turned his car engine on in his sealed garage while his wife and two children were upstairs, I thought somehow I was responsible—after all, I had not seen him for twenty years. When one of my first and most promising students ended his life, I thought I was responsible again—after all, I had very recently spoken with him. When suicides occur we all claim responsibility or feel we share in the failure of the social fabric to support the person in need. Suicide is a violent challenge to our general complacency about the extraordinary value of life. To be sure, suicide is not only violent against the community but also against the survivors. It stuns the reflexive optimism of most communities as they proceed without searching cosmological analysis. Yet the suicide forces such a cosmological analysis on us—those who feel guilty and those who feel innocent—all must reflect at least for an instant on their response. "To be or not to be?" What does it mean? In a perverse way the rededication to the living entailed by a reawakened understanding of the nearness of death provokes a forceful injection of the optimistic sociohormone into the social body.

There are two apparently contradictory thrusts in the modern science of behavior. One reveals the way in which large, complex systems involving countless people may affect individual states of being—for example, Brenner's demonstration of the relationship between poor and unsettled economic conditions and personal mental illness. (Brenner, 1973.) The other shows

with increasing refinement how private experience is composed of processes linked to internal personal chemistry—how
brains, glands, perceptions, tissues, bones and resources all
interact to provide that composite: experience. In this chapter I
focused on the latter problem. In my view, it is the more allur-
ing to scientific inquiry. Imperfect as the data seem to be, they
seem to me of great significance. Both in the therapeutic sciences such as psychiatry and the more abstract social sciences
such as anthropology or political science, it is essential to recognize the kinds of connections which may exist between
bodies and behavior and what goes on inside bodies and outside them.

I have tried to show how a psychological state nearly opposite
to optimism—depression—displayed some clear physiological
indices and how these related to various behaviors both in
humans and other animals. I tried to relate this to what is
known about the structure of the brain and how different parts
of the brain respond differently to the internal secretions which
wash it and engulf it. In particular I focused on the internally
secreted opiates, the discovery of which may well turn out to
be of inestimable importance for the understanding of human
pleasure and the avoidance of human pain. The discovery of
these substances occurred after I had begun my work for this
book. Not only did they fit neatly into a theoretical place I had
assumed was necessary for them, but the strength and complexity of what they do in bodies went far beyond what had seemed
to me even theoretically possible. On reflection, however, I can
understand why my conjectural approach to internal opiates
turned out to be less adventurous than the one finally urged on
us by the emerging data. After all, the work in this area occurs
largely in the therapeutic professions concerned with the avoidance and remedy of pain, and also within a Euro-American
cosmological tradition suspicious of ecstasy, committed to so-
briety and in religion and morality very careful about delineat-
ing the proper sphere of physical pleasure.

A feature of the optimistic phenomenon well known, though
hardly adequately researched or taught about in medicine, is
the placebo response, and I tried to show how this was con-

nected with the overall story I'm telling. The same effort was made in regard to survivors, to victims of extraordinary duress, and even, finally, to those unfortunate persons, suicides, who conduct the least-promising experiment in mortality. In all of these people doing all of these things—being depressed, being deliriously hopeful, using placebos, destroying their bodies—blood courses in the veins and substances in the blood. The connection between body chemistry and the great events of human hope and failure may be puzzling and the substances involved seem trivial. Yet however much some may resent seeing the origin of grandeur, or human folly in what is tiny, the pressure of a provident science is unremitting and we must continue to look, and look again.

5

The Great White Whale

The most self-denying monk of a self-denying Asian monastic order has a particular robe of a special color. The half-naked Indian holy man testing his body's limits boasts a particular bed of nails. The rootless sailor signing on as deckhand for ship's voyage after ship's voyage has his tattoo. Babies clutch dolls and blankets so long they practically vaporize, and bourgeois people fleeing advancing armies try to hide small mementos of their families' past in their clothing or the crannies of small baggage. If only to reject them as an act of moral rebellion we respond to things. More often we embrace them, seek rather than shun them, find them attractive.

We all are connected to the substances we take into our bodies and to the other living and inanimate components of the universe. If we love or care about our existences we must appreciate the manifold transactions we conduct with the external world. Like any living thing, we contain within ourselves the energy of a genetic program which broadly determines not only ways of life and time of death but what we need of food, water, air and light to survive. The food and drink we take into our bodies are turned into sound, heat, odor, excreta and, most dramatically, behavior. Like other animals, we have abiding and deep concerns about food and its availability. But unlike other animals we surround the food and drink we consume with stories and forces; we cook foods or otherwise prepare them in an amazing variety of ways and modify their taste and appearance with endless skill. Moreover, food is never judged apart from its ambience. The setting, time, ritual implements— all are part of the ceremony through which we affiliate with the substances the world provides.

Food deeply concerns us. It is perhaps the most reiterated of our concerns apart from the weather. But clothing also concerns us, and shelter, and the various items of pure adornment which, whether reposed in museums or vended in dimestores, constitute part of the almost universal apparatus of our existence. Each of us is distinguished by some symbolism of costume, some greater or lesser flamboyance of personal heraldry—in short, some arrangement of our personality, portable as clothing or fixed as furniture, which marks us as unique.

So far I have written about very intimate and principally internal processes which relate to our sense of the future, of well-being, of malaise, of skepticism, of conviction. These, I claimed, were connected to reproduction, what one enjoys as a child, and how one functions as an adult. I also tried to show how the endogenous processes of the body affected and were affected by ideas of hope and misery and how all of these rested on a substantial platform—either of substances themselves, as in the form of drugs, opiates, or sedatives, or as guiding ideas—of voodoo, of miracles, of total hopelessness. All of these affect the very health of bodily tissue and even its survival.

Now I want to turn to the way in which individuals behave in small ways to stimulate and support what I will call "little optimism." In the final chapter I will necessarily turn to "big optimism"—the business of big business, big politics, large movements, great religions, etc. But for the moment I want to restrict myself to optimisms at arm's reach, which may come from a diet book, a telephone call from a stockbroker, playing the numbers, buying a Pucci silk scarf, using sugar and eating deviled crab on a bed of rice. I want to show how bits of behavior can be lifted out of the course of events and shown to contain optimism—that element I so firmly believe to be necessary in even apparently unimportant details of the human scheme. Is there a vital connection between inflation and vacations, radical chic and dinner parties, rebuffs and diets? I think there is.

Cash Flow

For most people on earth today money measures survival. Time on earth is bought with money. A few coins equal a few days; the connection with mortality jingles in the palm of the hand. For the poorest money may mean the difference between life and death. For the richest it becomes a calculus for immortality; landscapes and cityscapes are strewn with monuments to the possessors of far more money than was needed to see a life through. Between these extremes money can provide a very volatile index of personal status, and it appears to permit people to rank themselves in relative statuses quite rapidly.

Like all human constructs, money—for all its remarkable, bewildering, practical importance—embodies a wealth of symbolic meanings about personal states and the forms the future takes. Because it is an arbitrary and formalized construct, it can be used as readily by groups and governments as by people. Since the rise of agriculture an important means of transaction between government and people has been money, usually in the form of expenditures for taxes going to governments and expenditures for benefits going to people. If money is as central to the conduct of contemporary communities as it appears to be, and if optimism is as important to the constitution of society as I've claimed it is, then there should be something to say about the relationship of these two things—money, the hard fact, and optimism, that will-o'-the-wisp.

Well, is there? Let's ask, why do people celebrate? Why do people mark occasions which are already favorable and happy enough, such as anniversaries, birthdays, graduations, births, promotions and publications, by purchasing gifts which are unduly luxurious, by providing food, drink and settings which are extravagant, and by ingesting substances such as alcohol and drugs which substantially alter their and their guests' perceptions? Is bread being cast upon the waters? Is a demonstration underway to show the faith of the celebrant that occasions for this kind of celebration will appear again—that the frailty of human kind and its mortality have once again been overcome? Why is the birth of a child an occasion for celebration? After all, the money and time involved in supporting the child could otherwise be spent supporting the freedom and general pleasure-seeking of the parents. Is this willingness connected with the difficulty governments have faced in stemming population growth and, alternatively, with governments' surprising unease when their populations appear to be stationary or declining, e.g., the French government's consistent pro-natalist policy and the Japanese government's establishment of a study group to determine reasons for a decline in the Japanese birthrate and to consider means to reverse this decline?

What purpose does conspicuous consumption serve? What, for instance, is the function of vacations? Why did the Lord set aside one day as a day of rest and why, even in communities where work is an important ethic, is an increase in holidays and leisure a sign of improvement and plenty? How, if in any way, is this connected to the existence of feasts, ritual celebrations, even national days of dedication and rededication? In what way is the human connection to prosperity different from the same connection in other mammals? I've already asked what will happen when the species must either not grow or contract in numbers in order to survive—with the consequence that large numbers of people will have no children or very few. Do declining birthrates imply declining economies?

These are all questions about the biology of human behavior which has bedeviled the study of human biology in general since social Darwinists claimed that owning money and property was a sign of biological superiority—a kind of fiscal version of the Calvinist notion of predestination. This foolish notion was self-servingly convenient for the group which by and large controlled and benefited from Victorian economic life. There is a more recent rendition of the same confusion, which appears to rest on the judgment that there has been no improvement in the quality of biological thought since Darwin; some writers, such as Sahlins (1976), appear to regard present biological efforts as merely an extension to other animals and to genetics of capitalist economics. However, the problem of establishing a "human nature" baseline for economic theory has only recently been approached, apart from the Marxist effort, which treats human economic nature as an artifact of, not a producer of, the economic system. Some Western economists, such as Becker (1976), are prepared to examine the relations between economic behavior and biology, while others, such as Samuelson (1977), see no useful connection between the laws and analyses of economics and those proposed by some biologists. My intention here is not to explore these various minefields but rather to comment ethnographically and descriptively upon some critical economic behaviors.

A first step must be to ask what we can surmise about "natural economics" from our evolution as an economic species. I've already cited the effort Fox and I made to try to draw conclusions from information about our extensive hunting-gathering history. For my purpose here perhaps the most significant feature of this history is that as hunter-gatherers humans were predisposed to economic equity if only because owning property—for example, land—would produce little wealth beyond the resources needed to maintain its producers. Furthermore there was an interdependent connection between humans and their environment; in the absence of preservatives or refrigeration there was no way for humans to accumulate extensive surpluses of foodstuffs or possibly indeed of anything else.

Prosperity meant "enough." The shift to agriculture and then to industrialization changed this. Now prosperity means "more." Often it means "more than enough." I am not suggesting that hunting-gathering peoples did not or would not try to acquire beautiful or useful objects. But their circumstances made it difficult to do so, and it was certainly inconvenient for

wandering hunter-gatherers to retain any possessions. Whatever their property, like us they had to make and execute economic plans. With settlements, pastoralism and agriculture,
once the constraints of very simple economics were removed
the same planning and executive skills were employed in enterprises which grew in scope. Now they are of global range. The
means of production may be owned by the community as in
socialist and communist countries, or private investors as in
capitalist, but certainly technology coerces particular forms of
conduct of industrial organization. How the surplus or profit of
an enterprise is distributed is basically a political question;
there may be some differences in efficiency which result from
one procedure rather than another, but these do not concern us
here. For example, it may not matter much if on the one hand
central planners require an organization to generate an additional 10 or 20 or 30 percent of production each year or whether
the impetus for this arises from the scrutiny of bankers and
investment analysts or the desire for greater profit of an entre-
preneurial family. In both cases the net result appears to be
roughly the same; there is a consistent commitment to growth
and presumably surplus.

Perhaps the most liberating feature of the shift away from
hunting-gathering was not solely or even principally that communities could focus enthusiastically on making exquisite objects, satisfying curiosity, or creating wider social networks.
Rather, it likely permitted the free exercise of optimistic productivity, to create the economic base for acquiring larger
herds, more farmland, more factories, buildings, tools. This is
a melancholy but I think correct revision of the idle if benign
sentiment that emancipation from immediate economic need
leads to decreased concern with economic activity. The contrary
seems true; people in communal regimes may be as coerced by
demands for successful productivity as are the workers in the
crassest of exploitative systems. The same pattern seems to
apply when no calculable profit is involved. So, bureaucrats
who manage government-owned enterprises appear to be as
incapable as private owners of reducing their volume of activity
and their income. Both groups will do so with equal reluctance

and only under the most rigorous of compulsions. It is also ironic that those concerned with the ceaseless growth of capital enterprises and businesses are surprised by the consistent and similar tendency to grow of official bureaucratic enterprises supported by taxes. But why? There is no reason to believe that bureaucrats are less coerced by optimistic zest than investors. Indeed, because they possess what may seem to them the moral advantage of working for the common good rather than striving for private profit, they are more likely to assert a commitment to growth. From this perspective, so-called zero-base budgeting, which requires that bureaucratic units justify their entire budget over each year, is as radical a proposal, given the way modern economies consume bureaucratic wealth, as the expropriation of private property would be. As a citizen, I happen to think that this is a very desirable procedure for bureaucracies to follow. I also suspect on anthropological grounds that it will be enormously unpopular with bureaucrats, if popular with taxpayers, and difficult to achieve for reasons I've already alluded to and will deal with further as we proceed. The principal threat of such a budgeting pattern to a bureaucrat is that he will suffer a reduction in the volume and scope of his activity. Even if he is guaranteed by civil service procedures both income and rank, there may be a traumatic effect on morale and self-conception—the individual may appear to be as wounded as if he had been actively dismissed and not merely curtailed. What is remarkable about zero-base budgeting is that it should have been hailed as such an innovative concept and that it should have taken so long to be suggested as a guiding principle for financing government agencies.

The problem is real in part because human beings appear to possess few effective control mechanisms on their senses of growth and prosperity. In the name of economic efficiency and growth at least some people are content to design and produce extremely effective weapons of destruction and sell these to governments or even individuals who plainly have in mind plans of questionable civility. More prosaically, but as dreadfully, entrepreneurs and state monopolies systematically continue to produce and market substances known to have vicious effects on their fellow citizens—particularly producers of alcohol and cigarettes.

Let me restate my position. I'm suggesting that greed is a pathology of prosperity which in turn is a component of the optimistic syndrome. But what reason can there be for the persistence of such an obviously unpleasant and socially disruptive kind of behavior—greed? In a nutshell, I believe that greed as a potentiality or possibility was contained and managed and even used constructively when the redistributive system of the hunting-gathering ecology kept everyone in a state of communal interdependence and mutual obligation. As well, the intimate connection of the kinship system to economic life could well produce an additional control on greed; at the very least because of the loyalties of kinship, funds taken illegally from the public sector would almost inevitably be funds taken from one's kin, and there is some reason to believe that such greedy dishonesty is less likely to occur than the theft of resources from impersonally owned public funds. Indeed, we know on the basis of ample evidence how readily police officials, jurists, criminals, politicians and others will from time to time and from place to place engage in elaborately corrupt subversions of correct public practice in order to secure private gain for themselves and their immediate kin. For example, the corruption surrounding the importation, distribution and use of illegal drugs in the U.S. and particularly New York City is profound in the social system of the city, to the great cost of its overall economy, the sense of moral dignity of its citizens, and of course the wrecked bodies of addicts and the destroyed ones of individuals no longer useful or too dangerous to the conspirators involved in this lucrative trade. It is unnecessary to catalogue extensively the dispiriting amount of bold and unjustifiable criminal behavior which serves to enrich some individuals at the expense of the wider public. It is enough to remark that the acquisition of wealth seems so important, even wealth vastly beyond any known need for it, that individuals will violate their communities' norms of decency and mercy, let alone the communities' laws. (A Professor of Law at the University of Houston, A. A. White, has written an intriguing analysis of legal aspects of this problem in an essay with the grave title "The Intentional Exploitation of Man's Known Weaknesses," 1972.)

How does prosperity work and where is it to be found? There is certainly a sheen to the prosperous. Indeed the accoutrements of the rich, usually including their own skins, generally have glisten as a component—from the sparkling jewels to the precious metals to the polished cars to the silk and the almost electric hair. These and other characteristics mark the prosperous. A glow of control, effortless but decisive, surrounds them. This needn't involve only the authentically rich, those with certifiable wealth, but also those who feel prosperous or rich in the context of their origins and strivings. Thus the capably self-supporting ghetto female who has earned a good income will select mass-produced fried chicken or other food for herself and her children with the same sense of bounty, importance and efficacy as the industrialist choosing among limousines. Likewise, the same sense of prosperity appears to exist at the tables of the large families with children, aunts, grandparents, parents and cousins at a Sunday morning tea-lunch in a Chinatown restaurant as exists in the smaller family of the South Vietnamese general whose stolen gold was transported from his country before the Americans yielded control of the airport and who shares the benefits of his cunning in one of the very costly, punctiliously adept, Vietnamese restaurants in Paris.

Jewelry shops also are prime symptoms of that pathology of optimism, greed, and exist everywhere. They attract people who have a sense of prosperity, and who wish to reflect it in the shine of precious objects or preserve it in the highly portable certainties of metal and gems. It is amazing to consider one consequence of jewelry shops—that wealthy women will attend social functions bearing on their bodies thousands of dollars worth of jewelry that otherwise has to be kept for security in bank vaults. This is indeed a pathology of prosperity. Like candy shops and bakeries, jewelry shops reveal a psychological sweet tooth unhealthy and thus pathological—but, in terms of their widespread occurrence, seemingly totally normal. In the context of equity, jewelry shops are a wound in the social body.

They are incitements to outrage, as are the limousines and *dachas* of Soviet notables and amenities of white African colonials. All such privileges based on greed—and there are countless others—are depressing affronts to those in the world who seek to enhance rather than weaken the power of the principle of human equity.

But what stimulates the onrush of need and want which constitutes the greedy action? Does the greedy person desire more and more because he fears there will be less and less? Conversely, has he decided that he is particularly fortunate and worthy and therefore deserving of unusual bounty? Gluttony is greed of a particular kind, in part because it may have a relatively definable physiological substrate—there are reasons to believe that obese people lack the "switch-off" mechanism which for most people indicates that ample has been reached and surfeit impends. Of course greedy eating and the obverse, dieting, affect people's conceptions of their bodies and hence themselves and may also betray a clue to their sense of personal wealth.

I will shortly turn to the question of the small optimisms involved in dieting and eating and drinking. But, before doing so, I would like to examine several features of economic activity which involve big optimism—institutionalized forms of optimism which affect large numbers of people in a widespread way.

I think that one of the critical problems facing the human species arises from this possibility: that in the absence of the natural constraints on consumption imposed by the hunting-gathering system the genetically based optimism of people produces a desire for ever-increasing consumption of goods. And it is not clear how the economy of the world can satisfy this demand. In his fine book *The Limits to Satisfaction*, William Leiss has noted: "The principle of legitimacy for modern society, which simply stated, is the rationale for the acceptance of the prevailing distribution of rewards and power now consists in a permanently rising level of consumption. This principle is today at work not only in government-managed capitalist societies (North America and Western Europe), but also in the industrialized socialist nations (Eastern Europe and the Soviet Union). . . . A permanently rising level of consumption is the single most important element in the network of popular hopes and fears whereby the citizens of industrialized capitalist and socialist societies register their belief in the legitimacy of those social systems." (Leiss, 1976:4.) The situation to which Leiss points is in its way even graver than he suggests if the hypothesis here is true about the natural quality of optimism. But even if my hypothesis is wrong, there are some very basic socioeconomic practices which institutionalize optimism, and these are worth noting.

It is often fruitful to look first at what is taken for granted in a social system—it may most centrally reflect the system's assumptions. Economic optimism is most directly enshrined in the "cost of living bonus" which is widely distributed to employees in many countries. Because the emotional and other satisfactions of employment in industrial societies do not match the excitement and vividness of the hunting-gathering way, it almost seems as if one light solution to the heavy plight of being industrial is to look forward to a constantly expanding income. There are other forms of this promise of expansion, such as the widespread practice in official government bureaucracies of providing annual increments in salary. Presumably these are based on the assumption that the individual employee becomes more skilled with time and therefore useful to the organization; on economic grounds alone an increase in salary is held to be justifiable, though it is scarcely clear that the size or very existence of these increments is ever carefully related to perceived improvements in services provided. A similar process of relatively automatic increments occurs in private business, where one would have thought at least the requirements of bankers and shareholders would have dictated that increase in emolument was accompanied by increase in production—a relationship scarcely certain, given the automatic nature of most salary increases. So strongly rooted is the notion of almost inevitable increase that the logical basis for this practice is hardly examined.

In an even more bizarre version of this process some communities, notably Brazil and Israel, have made a pattern of "indexation" in which all values—for example, of money in savings accounts—increase as currency is inflated. That is, if a saver has 1,000 pounds in a bank and the government reckons that the value of a pound has declined by 15 percent in terms of purchasing power, then the saver is credited with 1,150 pounds rather than 1,000. It had been the case in Brazil that "practically all economic areas from savings accounts to corporate balance sheets to business contracts were automatically adjusted to compensate people (in Brazil) for the Brazilian currency's persistent loss of value because of inflation." (*The Wall Street Journal*, October 20, 1975.) The remarkable foolishness of such a scheme has apparently been perceived and some modifications of it are underway.

Originally such "indexation" was thought necessary to induce people to remove funds as savings from the consumer economy where their presence would inflate an already excessive demand—or so goes the reasoning. But the net result of all these schemes is of course precisely that government and labor costs increase in general and this in turn causes cost of living bonuses to become necessary. With stunning irrationality the cure for the disease of inflated costs of living becomes itself the cause of the disease. Furthermore the entire process is incremental, not just absolute. That is, once a cost of living award has been made or an increment for merit or seniority received then the new level becomes the fixed state. The activities of employees and their representatives are directed to further increase in the future. However, now the gain is a percentage of a larger sum and so the escalation proceeds. Furthermore, increases are frequently based on percentages, which means that differences between salary levels already in existence are further exaggerated. After negotiations for increases at my university, the conclusion is usually a fixed percentage of award given to all employees with the few very minor variations at the very top of the scale and at the bottom. The general pattern is that the people receive five or eight or whatever percentage more this year than last. But eight percent of $30,000 is a much greater increase than eight percent of $13,000, and the award thus expands significantly the dichotomy between junior and senior employees. The apparent equity of an equal percentage increase for all is in fact a producer of increased inequality. For example, in a settlement arrived at in 1978 the faculty team negotiating with university representatives came to the conclusion that the distinctions between high-paid and low-paid people were woebegone indeed, and in a display of surprisingly transparent inefficacy, determined that all members of the university would receive an equivalent increase of salary on a percentage basis of either $30,000 or $10,000, but that people currently paid under $15,000 would receive an additional $75 a year over a two-year period!

Of course there are numerous schemes for providing pay increases. But to be effective they must boast the essential characteristic that the pay increase be perceptible. For that reason relatively highly paid persons may require larger pay increases than poorly paid ones—only a large increase would be appreciable if only because of high taxation, and thus contribute to the contentment of the employee. Following Leiss's assumption about implacably increasing wants, one would assume that governments and employers will try to maintain political control over their systems by continuing the practice of providing perceptible increases, even though a consequence is the enlargement of inequity and the unchangeable commitment of larger and larger blocks of organizational funds as time goes on. In effect, what happens is that enormous sums of money are redirected in the economy for reasons which are poorly formulated, inadequately scrutinized, and perhaps as much related to the semi-occult manipulation of the opiate of optimism as to any systematic plan for reasoned management of the communities' resources and its peoples' time. My point is that only rarely does the optimistic impulse receive the analysis it requires. The result is that random extrapolations from it come to dominate aspects of social policy allegedly unconnected with such a basic-level psychological response as the optimistic one.

One justification frequently given for the cost of living bonus is that it is supposed to provide what an individual "needs" to "keep up with" inflation and thus ensures some equity over time. However, this does nothing to ensure equity within organizations or to provide adequately over the life cycle for "needs." An anecdote may illustrate: When I was a teacher at the University of British Columbia, the pension plan that all who worked there shared was controlled by the members of the faculty. At a faculty meeting a motion was proposed that additional payments on retirement be given to the oldest members in the plan when they retired. This was because they had entered the academic profession at a time when salaries were very low and when pension contributions were small or indeed nonexistent. So, when they came to retire, the discontinuity between what they had been earning as full professors and their retirement income was severe. Hence the suggestion that they be given *ex gratia* payments. I spoke in favor of the proposal but noted that since what was being introduced was the notion of economic equity this presented the possibility for review of the entire salary structure in these terms. I made the following suggestion: that if income were to be based on need—the rationale for the contribution to retiring persons—then salary allocations in the university should be changed to reflect that need. Accordingly, young faculty members seeking to establish families, purchase homes, and acquire furnishings and appliances should be given larger salaries than senior members of the university whose family-raising responsibilities were complete, whose mortgages were paid off, and whose declining range of activities because of age could be reflected in lower income. Needless to say, this half-serious proposal was welcomed by those who, young like myself, would benefit from this equity. But it was roundly rejected by the disproportionate number of senior faculty attending the meeting. My naïve plan to provide income to people in terms of their needs was doomed to failure not only because it departed so drastically from the existing practice but also, I now realize, because it would have made impossible the translation of the optimistic urge into money.

This was not a unique situation. Government after government has experienced immense and vexing political difficulty whenever it has tried to control rising prices and incomes. The words "wage and price freeze" are commonly invoked by governments as solutions to the obvious problems of inflation but instantly become the cause of endless and usually heartfelt and bitter acrimony and manipulation. It appears quite clear that consumers as well as producers see economic welfare as an increase in quantity. It also appears that the phenomena of increase and decline are as salient psychologically as the absolute value of what is increasing or declining. Perhaps this is one reason for the widespread use of percentages, changes upward and downward, and the calculation and projection of trends in financial reporting: "Dow Jones up 6.28," "Unilever boosts dividend 12 percent," "Money supply up 1.8 percent in August," "New car demand on upward trend." I think it is scarcely accidental that there exists this preoccupation with more and with less in financial reporting because it has very much to do with basic human responses to wealth and its uses. We are calculating organisms exquisitely equipped to desire more and truculent and grim about enduring less.

Surely the attitude people have in this connection toward their income is a factor in the development of inflationary economies, indeed a strong reason for the tendency toward inflation. There are several structural reasons for this; control of the money supply offers governments an opportunity to pay their own debts with paper they themselves print, whatever may be the consequences for their currency in international terms. As well, since many tax systems are progressive, governments are able to extract increasingly large sums in income taxes from people whose tax bills rise as their inflated income falls into ever higher tax brackets. Nonetheless, psychologically, at least a semblance of "keeping up" or "getting ahead" is maintained. As Tibor Scitovsky has commented, ". . . not surprisingly people's self-rated happiness is positively correlated with their income in each of . . . ten surveys. . . . Over this period of almost 25 years per capita real income rose by 62%. . . ." However, supporting the suggestion that the theory of relativity applies as well to money as to matter, Scitovsky notes that ". . . the percentage of people who consider themselves very happy, fairly happy, and not too happy, has hardly changed at all. Our economic welfare seems to be going up and up but we seem to be no happier as a result."

How is one to explain this? The most obvious explanation would be that one's happiness depends not so much on one's absolute standard of living as on one's relative one—in short, on how one stands in relation to the Joneses. (Scitovsky, 1973:17.) In a series of surveys of a sample of the American public, Daniel Yankelovich and his associates have concluded that their respondents had over time escalated their notion of what was due them in their community. Now they regard as "entitlements" what had formerly been seen as privileges or in any event goods or services purchasable only by the fortunate and wealthy—such as good-quality higher education and low-cost and full-scale medical treatment. (Yankelovich, pers. comm., 1976; see also Heilbroner, 1978.) In effect, citizens of capitalist America are increasingly taking for granted those educational, medical and other facilities provided to citizens of socialist and communist countries. At the same time they continue to claim their rightful and expanding share of consumer goods and services, the very things which consumers in the socialist and communist countries may be prevented from enjoying by the governments of their communities.

Lead Us Not into Temptation

Government policies always have a great deal to do with people's attitudes toward their own consumption. Such policies reflect basic values of societies. For example, England in the 1970's, virtually all of the belligerent countries during the Second World War, the United States under the Nixon administration, and Canada for several years in the mid-70's have all made efforts to control wages and prices. Though these were controls imposed largely by capitalist societies, instituting them required an apparatus of administration reminiscent of the controlled economies of Eastern Europe and parts of the Third World.

Price and wage controls represented a centralist effort to cope with the problem of individual desires for a greater share of the community's wealth or at least for greater income. However, they were firmly embedded in a capitalist context, and there are major differences in how capitalist as opposed to communist countries deal with the problem of human economic optimism. Capitalist countries at most times seek to maintain control over their populations by stimulating their optimism, by persuading them that they will fulfill their economic hearts' desires. Communist countries seek to maintain control over their populations by reducing optimistic stimuli: information is restricted; advertisement of desirable goods and the media of communication about merchandise are carefully controlled. The credo of the capitalist optimist is: If you know you can buy it you will work hard for the money which you need. For the communist: If you don't know it's available you'll be content with what we give you—with what is available. This is an extreme caricature. Yet the contrast is itself extreme between the hectoring bombardment of advertising stimuli to which potential consumers are subjected in capitalist countries and the controlled, usually censored arrangement of consumer information in communist societies. An exceptional case, and it is a major one, is of the so-called Third World communities which may have socialist and centrally controlled governments but which may nevertheless permit open access to the mass media of rich countries. The effects of this on their populations, on their attitudes toward progress and modernization, are immense. The explosive information of the remarkable privilege enjoyed by the world's rich is almost flaunted to people who can barely afford the price of a radio or television set.

As is well known, efforts to inhibit individual consumption in communist countries have succeeded principally because goods have been limited or unavailable, not because people's interest in them has been deflected. The passion for goods in Eastern Europe, for example, is untrammeled. The skill, zest and success of various communist élites in acquiring material possessions are well known. The materialist fascination of the citizenry and their devotion to shopping (which is often necessary because of inefficient distribution) remains striking. Perhaps the communist system has succeeded in altering crucially the attitude of people to the ownership of the means of production. But it appears to have had less success in changing their commitment to the products of the means of production. The same is true in the Israeli kibbutz system, in which the totally communal productive system has also been accompanied by a considerable concern for consumer goods, such as small items of furniture, apartment décor, and electronic equipment such as stereos, radios, etc. I note this without an implied criticism; it was and remains one of the intentions of collective societies to make available the fruits of production to all citizens. That people are interested in these products is hardly surprising and presumably, given the moral structure of the community, also desirable. (Tiger and Shepher, 1975.)

Whatever the larger overall system of economic activity in which people find themselves, their primary personal economic wants, sense of need, and behavior will be directly affected by the optimistic urge as well as by conventional notions of fairness. Even in the relatively structured economic environment of communist China, suggestions as early as 1975—more recently reflected in the political changes there—indicate a concern with private income and benefit. For example, in a report in the August 1975 *New York Times,* Fox Butterfield noted that there was emerging ". . . an important drive to end factional bickering and labor unrest like the event that recently led Peking to send more than 10,000 troops into factories in the coastal city Hang Chow." It appears that ". . . in Chinese communist parlance the drive is aimed against what is referred to as 'bourgeois' factionalism." This broad phrase apparently encompasses not only factional strife of a presumably conventional kind but also workers' demands for higher pay and other material incentives, both of which stem from a selfish individualism which, as Butterfield reports a radio commentator having said, ". . . is a sharp manifestation of the bourgeois mind." According to Butterfield, people traveling in China have noted that party officials managing some factories are reluctant to confront workers who demand higher wages and who have been staging slowdowns or in effect striking because of dissatisfaction. "Although there has been no inflation in China, where wages and prices are government-controlled, most workers have not had raises in years and their bonuses were taken away last year as part of an effort to prevent backsliding toward capitalism." In this context the controversies in China following the death of Mao and the removal from power of his widow and the other three members of the so-called "Gang of Four" as well as the return to power of Mr. Teng are presumably not unrelated to public concerns about private consumption—it did appear that the return to power of Teng was popularly greeted and his emphasis on economic efficiency and productivity welcomed.

It would be foolish to make any comment on these situations in the Chinese economy and how it is or is not affected by consumer demand. However, the relationship of the "little optimism" of personal consumption with the "big optimism" of the Chinese revolution and national development may well prove to be very volatile. It may not therefore be insignificant that 10,000 soldiers were needed to deal with the effects of what was described as an ideology imported from capitalist centers—"bourgeois" materialism. It is well to recall that China has been extraordinarily well insulated from such centers, and from their propaganda and other products, for nearly a generation and a half. Will the notion of personal economic growth be a fatal or dangerous virus when introduced into a country which has for centuries been faced with no more appealing prospect than basic survival with few perquisites except for the few? Given the perspective I've sketched here, it seems likely that pressure for increased personal consumption will provoke important responses by the Chinese government. Consumer demands, together with the incipient regionalism of China—a poorly understood but probably immensely underestimated force—possess the potential to stimulate larger and larger military cadres, as much for internal purposes as external. From a political point of view Mao was sensibly prudent in seeking to immunize the Chinese people from consumer demands. I believe, however, that even the tentative introduction of the virus of consumption will have rapid and powerful effects which will produce increased reliance on military strength to maintain political hegemony. (It has been estimated that the Chinese currently spend a relatively modest eight to ten percent of their gross national product on military matériel and services.)

The use of military force to restrict the passion for increased income is scarcely unusual. The procession is now a long one indeed, of relatively poor, allegedly modernizing countries which began their independent existence with political leadership only to be overtaken by military control. It is hardly surprising that under these circumstances the purchase of weapons by poor countries controlled by military cadres has increased drastically in the 1970's and has now in fact become one of the most serious moral, economic, and political problems confronting the world; in 1977 the United States alone sold 11.3 billion dollars worth of armaments to foreign countries. Militarists seem intent on increasing the resources at their disposal. They appear to want a collegial connection to the dominating military forces and hence technology of the military world. They want planes, missiles, tanks, boats, communication systems, as good as anyone's and preferably better, even if the economic base supporting their countries is unable even to service the technology. When militarists of poor countries are impeded in their self-aggrandizing plans they may simply appropriate the civilian governmental machinery which exists. After all, they are trained to use force and have a structure of authority and property with which to do it. Furthermore, having achieved power, militarists possess an important advantage of controlling the money instruments of a community—in particular its printing presses for money. This provides them a significant edge over any civic group seeking to return to political power. In general the ease with which money can be printed involves a new order of centralizable control over peoples' lives, one which has been quite underestimated for the political weapon it is by theorists of economic, political and social behavior. Of course, I'm not arguing that it should be an instrument of such control, but it is. If the money machine can affect for the better how people perceive their short-term circumstances, it can also lead in the long run to immense dissatisfaction and disarray in communities as the fabric of social and economic interaction is stretched paper thin by the profligate production of paper money. Unfortunately, a military government is best prepared to deal cruelly with people who may ultimately seek reform.

Air in the Money Machine

Now I want to turn to how individual perceptions of the economic future become integrated with and reflected in how an economy operates. The discussion must focus principally on non-centrally managed ones, the capitalist ones, because in controlled economies the relationship between individual behaviors and central plans and responses may be leaden and imprecise (though during particular periods the public may be able to make its dissatisfaction with its government's policies about consumer goods explicit indeed). An important open question about economic behavior in the non-managed economies has to do with the link between individual perceptions of the economic future and how the economic system as a whole functions. What people think about an economy helps determine whether economic activity will improve or deteriorate. The result of individual economic decisions and moods may well be a thriving economy in which people feel prosperous and confident about their futures or one in which people feel poor and disconsolate. There are real effects of an often major financial kind of evanescent moods. For example, the attitude collectively shared about the future may decisively affect how shares are valued on stock exchanges. Anyone who has had even a minor connection with the stock market, as a trader or student, will know of the persistent miasma of opinion, rhetoric, assertion, confusion and pretentious necromancy which characterizes the process of predicting what the stock market will do as a whole and how individual issues will move. Often, to be sure, there is a firm infrastructure of serious analysis of how changes in costs of goods and services, technical developments, government policies and shifts in taxation patterns will affect individual companies and thus the stock market as a whole. But fluctuations in prices finally appear to respond to a perplexingly important element of contagion. Investors come to respond not to specific economic circumstances but to the general ambience of the financial community. Rather like a collective manic-depressive, overall investment appears to exaggerate the implication of pessimistic outlooks and optimistic ones as well. Success or failure in the stock market may depend more on an assessment of the probable behavior of investors and the framework of mood within which they act than on any "bottom line" analysis of definite economic matters. Such phrases as "investor confidence," "investor uneasiness," "consumer confidence" or "consumer caution" all reflect an understanding that money decisions are being made in the context of mood. Therefore, the disposition of enormous sums of money becomes heavily burdened with problems of making estimates which are partly psychological—a task for which conventional economic training fully fails to prepare its students in formal terms. Indeed the pious responsibility and academic firmness of economic training may well militate against attention to those matters of mood, which may seem frivolous or pathetic to financial personnel who stalwartly reject even a whiff of whimsy in their work.

There is even a semantics for the management of optimism or pessimism in the stock market; the words used to describe a situation may be biased to suit the mood of the moment. When the market is rising and then drops because of a sell-off this is not immediately considered a clear fall. Rather, "profit taking" has occurred. By this definition the market has not really moved downward; it is just that some slightly devious individuals have taken advantage of a generally favorable trend. Similarly, when the market is down, and yet rises slightly although the general ambience of the stock market is negative, the rise will be attributed to the actions of "bargain hunters" taking advantage of the depressed situation—people who are clearly not serious guides to the future of economic activity. (Matlin and Stang [1978] have noted the preference people appear to have for optimistic words rather than gloomy ones, which puts the occasionally lurching up-and-down movements of the stock market in even greater relief.)

Then who is? A smug but pervasive cliché suggests there is an antidote to contagious thinking: "Buy on bad news, sell on good." This expresses the view that professionals—persons in the know, those above the impulsive behavior of the herd—can do better than the market by operating against it. And yet this presents two problems—one technical and the other comical. The technical one is that small private investors now play a relatively small role in the stock market. So most transactions are conducted by professionals representing large funds of money. Then whose market are the wise ones contradicting, if not their own?

The funny aspect of all this is that other things being equal, 50 percent of the participants in the stock market are wrong at any one time. Every buyer requires a seller, every seller a buyer. Now obviously individuals will differ in the amount of spare cash at their disposal. From time to time individual's companies, pension funds, etc., will require funds for some purpose or wish to invest some for another or merely wish to organize their accounts in a good-looking way. But this must all balance out overall, and finally all buyers and all sellers must assume that they are acting rationally in terms of the overall future of the market and of the particular stock they're dealing in. Yet one of the two is making an empirical error in terms of the next move of the individual issue and of the market as a whole. In effect half the participants are wrong all the time or all of the participants are wrong half the time. In that sector of society with clear units of exchange, dollars, and clear principles of accounting for these units of exchange, one would therefore expect finesse and accuracy in prediction. But half the participants in this important system are making wrong moves. This is particularly the case during rapid movements of the market when these volatile contagions become much more influential. And so the covetous miscalculation called "greed" or the fearful suspicion that one's security is threatened, which sometimes becomes "panic," may govern the behavior of people supposedly measured and sage as they handle nothing less than a community's wealth.

On the other hand, sometimes there is an extremely clear relationship between the price of a stock, its dividends, and its future movement so that there is in fact little opportunity for contagious error. Such a stock may not be of great interest to the market if only because the opportunity for error is limited and hence so is the opportunity for profit by some at the expense of others. Much more interesting to the market as a whole are those stocks with extremely high symbolic meaning; they may be shares of companies which are expanding rapidly and have considerable book value but may pay relatively low dividends if they pay them at all. Nevertheless these psychologically volatile stocks appear able to provoke optimists into hopeful investment.

Two professors at the University of Chicago Law School, John Langbein and Richard Posner, have reviewed the results of the money management of a number of concerns and conclude that "it is not only futile to attempt to beat the market averages but also unduly costly." (Metz, *The New York Times,* October 22, 1975.) They found no empirical evidence to suggest that "large investment plans can consistently outperform the market." Despite the substantial and costly amount of market analysis now employed, data show that success rests largely on luck, the professors argue. Langbein's and Posner's solution to this problem is for investments to be made in funds owning shares in some 200 central companies which would then benefit from the general movement of the stock market without real possibility of greater than average loss or gain. There would however be an advantage in the reduction of commission costs and taxation which would more than compensate for any gains made by outwitting the market. Professors Langbein and Posner may be correct in their general analysis. But the first consequence of the procedure they recommend would involve the unemployment or reduced employment of large numbers of people involved in the security business. The investment strategy they recommend is likely to be unpopular within the investment community for that reason at least. But perhaps more important, their investment mode would provide no amusement whatever for the people involved and is therefore likely to be found unacceptable for purely psychological as well as economic reasons.

The analytical literature about how investors approach and use information has been described in psychological terms by Hughes and Downs (1976), who point up the complex uncertainties implicit in the process of making investment decisions. However, I'm not singling out stockbrokers and investors particularly in this discussion of how personal optimism or depression may affect rational perceptions of presumably calculable matters. I've already suggested that optimism as such may reflect a "design defect" in the analytical capacity of humans and indeed in a modified form may exist among some of the other vertebrates. But in the human case the matter becomes the more critical since human beings can amass control over many resources or other people. Hence decisions made by individuals may have implications ramifying infinitely beyond the usually intimate circumstances of other animals.

The problem of error as I have described it is by no means limited to those in economic activity; suggestions have been made about the likelihood of error at the very level of neurophysiological responses (Granit, 1972) and significantly by Tversky and Kahneman, who have conducted a series of searching inquiries into the general phenomenon of erroneous judgment under uncertainty. (Tversky and Kahneman, 1974, 1977, 1978.) They have now extended their study of such misjudgment to include military strategists and planners, who they conclude, operate with similar judgmental inefficiency. It is scarcely encouraging. Their quite remarkable work suggests the magnitude of the problem faced in producing intelligently correct analysis of situations ranging from the price of a stock tomorrow and the costs of war today.

The Theory of Relativity

I've already noted the importance of previous experience in governing assessments of future behavior. This is particularly the case in reportage of the financial events in which there is constant attention to numbers relative to other numbers—to numbers that are more than, less than, the same as, decisively more than, decisively less than, numbers of the past. Thus charts, trends, cycles, increases or decreases in volume, number of stocks that rise, and numbers that fall are all documented extremely carefully by brokers, investors, and others concerned with this world of relative and fixed values. This obsession with relative changes is institutionalized by the common practice of daily newspapers in reporting on economic matters by stating whether, for example, a stock's closing price was greater or lesser than on the day before or whether the earnings of a company increased or decreased. What applies to a stock may apply to a country and, in economic reporting of the planned economies of the communist world, production figures may be given as a percentage of the previous year's—constantly increasing figures are of course better. The result may be that poor-quality goods may be produced simply in order to achieve a larger numerical result in the year's production. Or, to maintain optimistic tonus, the figures themselves may be altered in mid-plan to produce encouraging numbers even though the reality the numbers describe may be discouraging. For example, in a report about the Soviet economy, "Soviet, growth slack, seems unlikely to hit '80 goals," we learn that "Although *Izvestia* published percentage figures indicating that production in many fields exceeded the 1977 plan, the comparison of the absolute amount of production with the goals announced in the 1977 plan showed failures in almost every one. Apparently the goals were reduced during the course of the year as production lagged, enabling *Izvestia* to announce overfulfillment." (Shipler, 1978.)

This is simply comic; the procedure by which dour, grimfaced economic planners seat themselves round a table in order to confect spurious sets of figures to deal with nothing less trivial than the Soviet economy reveals plainly the human obsession with optimistic flair. It is completely consistent with this comedy that the overall point of the economic system—to produce goods and services which people will benefit from and enjoy—may be thoroughly subverted by economic bureaucrats committed to furthering their bureaucratic careers even at the cost of producing just good numbers, not good products.

Indeed it is one of the not-so-incidental tyrannies of industrial society, particularly of the centrally managed kind, that playing the optimism game can be done with numbers to which realities may be suborned. Because accurate inspection of the activities of large-scale enterprises is extremely difficult, if not impossible, the only practical control is one based on inspecting numbers. But this is a form of control dangerously susceptible—in the short run at least—to questionably accurate mechanisms of reporting and evaluating what is going on. The process of evaluation may be powerfully suffused by important elements of numerical romanticism. And in the most extreme version of this, since currency parities have been allowed to float with market forces, the activities of whole countries are monitored by these numerical representations and the value of a nation's wealth, its debt, and its future credit can be affected very markedly by reevaluations of the meanings of numbers. So the value of the Canadian dollar drops 15 percent over a period of less than two years—an absolutely enormous shift involving fundamental aspects of North American life. Whole countries become like the households of individuals, which the sophistication of economic assessment based on contemporary control of apparently realistic numbers has made possible. It may also cause increasingly wide-ranging rearrangements of economic circumstance.

If the up-and-down numerical ballet of financial reportage travels well so does the same low-level folk theory of economic relativity which produces the frequent confusion of prediction with extrapolation. Prediction depends on an assessment of figures and an assessment about what will happen about them. Extrapolation simply involves a statistical extension of what happened before. Extrapolation of course suffers from the "Monte Carlo" fallacy. This is the commonplace but incorrect observation that in events such as tossing coins and drawing lots the next outcome is influenced by previous ones. The fact is that if I am tossing coins and turn up heads nine times in a row, the likelihood that heads will turn up for the tenth time is as great as it was on the first. But this fact appears to be difficult to accept. As the psychologist, John Cohen, has shown, there is a frequent connection made between what has happened in the past and what is likely to happen in the future. Logically and mathematically there is no such connection (Cohen, 1960:31); people have made immense reputations as gamblers simply by understanding the Monte Carlo fallacy and courageously persisting in betting on either winning or losing numbers in the face of what appear to be the odds.

Now of course extrapolation is not necessarily incorrect when there is a real connection between one event and the next—for example in the economic realm where a highly productive firm may be expected to continue its productivity because of the skill of its systems and the desirability of its product. This is unlike the case of the tossed coins where nothing except the law of probability connects the events. However it is perhaps an undue devotion to the law of extrapolation which leads to cycles of business and economic activity. In "boom" times the cycle may go beyond the capacity of the community to consume the goods and services it is financially committed to produce— what is called "overheating." But in "bust" times it may be inadequately confident to lend for investment even those funds required to maintain a dignified level of economic welfare. Quite without anyone wanting it, the economic system unduly responds to forms of economic contagion. These may become predictions about the future and then the basis for actual individual and corporate economic plans: this cyclicity based on extrapolation stimulated, among others, Maynard Keynes to develop theories of deficit spending which have since become rather widely accepted in many governments, and which constitute an important prop for much current official regulation of economic matters. I am not competent to judge the technical merits of the Keynesian position, which seems to provoke periodically as much dissent as acceptance, but I am persuaded that it may well be useful if only because it contravenes the normal "design defect" that I've claimed as characteristically human. The entrails of the economy are inspected almost daily through computerized revelations of money movement, bank debt, share volume, car loadings, balance of payments, etc. To the extent that these are accurate they may propel overall economies in directions quite undesirable politically and socially; hence the value of the Keynesian antidote. (For a discussion of the background to and response to Keynes's *General Theory of Employment, Interest, and Money*, see R. F. Harrod [1972]. Keynes's own ability to outwit economic movements was not infallible—during one period of his speculation on currency appreciations and depreciations he was driven almost to bankruptcy, to be rescued by a loan of 5,000 pounds from a financier who admired him and unexpected royalty checks from Macmillan of 1,500 pounds for sales of his book, *The Economic Consequences of the Peace.*)

The Preservation of Optimism in Everyday Life

I have tried to sketch briefly some relationships between private moods and the conduct of financial matters large and small. However, the distribution of human power is unfortunately very unequal. The small optimisms of important people are not kept to themselves. They become translated into big ones as in military, economic, or political misadventures or adventures. Small pessimisms may do the same as they become projected into the larger scheme of things. This is merely to say there is always a personal basis for actions which may have impersonal consequences. But humans are not solely constrained by numbers or abstract patterns or even abstract passions. They are not automata but rather living beings subjected to the consequences of their own experiences; they are also influenced by those experiences of their own species which remain somehow lodged in the genetic information which constitutes the basic energy system through and with which we live.

Now I want to take a somewhat different point of view and turn to individual personal connections with economic life to try to show how a recurrent and persistent need to produce agreeable outcomes for one's personal drama results in behavior betraying the optimistic syndrome. In particular, I will concern myself with the uses to which objects and services are put and how practices of merchandising and consuming relate to optimism.

I should state two assumptions at the outset: people will seek to increase their pleasure and sense of dignity or pride of place; and they will try to reject situations and experiences which debase, deprive, harass or trivialize them. I recognize that these assumptions involve a graft onto the psychological idea of the pleasure principle, of the additional notion that much of what motivates people, certainly in capitalist and to a considerable extent in state socialist economy, is the desire to increase their personal property, their control over resources in general and their personal autonomy. Moreover, I think that in individualistic communal settlements as well, such as the kibbutz, or Mennonite or Hutterite communities, there is considerable concern with increasing production and property, albeit communal. In fact, among the Hutterites, it is precisely their productive habits and abstemious ways which generate capital continually. This enables them to buy increasing amounts of land, which is a source of great resentment toward them among surrounding farmers who elect to focus on private consumption not on public saving for this kind of expansion. I do not think there is strong evidence for the view that fundamental changes in attitudes as to who owns property, the commune or the person, necessarily affect how people feel about their individual lives in terms of the food they eat, the books they can read, the music they can hear, the clothes they can wear, the toys they can give their children, the confidence they can have that when they become old they will be secure.

Even in organizations with a religious mission and who abjure wealth as an important factor in life there are examples enough of the sumptuous living conditions of leaders or ruling cadres to suggest that what one part of the organization yields the other part retains. Think of the wealth of the Reverend Sun Moon, even of such as Father Divine, or the Mahareshi and similar religious luminaries; one may understand that the net effect of such a renunciation of material goods is to have the central focus of the beloved group serve as collective status symbol. Furthermore, it is also the case that it may cost a considerable amount to participate in such religious or neo-religious activities, particularly when serious attendance of the rituals of the group requires lengthy voyages, costs of lodging, and fees to organizations. (I'm not mocking or calling into question the sincerity of purpose and execution of such groups and their membership, but rather noting that there are costs even in sustaining an attitude of renunciation of property and what goes with it.)

In his discussion of human needs, Leiss stresses the "indissoluble unity of material and symbolic correlates" in every human system of needs in every culture. Furthermore, he insists that this complexity is a reflection of a process that reaches back into the evolutionary origins of our species. The available evidence shows clearly that there is no aspect of our physiological requirements (the famous basic needs for food, shelter, etc.) that has not always been firmly embedded in a rich tapestry of symbolic mediations. Likewise what are called the 'higher needs'—love, esteem, the pursuit of knowledge and spiritual perfection—also arise within a holistic interpretation of needs and are not separated from the material aspects of existence." (Leiss, 1976:65.) Each human possession, each choice of color, each drape of fabric, each vehicle, each crystal wineglass, each Formica dinette, each pair of faded jeans, each fruit salad is a marker and counter in the web of human interaction. Even the most elemental of goods—perhaps bread is the classical example—are rendered and distributed in a context of greater and lesser value.

Sometimes we may achieve desirable positions by making others feel worse, but usually by simply establishing ourselves as persons of skill or taste or status or dignity or power or moment. This happens at every level of the social system, in remote backwaters and their quickly running mainstream. Responding complexly to material objects is one of those things which the species appears to find "easy to learn." In general that is why advertising works and why human beings, nearly all of whom have to work with some seriousness for their money, are prepared to spend some of it on objects and services which have little other than symbolic value. For example, compare the cost of fish and chips at a corner shop in a working-class district in Newcastle with fish and chips served at an elegant London restaurant. The nutritional value and indeed even quality of the cooking may not be markedly different because deep-frying is a process which can be done very well and cheaply if the oil used is good. But the investment of money in symbolism in the expensive case may be tenfold compared with the act of feeding one's self at the corner shop on very similar food.

When I was a student I was fortunate to be chosen to represent my university on a study tour of West Africa, which I made with a group of Canadian students in 1957. One country we visited was Ghana, and as part of our experience we toured both small villages and the larger centers. In one of the former we were invited unexpectedly to meet the chief, an invitation we gladly accepted. The chief, it turned out, lived in much the same kind of extremely rudimentary mud dwelling as did his subjects, though his was perched slightly higher on the hill on which the village was situated and there was an additional design over his door which the others lacked, a design of branches and mud worked together. The chief was seated on his throne when we entered and he offered us all a fruit drink. The principal decorations of his throne room were three travel posters advertising West Africa and a few odds and ends of bric-a-brac from industrial society. Shortly thereafter we made a formal visit to the important Ghanaian who was the chief of the Ashanti tribal group, a wealthy and powerful group; his title is Asantehene. He too had a throne room, but with a throne fabulously inlaid with gold. Because the Ashanti had had a long connection with gold mines and traditions of gold-working and were wealthy cocoa farmers as well, the amount of display and the lavishness of the décor were altogether different. But the processes were the same and the effort at adornment and self-enhancement by both chiefs was dictated by the same urgency. Similarities of behavior in cultures very different from one's own can be easier to perceive than such similarities in more familiar ones; moreover, appreciating the similarities is at least as intriguing as spotlighting the differences. For there is far more unity in the cross-cultural record than appearances would suggest.

I now want to discuss two particular aspects of consumer behavior which may elucidate the more general process I'm trying to describe. The first has to do with vacations and, more specifically, travel. The other has to do with food—its preparation, ingestion, symbolization, and occasional rejection because of the private militancy of diets.

Is it not curious that doctors and others so frequently contend that people's health and sense of welfare will improve if they have the opportunity to travel to different places? Why? What are the psychological implications? What can possibly be the function of vacations from the point of view of personal health? After all they are normally costly and involve vacationers in expenses over and above the normal costs of rent, taxes and household maintenance. Indeed, vacationers may incur expenses for luxuries and inordinate personal comfort and entertainment out of all proportion to their usual needs. Thus, to enjoy themselves, they must bear the considerable inconvenience of transporting their bodies and certain belongings from one place to another—usually the farther away the better—and then engage in a program of expenditure which if practiced in their normal routines might well cause them considerable psychological grief, to say nothing of financial.

But it appears that people do deprive themselves on their current accounts by saving money in order to enjoy vacations. Is travel, then, as grim as Graham Greene has said? "That is really the only thing that journeys give you—talk. There is so much weariness and disappointment in travel that people have to open up—in railway trains, over a fire, on the decks of steamers, and in the palm courts of hotels on a rainy day. They have to pass the time somehow, and they can pass it only with themselves. Like the characters in Chekhov, they have no reserves—you learn the most intimate secrets, you get an impression of a world peopled by eccentrics, of odd professions, almost incredible stupidities, and to balance them, amazing endurances." (Greene, 1939:19.)

There must be more to it than that. Surely one important characteristic of vacations is precisely that they can be anticipated—planned and prospectively enjoyed during the routines of daily life. The vacationer can see beforehand the expected period of openness, delight, and ambiguous irresponsibility. Never mind that the vacation itself does not provide what was promised; at least for the period beforehand it was a useful means of spicing the daily round. And even if during the vacation itself events go badly or tediously, there are remedies. In literate days one could write long letters—analyses of local customs, soundings of one's heart, reiterations of affection, contemplations of human variety. Travel correspondence in the past was itself a significant part of the world of letters.

Now the vacationer is far more likely to take photographs or films. My suspicion is that much photography is not employed primarily to record delightful events but to capture events and places which, although boring in themselves, can be reexperienced later on, embroidered and vivified with a kind of retroactive optimism which justifies the vacation as a whole. What can be seen as sentiment may be in fact the application of optimism to personal history, an effort to turn what is banal or unpleasant into something memorable and pleasing. One hesitates to acknowledge that one has purchased boredom at a great price and willingly chosen a cheerless holiday. But the same urge which impels one to the holiday presumably permits its reconstruction as a cherished memory.

When Daniel Boorstin, in his memorable discussion of the "pseudo-event," told about the vacationer at the Grand Canyon looking at Viewmaster slides of the Grand Canyon, he intended to assault the vacationer's aesthetic integrity, and of course he did. But he also made a mordant comment on the ubiquitous use of photographs, and by extension on the symbolic uses to which vacation snapshots are put. The countless photographs of the same statue of David, the same Leaning Tower, the same cablecar, the same Sphinx, the same whatever—all are in technical respects inferior to the postcard photos taken by experts.

However, by taking the photos themselves tourists acquire an irreplaceable means of savoring usually short-lived events. Moreover, they may thereby tame events. Photography is epidemic among tourists not because it captures reality but because it bends reality to their needs. When the vacationer is installed next to a famous monument and recorded there on film, one scene of an intimate personal epic is created and then fit into a larger scheme.

Is tourism a form of secularized pilgrimage? Is that why people accept the expense and inconvenience of travel to the great shrines of the secular realm? We profess to understand why people endure the cost and travail involved in pilgrimages to Mecca or Lourdes. Is it not possible that secular travel fulfills a similar urge, for connection in the secular world? Conversely, is it possible that people who travel to religious shrines use the pilgrimage to justify an expenditure which would otherwise make them feel improvident and foolish? And in this connection, are the jet set the bishops and abbesses of this system, who live out for others a fantasy of utmost seriousness? There are numerous parallels between tourists and pilgrims.

Nevertheless, there is a difference between the two, one having to do with status and pretension. It is always amusing to watch foreign tourists make their way around New York and the area where I live, Greenwich Village. They usually are better dressed than the natives and somehow more self-important. They snap their photos and survey the scene with all the confident pleasure of powerful primates picking the fruits of vast ranges where their power is supreme. Wherever the shrine, the tourist tries to seize the advantage, although much depends on the relative prosperity of himself and the natives and on their relative sense of personal style and savoir-faire. Frequently, to heighten their advantage, in this respect and in others, tourists will choose holiday communities much less prosperous and expensive than their own. The bargain seems to produce an augmented sense of pleasure quite out of proportion to the savings achieved (bargains are curiously powerful stimuli in general; they reaffirm at once one's largesse and prudence—optimism and realism achieved in the same instant!).

So the powerful tourist confronting the less affluent native is engaged in a different process from the pilgrim's. The true pilgrim is necessarily a needy person in thrall to the powerful—the poor traveler in a rich country, the colonial in the metropolis, the hick in the capital. Otherwise the system to which he is making appeal could not imbue him with the religious or secular perfection which he seeks. All true pilgrims must acknowledge their frailties and their neediness if they hope to improve their lives. They must concede that they cannot succeed on their own.

But let's not unduly complicate what may be quite simple. People on vacation after all do not work. If they are staying at a hotel they may have their food prepared for them by others. If they have traveled to a warm climate they will need fewer clothes, and formality in general is likely to be relaxed. If the vacationer is astute he will find himself an ambience which is attractive to him and consume food and drink to which he can quite properly look forward and which he will recollect with real pleasure. Clearly museums, cathedrals, interesting *quartiers* of ancient cities, religious shrines, powerful fortifications and scenic beauties are understandably attractive to the tourist. Similarly, opportunities for social and sexual intercourse with either natives or other tourists offer a convivial option to add to the mix.

The Presentation of Self across State Lines

Whatever its attractions, travel entails certain problems to be faced by those seeking to assert their dignity and prosperity while abroad. How can they produce signals readily understandable to members of different cultures? In particular the traveler faces the problem of providing enough generalizable markers of well-being so that his peers in other cultures and those who serve his peers and who must now serve him will readily recognize they must respond in a particular way to this person. This helps explain the importance of, for example, such readily acknowledgeable totems as Vuitton luggage. This instantly defines the owner as someone possessing the considerable funds required to purchase it, as somebody with notions of taste which may be readily shared by similarly affluent people in other cultures, and as a person concerned enough about the emblems surrounding him to add a sense of éclat, even to the containers of his personal effects. Thus when one purchases such luggage one acquires not only a container for clothes and other objects in transport, but also a place in the self-defined worldwide bourgeoisie which recognizes and responds seriously to such a powerful symbol of personal prosperity. More recently of course this has become more complicated because the implications of the luggage are also known by thieves, and in view of the quite remarkably casual control of baggage at airports the social and personal benefits of carrying ostentatious luggage are now for many people perhaps outweighed by the risks of being plundered—a smaller version of the larger problem rich people have always faced in leaving the protections of their own systems.

In part because of a tendency toward the metropolitanization of systems of taste, but also because of the considerable increase in the numbers of people traveling beyond their own particular ponds, a series of cross-national symbols has become more and more important since the early 1950's because they radically widen the arena within which personal assertion may occur. This development has provided an economic opportunity for producers to make readily identifiable goods which offer a sense of luxurious quality and value as well as an immediate assertion of who one is in socio-economic terms. Perhaps this accounts in part for the burgeoning success of such organizations as Gucci, Hermès, St. Laurent, Dior, Cacharel, etc., all of whom can provide a certification accepted in many cultures of the taste and economic power of the purchaser. The importance of the brand is painfully demonstrated by the manufacturer's practice of signing the article in question either with a recognizable symbol or, more recently—lest there be any slightest ambiguity—with the brand name emblazoned as part of the design.

When travel was mainly a luxury of the rich or a necessity of the migrant poor, it was less important to make symbolic statements of a material kind than simply to be an American in France, an Englishman in Italy or a Swede in Japan. A benign sense of self and of one's status came with simply having moved one's body from place to place within the ambience of whatever circuit of hotels, restaurants and carriers one chose or was able to choose. But since the expansion of the machinery of travel because of jumbo airplanes and their associated jumbo developments, the stamp of commercial approval has been increasingly in demand. Apart from the economic factor, what is fascinating about this is how readily people are willing to enter into the realm of heraldry and comport themselves in terms of some hierarchy of insignia which has nothing to do with their own station or family. Indeed, the emphasis on displayable brand names involves a commitment to heraldry of an almost Renaissance kind and which involves males as much as females.

The same principle governing the choice of consumer items by people who travel applies to people who remain at home. I refer to the development of a system of "branch plant consumer outlets" providing consumer cachet, such as the department store boutiques throughout America for such prestigious New York stores as Saks Fifth Avenue and Bonwit Teller. The same pattern is seen in the prestigious stores themselves, which house other outlets, usually for European talismans made by such as Fauchon and Turnbull and Asser. Such a fragmentation of the symbolic force of the host shop reflects a complex symbolic process of, again, metropolitanization of cultural symbols. Thus, persons residing in smaller communities of the larger system may appropriate in their own department stores tokens of participation in the grand system to which they wish to adjust themselves. Traditionally, appropriating metropolitan symbols was achieved by a relatively ritualized shopping visit to the capital or major center, in this case New York City. The returned prodigal would then exemplify in his or her person the standards of achievement of the fashion leaders and producers of the foreign or distant centers. Of course this continues. However, it has presumably been found more congenial and profitable to merchandise goods by widening the grip of centrally derived symbols through the colonization of taste produced by the branch plant shops to which I have alluded.

As more people travel more often new forms of heraldry and privilege emerge, at least several prompted by the availability of that most impersonal of machines, the computer. In a perverse reversal of the Calvinist principle that by good works shall ye be known, it may now be equally the case in certain milieus that by good consumption shall ye be known. Because computers can rapidly scan patterns of consumption by individual holders of credit cards, a class of individuals is discernible whose consumption habits are of particular interest to producers. Allied hierarchial devices have emerged such as VIP lounges, special grades of credit cards and similar efforts to marry status-markers with cash flow. The central point here is that it appears to be important to travelers to possess means to somehow assert their personal status—even among total strangers in communities wholly remote from and unconcerned with their own.

Used Furniture and Genuine Antiques

I have commented on the relationship between vacations, travel, symbolic statements about one's self, and contriving to make one's self feel good. The connection between these apparently quite different phenomena illuminates the overall pattern of optimistic mood with which we are concerned. In effect I have tried to show that there is a surprising amount of symbolic meaning to the prospect of vacations and to the recollection of them either through photographs or directly, and that the décor surrounding people during travel is a special and somewhat extreme case of the more general process of flattering self-assertion through which personal optimism is reflected in the wider and perhaps impersonal world. In a moment I will turn to the most intimate of locations for one's sense of one's self, one's body, but before then a brief comment may be in order about

another form of travel, or removal, which affects self-percep-
tion—travel through time and the purchase of objects revealing
it. I mean, of course, antiques.

Just as one can assert one's place by wearing clothing which
is clearly status-marked and similar to the clothing of peers,
one can assert one's place by possessing things which other
people simply cannot have because they are not available—
one-of-a-kind works of art or very old things called antiques.
Such objects have somehow passed through the purgatory of
simply being "used" or "secondhand" into the quiet glow of
the world of desirable old objects. Several aspects of this process are clear at once; the first is that when this is associated
with property maintained and transmitted in a family there are
implications quite beyond the relatively simple ones of owning
property. We will return to this in a moment. As well, antiques
are held to be useful investments of currency which is likely to
depreciate while they themselves appreciate in value. In some
cases this is decisively so, in others there may even be a loss
over time, for example, the break in the prices of antique silver
around the turn of the seventies. There are also costs involved
in storing, insuring and properly maintaining objects which
are usually made of perishable substances. Indeed, it is a characteristic of many antiques that they are made of perishable
substances such as wood, leather, cloth, or some metals.

The most dramatic and perhaps financially most interesting
antiques are those which were manufactured as works of art
and/or designed to be ostentatiously valuable properties of notables—for example, the Louis XIV desks which nowadays circulate among a relatively small coterie of shipping fleet owners,
dictators, cosmetic manufacturers, and ministers of finance of
oil-rich countries. It is easy to understand the appreciation in
value of such objects, as of paintings and sculptures which are
attributed to well-known artists. The value of any of these objects, functional or artful or both, is enhanced when their history of ownership can also be traced. "This ormolu-inlaid escri-
toire was owned by Marie Antoinette or Fredrick Chopin or
Mark Twain" brings with the objects and presumably gives to
their current owners a sense of not only power in the present,

but a reach of this power into the past. The current owner becomes important in association with the much-heralded predecessor in ownership of the noble item.

More problematic are those objects which were relatively workaday and meant for the petite bourgeoisie rather than more elegant families, or those used principally by humble persons—for example, Shaker or Pennsylvania Dutch or much of Tudor public house furniture. There are, of course, a number of reasons for the interest which these old objects hold, not the least that they may reflect attitudes to design and the relationship of form to function which have become highly prized. Insofar as they have been made by hand rather than machine, the visual interest and textural complexity of the object may be comparatively rich and thus more appealing to people who wish to surround themselves with aesthetically intriguing objects. Furthermore, acquiring antique objects may be part of a claim an individual will stake in the past of his community. The individual is asserting that his present income earns him a retroactive position in the past. This historical access has a value reflected in the cost of antiques.

Finally, there is the even more general direct connection between antique objects and personal histories when these objects are passed down from ancestor to children. Thus they represent not only stored wealth and its elegant and impressive display, but also a serious connection to one's own past and the past of the community at large. For noble, royal and aristocratic families, antique objects, as well as houses, are highly explicit advertisements of their lineage and communal position as well as very useful forms of economic security. For less exalted persons as well, indeed for any family with heirlooms of whatever value and importance, transmitting objects through the generations becomes important as a source of historical depth and kinship continuity—regardless of the aesthetic qualities of the items in question. This can take astonishingly extensive forms, as in some ancient houses of Europe where continuity for centuries can be traced through property and objects. I once visited a monastery in the company of a Tuscan baroness who, when I asked about the history of the property, said, "Oh, it is ours—

or should be—we foolishly gave it away to the monks in 700." This woman's connection to her family through their extensive properties was evidently complete. Beyond the comprehension of most people was the sense of privilege, wealth and continuity which she had.

The final general aspects of the attraction of antiques may lie in the restrained but effective "glow of prosperity" of the patina of the objects—which is so valued and carefully maintained. Why objects which have been waxed and cleaned and polished many, many times shine with a subdued certainty is in itself interesting, and that it is assuring or reassuring to people with enough control of the present to afford them is an intriguing problem in terms of my argument here. This is all related to the sense of well-being about the future, which control of the past through objects may give to people who formulate their lives in this way. Indeed, for such people a sense of continuity with the past through objects may also betray a promise of the future because the very stability and durability of the objects suggests their owners will themselves enjoy the longevity and elegance the objects themselves are held to contain.

What is the evident lure of the sheen of which I've spoken—the yellow of gold, the crisp shine of diamonds, the play of light through crystal, the luster of oak tables and old silver and the peculiar hushed reflection of old mirrors? Is the light reassuring in some serious archaic sense? Does it connote the hearth, the flame, the fireside, security during the night? And is this quiet sheen again a reason for the association of celebratory eating with dimmed lights, candles and the quiet shininess of the items I have described?

When the past has been extraordinarily oppressive the objects representing it may be destroyed, as after revolutions or by children reacting against parents by abusing or destroying or selling what their parents leave. But the willingness of people in general to maintain museums in which objects of the past are housed and maintained, and their willingness to do the same thing privately in their own homes, suggests that these objects have to do not only with beauty and continuity with the past but also with persistence into the future. Sometimes that flowing and imprecise ghost which is time can be captured and enjoyed in objects which have defied it and whose very existence therefore is a source of nourishment for people who must somehow challenge, confront, or anticipate time to come.

Programmed Flesh

If people seek durability in material objects they know that they cannot overcome the fragility of the flesh. The instrument of their lives, the body, is constantly subject to change, deterioration, and death. Anyone who disbelieves the power of genetics must simply reconsider the life cycle of the body—how it begins as a speck and then grows within another body and finally emerges to take a series of predictable shifts in size, appearance, function, shape, health and, finally, viability. It is the genetic program which insures that the composition of the hair of the eyebrow differs from the composition of the hair on the head or the eyelash. The refinement of the pattern is exquisite, the effect of it is extensive. It is small wonder that there has been such extensive preoccupation with the human body as an aesthetic object—recall the early representations in the Dordogne, and the earnestness with which people attend to the state of their health and the prospects for its continuation.

Complex and resourceful though the inheritance of our bodies is it is not equal to the manifold interference with health brought about by accidents, fires and internal and external misdemeanors, and it certainly is not able in every case to suit the particular vanity of the inheritor. I've already discussed how certain objects are used to create particular "looks" and impressions, to affirm that their possessors are people of a certain style, class, and attainment. "Outfits" become properties of a carefully directed drama of subtle changes of self, all part of a larger and recurrent endeavor to fill one's experience with agreeable self-presentation. The most decisive of such efforts has to do with the discipline and care of the body itself. Whether done well, badly, obsessively or with imprudence, this effort is never a matter treated lightly, and I would like now to turn to a discussion of the relationship between bodies and foods in order to approach the more general problem of how we face the facts of life in the context of both our vanity about appearance and our fear about mortality.

At the beginning of this book I tried to evoke the meaning of the castles along the coast of West Africa where the slaves were kept before they were shipped to the New World. The principal work of those who survived the trauma of separation and the indignity and misery of the voyage was to grow sugar. There quickly developed subsidiary trades, in rum, Canadian saltfish, later on manufactured goods, but it was the explosion of greed for sugar, a foodstuff of evidently incredible appeal, which led to the unprecedentedly rapid creation of one of the most miserable social patterns of all human time—slavery in the New World. Community after community in the Americas was populated by means of the deplorable institution, while the communities of West Africa, which had already to contend with an extremely demanding and complex natural environment, were drained of many generations of able people. The eruption of slavery was in part a result of the wellsprings of human greed, evil and heartlessness. But it was also an artifact of the human sweet tooth. The sudden possibility of making available very widely very concentrated processed sugar wrenched the world. The consequence of a passion for sweetness, human slavery corrupted society after society.

So does sugar itself. Sugar is a highly concentrated source of calories and a great deal of it can be eaten or drunk without a feeling of satiety, which would occur with consumption of bulky foods—green vegetables, meats, or breads. The easy availability of sugar is surely a major cause of obesity, and of the widespread concern in rich societies about obesity. Frank obesity has been estimated to be as high as 15 percent in the American population, while 20 to 30 percent of that population are said to be overweight. Millions of inhabitants of wealthy societies concern themselves with losing weight or not gaining it. Books offering suitable diets appear to issue from printing presses as copiously as their enemy volumes, cookbooks. Organizations, guilds, and quasi-industrial resort establishments function to separate people from their fat. Innumerable magazines carry diets calculated to reduce girth and produce figures as fashionably emaciated as those of the models tantalizingly interspersed between the diets and the recipes; the tragi-comical aspect of the magazines' enthusiasm for diets is that they appear to realize that they serve little purpose other than the incantatory since a magazine which features a diet one month will almost certainly feature another a month or two or three later. The first one didn't work. Will the second? And the third? Obviously the natural system of control over ingestion is not foolproof and does not universally work. Why? Did we start with an imperfect mechanism? Are we in an imperfect situation? Are we merely greedy or gluttonous? Can it be that food is addictive, like alcohol or nicotine or opium? Of course not. Then what else is involved in this strange concatenation of need, tastes, artfulness, hunger, confusion, mise en scène, and excess?

All animals feel better for eating and we are no exception. Perhaps a temporary feeling of hunger is acceptable and even stimulating, particularly if it is part of an entertainment such as walking to an awaited picnic or preparing food to be eaten later or getting temporarily lost, with some amusement, on the way to a restaurant. But we know that that is about the limit of it, that private hunger and general communal famine are unyieldingly grim and desperate. (See Cecil Woodham-Smith, *The Great Hunger* [1962], for a poignant and full description of the Irish famine associated with the failure of the potato crop in 1846. Unfortunately there are in the literature descriptions of many other famines.)

My concern here, however, is not with the misery of unsatisfied hunger, the cause of which is usually maldistribution of resources, but with the peculiar phenomenon of why people eat too much when they know they shouldn't, and what it may mean when they do.

Konrad Lorenz once noted that in the human hunting-gathering past large animals, once secured, had to be eaten quickly lest they spoil. There was no advantage to having a built-in mechanism controlling the intake of food (Lorenz, 1966). That is, there would be an evolutionary advantage to gluttony; as much protein as possible would be ingested as quickly as possible and then a period of inactivity or "food hangover" could follow. Since Lorenz made this speculation we have become more aware of the importance of nut, fruit and vegetable gathering to the prehuman and early human diet; there need not have been so drastic a distinction between feasting and non-eating as Lorenz describes (Zihlmann and Tanner, 1978). Nevertheless his comments are provocative because of the very situation at present under discussion—overeating and its causes.

Some recent evidence suggests that the other primates, or rather at least the rhesus monkey, can regulate their caloric intake rather precisely. A skillful and shrewd experiment by McHugh, Moran and Barton, at the Health Sciences Center at the University of Oregon, involved giving rhesus monkeys food "preloads" of varying caloric value. It was discovered that when pre-fed with foodstuff as opposed to a simple salt solution the monkeys reduced the other food they ate—food which was readily available to them if they wished it. As the researchers note: "This system can be of such accuracy as to rival that of the controls of the vital autonomic functions such as blood pressure and respiration. The existence of such an accurately graded phenomenon for the control of caloric ingestion in primates raise questions as to how such a system operates in relation to available body stores, questions that are pertinent to such conditions as hypothalamic hyperphagia and the human disorders of obesity and anorexia nervosa." (McHugh et al., 1975:169.)

Even if humans share such a precise means of determining the relationship of how much food is eaten to how much food is needed, which is in any event questionable, our plight at the dinner table is very different from the rhesus'. First of all, as eaters of concentrated protein we may ingest too much food before we know it; the old saw about Chinese cooking may reflect the comparatively low level of protein in that cuisine compared with, say, the meat and potatoes consumed in North America. Perhaps more importantly, the rhesus monkey does not have to confront the chef de cuisine with all his colors, tastes, arrangements, recipes—the vast armamentarium of delight which cooks can marshal to please the mind and palate in a manner far more elaborate and delightful than mere nutrition requires.

There seems to be a genuine paradox here. On the one hand, many people eat too much food and furthermore eat too much of the wrong food—for example, fried carbohydrates which are frequently very tasty and satisfying but which are not by any means central to a so-called balanced diet. On the other hand, there do appear to be some mechanisms for assuring one's self a reasonably balanced diet. I recall some experiments done many years ago on young children who were given free rein of choice of foods to eat and who would prefer a particular food disproportionately for a period of time and then another and then another with the overall result that they ate what they should have eaten in nutritional terms. Some recent studies of rats and of human newborns suggest how effectively the value of nutrition can be gauged. For example, in an experiment with rats, their stomachs were injected with one of two samples of non-nutrient flavored water. When they were given nutrition along with one of the flavors within a ten-minute experimental session the rats chose the flavor associated with the nutrient, even though both substances had bypassed their apparatus for tasting and gone directly into the digestive system. In other words, these rodents' bodies "knew" which flavor accompanied substances injected directly into their bodies. Material from research on human newborns suggests that our own systems, even at the outset of life, are able to distinguish between more and less strong concentrations of sucrose and glucose; adults also possess this capacity and it is interesting that a skill such as this is included in the package humans begin life with. (Nowlis and Kessen, 1976.)

As with most important human behaviors a complex mixture of physiological and psychological influences appears to affect eating. But what goes wrong? Assuming there is a mechanism which can competently determine how much nutrition is physiologically necessary, we seem to have learned how to override the mechanism. Perhaps one reason sweets are served at the ends of meals, and not at the beginnings when they would too rapidly appease hunger, is that only the super-stimulus of sugar can overcome what may be an otherwise functional control on further eating. The Devil's portion must in itself be the most tempting, as it appears late in the game when satiety has already been achieved. Thus, although the human sweet tooth may have evolved to assure adequate consumption of food, its marriage to supersweet desserts appears to have produced a heritage of surfeit.

In a society composed of people nearly all of whom are aware of the problem of overweight and many of whom engage in dieting, there are still candy bars, bakeries, cans of sweetened fruits and kilometers of supermarket pastry counters to attest to the overpowering lure of sweet things. (A paper by Donald Campbell of Northwestern University which appeared as this book was approaching publication contains the following comment: ". . . the innate human taste for sweets has ceased to be adaptive and is now maladapted. In the ecology created by the abundance of refined sugars in the food supply and sedentary rather than physical labor there results an innate temptation to sin as far as the candy box is concerned." [Campbell, 1977:6.]) The desire for sugar fostered the development of slavery and collateral aspects of colonialism and imperialism. Sugar now being widely available, the imperialism has turned within; greed's attack is on the self and the health of the self and not on the hapless members of other cultures.

Suffice it to say greed in this as in other respects is amply reinforced by convention, ritual, status seeking and all of the other modes of behavior which bind individuals to their communities.

Fat Optimists

The physical shape of bodies has always had social and aesthetic implications. In parts of West Africa men are supposed to be thin, women plump. In some ancient communities it was the reverse. There exists an endless variety. What is intriguing about the fashions of social classes in countries sufficiently rich to make eating a function not of money but of taste, time or preference is a pattern of renunciation and denial which seems implicit in the current fashion for thin bodies. The most casual scrutiny of the figures of models in advertisements for clothing and fashion accessories shows the passion for thinness and the almost total suppression of superfluous fat. To be sure, fashions change constantly; but the more models change the more they seem to be the same.

However, one must keep some perspective. Our generation and Western society are not alone. Self-mortification in the name of fashion has enjoyed a remarkable ubiquity: mutilation of faces of men and women in West African tribes, foot binding of girl children in imperial China, breaking the bottom ribs of Victorian women to permit them to wear the wasp-waisted garments shown in fashion plates of the period. (Luria and Tiger, 1977.) Does this seem barbaric today? Then consider the earnest seamstressing of plastic surgeons as they revoke and reform faces, thighs, breasts, and ears of normal people. It gives pause. In a self-consciously progressive society an appearance of youth, however cosmetic, is regarded in some milieus as necessary, notwithstanding the certainty that organisms change and also change their appearance. The immense impracticality of attempting to reverse this unalterable process is striking. All things considered and if the Spinozan principle that "freedom is the recognition of necessity" is correct (which I believe it is), then it is the most slavish of obeisances to a grim theory of hopeless self-denial. Sisyphus and Ponce de León had much in common.

In all of this, of course, the diet is central, albeit various contraptions, such as motor-driven belts, stationary bicycles and vibrating instruments that reduce fat to oblivion, may be part of the regimen. An intriguing feature of dieting is that it almost always entails a recurrent sequence of renunciation, excess, renunciation, excess—so that the individual is frequently, if not chronically, in a state of commitment to improving his or her future by dieting. Judging from the regularity with which proposed diets appear in monthly magazines directed to women, their readers must not follow them successfully, although they presumably try them repeatedly. Thus the publication of diets must have a ritual element.

An anthropology student at Rutgers, Barbara Blei, and I once cursorily looked through back issues of a number of American women's magazines to learn what appeals they made to readers through diets. We were struck, first of all, by a major difference between the 70's magazines and those of the late 40's, when attractive self-presentation could depend on supporting garments such as corsets and girdles over which carefully contrived clothing could be worn to create at least an illusion of thinness. The demands of the early 70's for relatively revealing and untrammeled fashions, on the other hand, made this impossible and accordingly appeared to have stimulated a plethora of magazine articles about losing weight—articles very often featured on the covers. By way of contrast to female-oriented magazines such as *Vogue, Harper's Bazaar, McCall's* and *Good Housekeeping,* we then looked at magazines of general interest or directed to males, such as *Reader's Digest, Esquire* and *Sports Illustrated,* and in these publications there was, with occasional exceptions in the *Reader's Digest,* no attention paid to diets and dieting per se, though there was a consistent concern with gastronomy and sophisticated means of preparing alcoholic beverages. This is curious since males are by no means immune to the problem of obesity—in fact, Dr. Jean Mayer, the Harvard nutritionist, has noted that in the U.S. males are becoming obese more rapidly than females. A number of interesting aperçus emerged from our quick magazine survey. First of all, in more than half of the cases in which an article on diet was included in a magazine the article was given billing on the cover. There was relatively little seasonal variation, although August saw the fewest diets and January the most—presumably an aspect of prior Christmas and New Year's indulgence for which a New Year's resolution was required as the penitential price.

The diets offered not only the promise of better health but psychological blandishments as well. What might emerge from the ordeal of the diet was an "all-new you," a "miraculous change" or some other version of "Another Way of Being." A clearly redemptive quality was part of the diets' appeal. Dieting would liberate confidence and stimulate self-love. One might obtain a "mood change" from one diet and a "serene mind" from another, while even "spiritual awakening" or "enlighten- ment" would follow other regimes. The most effete of the pub- lications advertised an extreme form of dieting in which one might remove one's body to a beauty resort and have it wholly controlled and processed. Not only would one lose weight but also receive massages, hair treatments, manicures, and in gen- eral be rid of the accumulated attitudinal and physical detritus of a non-healthful, non-Spartan way of life. At considerable cost participants in this ritual would be deprived of the food and drink they craved under other circumstances and subjected to a degree of personal austerity they could never have at- tempted on their own.

It is extraordinary that the cost of deprivation should soar so high, and that presumably sophisticated and skilled persons should go to such extreme lengths in order—let me be simple— to eat and drink less than usual. Indeed the overall problem of dieting resolves itself to this tryingly plain formula: eat less. All the various strategies and plans surrounding the business of making one's self better by making one's self smaller are in good measure mechanisms to avoid "eating less." Were not so much human rue, personal unhappiness and waste involved, the entire matter of dieting and its consequences and causes could be seen for the comedy it is. Thrice daily a grim and predictable battle is joined with sweet provocations. Together with nature we have fashioned food far too effectively and enticingly for our own good. We possess an apparatus for en- joying food and drink which is now, like some of our other evolutionary adaptations, unsuitably enthusiastic and plea- sure-producing given the relative plenty which some people in the world live in all the time. Our skill with the wok, skillet, griddle and skewer handily overwhelms our sense of what we need to live.

Dieting is the negative or passive approach to the overall problem of controlling personal size. Exercise is another, more active way of outwitting one's taste buds and stabilizing the consequences of greed. Yet how bizarre and odd it frequently is. Regimens of bouncing, trouncing, dancing, jogging, fleeing, running, hopping, swimming, conniving with machines, modern dancing, ballet dancing, walking, hiking, and sailing are all thrown in the balance against half a pie a week, or a thicker steak, or three bars of good Swiss semisweet chocolate. Exercise, however, improves physical condition and possibly has a considerable role to play in reducing those substances in the body which operate neurochemically to produce depression. There exists a claim that running some miles a day is at least as effective a therapy for schizophrenics as the battery of available drugs (Arnold Mandell, pers. comm.). Indeed it is the common experience of people that systematic exercise or sport in general produces feelings of well-being and competence. Exercise and sport are two of the most important sources for "little optimism." If the fashionably dire problem of extra weight induces the carriers of this disease to indulge in adequate exercise there may be even a net advantage to the individual overall; without the penitential need for exercise the individual might, like Oscar Wilde, simply lie down until the desire to exercise passed away. Certainly there is a joy in physical activity which carries over into other realms of life, and it is presumably not an arbitrary or accidental matter that human cultures have consistently made a virtue of physical fitness and health.

But even stout people can enjoy some little optimism because of their size. Their solidarity with others provides an excellent subject of conversation. This can be formalized, as in weight-control groups which meet regularly and perhaps for a fee, or simply gather with no pretensions. Diet talk is a tolerable equivalent of talking about one's operation. Overweight people may communicate through the pounds of extra weight buffering them from the world—paradoxically, extra flesh binds them to the world and produces an opportunity for exchange, commiseration, understanding and conviviality. Being overweight may permit them an acceptable even if, to some, tiresome narcissism and, paradoxically again, it promotes as much optimism as despair. The obese person believes that at some point the weight will disappear. And that will be the beginning of something wonderful.

In this chapter I have focused on resources, how people seek them, which ones they seek, why, and what use they make of them. My effort has been to show the manner in which the human being is not merely an ecological conduit through which resources flow but is, rather, an active and highly biased seeker, finder and user of the stuff of the world. *Homo economicus* is neither only coolly rational and calculating nor feckless and passionate but an amalgam of the various appetites and moods which often lead to surprising consequences. The mood I focused on was that disposed to favorable expectations of the future. I tried to show how such favorable expectation affects actions in the present and plans about the future. This in turn I tried to relate to my earlier description of the evolution of some broad human responses and also to some particular and exotic uses of resources, such as dieting, by an animal far removed from the circumstances in which he evolved. Finally I argued that human consumption of resources need not be of any tangible material benefit to individuals in the ordinary sense, but may find expression in such conspicuous oddities as a particular cut of trouser leg, special ways of folding omelets, or creating surprising architectural perspectives through the use of dormer windows.

6

This Way Out

A colloquial expression in Britain for credit purchasing is buying "on the never-never." Even the word "credit" itself has a
tangled connection with ideas of belief—think of the Latin
credo, "I believe." The self-mockery implied by the phrase "on
the never-never" reveals an uncertainty about mortgaging
one's future and yet a suspicion that somehow the dreadful
business of having to repay money owed will never really ma-
terialize. The future is in that sense ambiguous—both intangi-
bly distant and yet perceptibly looming. We know it's coming
but we don't know how. I've tried to describe ways in which
we seek means of knowing what to do about what we can't
predict and of deciding how much to mortgage on a future
which is unsure. In this final chapter I want to address this
problem and show some of the implications of the material I've
presented. I also want to fill out the story of this mood and its
effect and show ways in which we use and abuse the future.

Tempting Fate Through
Art and Contest

The future is never left alone. Human beings constantly create problems for themselves which depend for solution on the passage of today's time into tomorrow's future. Some of these problems are ones of artistic execution, which I will turn to in a moment.

Others concern contests. One of the recurrent themes of human culture has to do with contests—with play which is given an effortful structure and in which some more or less entertaining activity takes place but with an uncertain outcome. Countless humans affiliate with teams, boxers, billiard players, gymnasts, skaters, racers, runners, divers and cheer for them to win and feel despondent if they lose. Small children wear crests, memorize statistics about sports records which they are unable to grasp in formal math, and conduct their own miniaturized version of adult contest. Contests have a great deal to do with the matter of optimism and they may well be one of the commonest expressions of a way of behaving which I have argued is common anyway. Contests are usually optional, except for professional athletes with no other source of livelihood. People needn't enter contests, and certainly no one is required to take the fan's role in the contest system. Contest is to optimism as flirtation is to love.

There is an underlying meaning in the ritual of contest and I would like to consider it in connection with one of the most vivid and extraordinary contests of all, the Palio of Siena. A horserace run twice a year around the magnificent main square of Siena—the Campo—the Palio originated in bearbaiting, Jew-baiting, and woman-baiting in the twelfth and thirteenth centuries, when it became transformed into a race of horses. Over time the horses were made to represent neighborhoods of the city of Siena called *contrade,* each of which had a military organization involved in the frequent wars between Siena and Florence and other states until the final defeat of the Sienese by Florence at Montapuerti outside Siena in the thirteenth century.

Each *contrada* has a heraldic symbol—the goose, tortoise, shell, giraffe, panther and eagle are some of the seventeen— and each July and August ten of the seventeen *contrade* race in the Palio. A rotation ensures all *contrade* equal chance to compete for the Palio—a long flag and silver platter which are housed in the major church of the *contrada* that wins them and which remain there until the next contest.

Rivalries are intense. Competition among the *contrade* engages the citizens of the city for almost the entire year. Elaborate deals, some legitimate, some not, are made among *contrade*, among their senior commanders, and sometimes on the day of the race itself, among the jockeys, who have their own wagers and other interests to look out for. The Palio is remarkable not only because it involves so many members of the community throughout the year but also because the net result of this involvement is simply the determination of winners of two races. There appears to be no benefit of Palio success other than the pleasure of winning, except perhaps what appears to be the immense collateral pleasure of seeing others lose. To be sure, there is a host of implications having to do with the politics of the city and its social life, educational life, and commerce. Since the institution is very old and many of the family groups in the city are also very old—the Chigis, Piccolominis, and Ricasolis, for example—there is an extensive web of connection among the *contrade* which presumably is the integument of both the contests and the overall social system.

Whatever the underlying social and political implications of the Palio, which may have to do with the prosperity and efficiency of particular *contrade*, the preparations and the race itself are brilliantly colorful and dramatic. The heraldry of each *contrada* is broadcast throughout the city by scarves—worn by women around their waists and by men slung over their shoulders and knotted at their throats, sometimes with considerable élan. Many houses display *contrada* flags; and shops and restaurants, which must of course cater to the wider public, all display the range of *contrade* symbols. Apparently bets begin to be made, a process accelerated after the *contrade* are assigned the horses their jockeys will ride. (This allocation is supposed to be made on a random basis by drawing lots. However, it is said that often such decisions are not as random as they appear, in part for financial reasons. For example, the captain of a winning *contrada* may be required to lay on celebrations and other perquisites for his *contrada* after the Palio, an activity which can involve him in expenditures of tens of thousands of dollars. Indeed, *contrade* captains have been known to offer financial and other assistance to competitors, whose horses may then win and spare the traitorous captains expenses they are unwilling or unable to bear.) Radio, television and newspaper reports foreshadow the event, and the heat of excitement on the day itself is fanned by these and other arrangements. For example, three practice races are run around the Campo on days preceding the Palio during which jockeys test themselves and their horses against their competitors to find their weaknesses and strengths.

In preparation for the race itself, the Campo is covered with mud, which dries into clay. The race accordingly is extremely dangerous, and there are frequently serious injuries to jockeys and bystanders. Sharp curves are made worse by the inappropriate grades. Thus pads are placed on some of the brick walls enclosing the Campo and teams of doctors are stationed at strategic points around it—though their chief activity appears to be rescuing people who faint in the Campo itself, where thousands are tightly packed for hours preceding the race.

The riders ride bareback and are permitted any maneuvering they wish and any tactic in order to win. They may cut in front of opposing horses, strike opposing jockeys with their whips, try to pull them off their mounts, or hit opposing horses in the face. Nothing is barred. And as a result not uncommonly only three or four jockeys complete the three rounds of the field in the minute or so the race takes. Not that the riders are essential—a *contrada* may win if its horse succeeds in coming in first with its heraldic feather intact. Occasionally therefore a jockey in a tight race will leap off his mount in the final seconds of the race.

The event itself then is quite brief, but it is enshrined in extensive pageantry. On the evenings before the Palio, youths from the various *contrade* dance and sing in the Campo and in the streets, waving heraldic flags. On the day of the Palio the city fills with visitors from far and near and spectators literally hang from windows, balconies, parapets and stairs. In the late afternoon the square itself begins to fill. It is already bedecked with flags, banners, and heraldic devices of the city of Siena and its various *contrade*. At six, a rocket is shot and the Palio ritual begins. First come drummers and flag throwers from each of the competing *contrade* followed in each case by the horse running for the neighborhood. All the participants wear medieval clothes, some of them hundreds of years old, others newly made in the ancient style. The men wear wigs—virtually all the participants are men—and there are elaborate displays of skill and strength by the men wielding twin poles from which the *contrade* banners are slung. Meanwhile the captains of the *contrade* assemble on a balcony at the top of the main entrance to the square. Throughout these preliminaries drums beat and medieval trumpets blare. The anticipation and foreboding in the square increase tangibly as the start of the race approaches.

At length the horses, drummers and flag throwers of the *contrade* pass in review, followed by the Palio insignia, borne in a cart drawn by white oxen. Then the victor's symbol is hoisted above the crowd to the ceremonial box where the *contrade* captains are seated—to remain there until claimed by the winning *contrada*. Throughout this there are constant interactions of the dominant males—gestures, shouts, handshakes, kisses, hands around necks, laconically precise gestures of who knows what meaning—a harvest for a student of the process of male bonding. Finally two ropes are drawn across the track, one to restrain the horses and one to contain them in the rear, and horses and riders enter the field, all wearing the exuberant colors of their *contrade*. A policeman appears with sealed envelopes containing the order in which the jockeys will rank themselves at the starting rope. The crowd hums, the jockeys shout at one another threateningly, and the saddleless horses, constrained only by bits in their teeth and their heritage as animals bred to compete, shy and start between the ropes. A cannon shot explodes and the race begins.

On the occasion when I was present at the Palio the horse and rider of the Oca (goose) *contrada* seized an early lead and the outcome became clear even before the end of the first lap. A boy of twelve behind me then burst into tears. As the winning horse and rider approached the finish line, the jockey already waving his hand in triumph, members of the Oca *contrada* at grave risk to themselves surged onto the field to grab the rider and hoist him over their heads. Then, ignoring the other horses hurtling across the finish line, they raced back toward the box where the captains were seated, where, convulsed by tears and laughter, they held up their hands for the precious trophy. It is hard to describe the earnestness of their gestures, or the utterly uncompromising commitment these betrayed. The men of the Oca clearly were in agony to claim their prize.

Thereafter the chief of the Oca *contrada* held the Oca banner, waved it and yielded it to the crowd which, screaming and crying, bore it triumphantly around the field. Members of the losing *contrade* began to disperse, leaving in each case a symbolic remnant to join the triumphal procession under the banner of the Palio itself. Many men and women were in tears, of joy and grief, the long period of their anticipation terminated by an extraordinarily sudden end. Whereas before the race the captains of the *contrade* appeared deep in private worlds of hope and calculation, now the formal conviviality of the city was reestablished and they congratulated each other and shook hands; the easy bonhomie of powerful males once again bound them together as the function of representing their heraldic districts came to an end.

The overriding question is, why bother? Why commit one's self to the expense of time, money, things—rehearsals for drummers, practices for flag throwers; armor making, costumes, elaborate victory feasts and the rest? To be sure, the Palio is a major tourist attraction, yet even that begs the question. Why do people from far and near come to see a brief horse race, especially when they do not understand its surrounding ritual and underlying implication except as they are revealed by the enthusiasm of the Sienese themselves? As an American friend who speaks fluent Italian and has attended for a number of years remarked, "It is for them, not for us." The connections between past and present are many and powerful and in the Palio of Siena they are amply demonstrated in what would otherwise be a quite trivial event. In short, it seems worth it to "them" if not necessarily to "us."

The case of the Palio is plainly an extreme example of a general process of contest, yet it shares with other strongly felt contests the exquisite piquancy of uncertainty, and of course the likelihood of defeat. For, whether in races, ball leagues, or tournaments, there are always many more losers than winners. But being a candidate for losing seems to be better than no candidacy at all. Even if one cannot participate directly—in the Palio or its equivalents on the ball fields and in the arenas of other societies—one can participate eagerly in the rigamarole of constant trial, frequent loss, and victory from time to time. The point appears to be: do it, share the clamor, the waxing and waning of fortunes, the anticipation, the surprise and turmoil of outcome. It is a matter of maintaining tonus, a sense of zest, and an alive concern with a basic process.

Accordingly we create not only contests but numerous other enactments, both real and imaginary, to remind us of the odds against us. For example, in the mystery "thriller" we voluntarily subject ourselves to quite extended uncertainty, about what is happening, who is guilty, who is bad, who is cruel, who constructive. The morality-play nature of thrillers and the frequent development of major heroes with technical forensic vision and unquestionable if complex rectitude, such as Hercule Poirot, Inspector Maigret, and Perry Mason, reveal a commitment to the restoration of a healthy, forward-looking society despite the depredations of antisocial and corrupting elements whose very presence, to say nothing of activity, is widely dispiriting to communities at large.

Apart from contests, other more explicitly artistic activities share the important characteristic that they challenge human limit and fix human experience and perception—immortally the artist hopes. Do you remember the comment I made about the narrowness of physiologists who saw the endorphins as substances which principally operated to reduce pain—that in order to make an appreciable difference on the behavior of an organism they have to be able to affect pain? But ideas are so much easier and so much gentler to manage and to persuade. Maybe artistic and intellectual explorations substitute large and energetically expensive real behaviors with imaginative ones based on small scope and delicacy of execution. Artistic, literary, and scientific criticism become functions interposed between natural human expression and the thought and skill with which this is undertaken. First we have to play the notes clearly (hard enough as any young music student knows)—which is just the beginning of a genuine quest for a level of skill and desire for achievement consistently lifted as each plateau is reached. Like athletes, whom they resemble in their attitude to their own energy and efficiency, creative persons, and the greatest ones the most, drive themselves to the extra bit of music, action, color, logic, assessment or whirl which creates the difference between those who leave their environments as they find them and those who make a difference. Whatever it is which drives the dozens of young aspiring dancers who stream in and out of the famous dance studio near where I live and compels them to exert their bodies and wills until they can't anymore, it is not pessimism.

Mens Sana in Corpore Sano

The standard Latin motto "A sound mind in a sound body" must still decorate countless secondary school gymnasiums. The obvious virtues of good health, exercise and sturdy physical condition need no recounting here. However, the relationship between physical being and cerebral process must continue to undergo important examination and reexamination. For example, how little is known about pain—take the case of terminal cancer and its control by drugs, hypnotherapy, etc.—continues to be surprising. (Holden, 1977.) Yet the beneficial effects of exercise, particular diets and other regimens on moods and cortical activity in general are either well known or suspected on good grounds. In a folk version of the scientific story many people subject themselves to the strictures of various diets or regimens, such as vegetarianism, health foods, macrobiotics, high protein, high carbohydrate, or whatever. Whether they do this for reasons of fashion, controlled private hysteria, or genuine assessment of the relationship between bodily intake and behavior is not as important as the fact that the very business of subjecting the self to the regimen appears to provide at least the illusion of achievement of the goals intended. When such procedures of self-abnegation are successful is it because they are self-administered placebos or is it because there is an actual physiological connection between the diet and the outcome? Or is any diet or exercise regime likely to have a benign effect on the relationship between calories taken in and calories expended? Since at least in wealthy societies more people are overweight than underweight, perhaps this is the case.

Perhaps, too, dietary taboos, culinary practices, and even elaborate religious attitudinizing about food are self-administered placebos. We know that people administer to themselves an unbelievably costly and diverse array of patent medicines, douches, mouthwashes, sedatives, stimulants, cosmetics, skin purifiers, skin tighteners, skin looseners, etc., and it is also clear that many of the substances involved are essentially inactive and some may indeed be harmful. Nevertheless, particularly in societies where most of the basic survival problems have been solved, it appears that, in order to improve their senses of self, individuals will subject themselves to these substances. Is this a rendition of the optimistic principle in private terms? It is too easy for sophisticated persons to scoff at the often empirically preposterous efforts of gullible people to feel better by ingesting or coating themselves with allegedly efficacious materials. They are doing it for a reason and I have indicated what I think the reason is.

It is quite possible that the optimism principle demands that a certain ration of such self-administered uplift be used if not indeed required by the organism. Perhaps in communities with comparatively unsatisfactory forms of social grooming and socio-medication, the purchase of vials, tubes and variously shaped bottles may provide a relatively inexpensive and generally harmless fillip to the battering routine of ongoing existence. It is mere humanism to leave oneself open to the possibility that the endlessly varied but extensive effort people make to improve their physical circumstances through the often apparently magical means I have just described represents something important if not grave about the human situation. It suggests the way people see the relationship between what they are and what they can do about themselves. Nor is this phenomenon restricted to wealthy Western societies; it is deeply rooted in the social schemes of traditional, less wealthy ones. Furthermore, members of these societies may elect patterns of care with considerable skill. In her dissertation in anthropology at Rutgers University, Katherine Gould-Martin, now of the University of Southern California Medical School, showed clearly and in fascinating detail how persons in a rural village of Taiwan made decisions about which type and intensity of medical care they needed, ranging from the completely religious-magical to the surgical wards of Western Taiwan hospitals. (Gould-Martin, 1976.) As Gould-Martin revealed, people allegedly unskilled in these matters were indeed quite astute about the relationship between cost in money and energy and result in the various medical procedures which they could select from. The persistence of the traditional means of curing reflected a not unwise judgment about health care in communities which, while traditional and rural, were alive to the value of essentially urban sophisticated medicine.

Of course the process can become nearly insane, as in the splurges of rich people who receive bafflingly expensive injections, often in Switzerland, of serums alleged to reverse the aging process or to provide them some mysterious cellular power which will fundamentally improve their lives. One recalls also the consternation about the use of monkey glands as adjuncts to the human system which surrounded W. B. Yeats and his circle at a time when it was thought that such interspecies transfer of tissue could actually make a difference. The same kind of belief is shared by those who purchase powdered bones or tusks or other ornaments of particular animals in order to cure a range of ailments from depression to impotence. From the small clearing in a Ghanaian market town where a man circled by onlookers attracts the attention of possible buyers of his syrup offering vitality by showing pictures of human genitalia, to the carefully arranged, exquisitely designed and lettered packages of herbal medicine in a traditional drugstore of any major Chinatown, to the Fifth Avenue New York beauty salon offering clients expensive formulations of beeswax or algae or wheat germ or protein to massage into their skin, transactions recur between people and the quick sense they have of their own bettered possibility. Do they work? Another question entirely. But surely the wish is parent to something which maintains the prosperity of these age-old mind and body crafts.

However, there *are* concrete actions which can be taken, and are being studied, to try to understand what governs illness and thus health and indeed what the aging process is and how it can be affected beneficially. It may turn out that the most important constructive contribution of American society to the second half of the twentieth century will be the American support of medical research, led by the National Institutes of Health, at a degree of intensity and sophistication unprecedented in human history. A vast establishment was created and is being maintained to probe malady after malady, pathology after pathology, and healthful balance after healthful balance. The optimism principle is expressed this way at its best. Persons at once committed to finding an answer but knowing for certain that they do not have it are energized and supported by a community's willingness to gamble resources or the possibility of knowledge. Of course there have been inexcusable abuses of accounting techniques, because of careerism, because expensive but trivial research has been sponsored and approved by pedestrian workers; however, the penetration by scientists of formerly mysterious features of nature now forms a rich portion of the species' patrimony, and it will continue to yield results for decades to come.

There have of course been criticisms of this institutionalization and what it means not only for the obvious reasons which I earlier alluded to but because of a disgruntlement often confused and sanctimonious, *e.g.*, Roszak (1975), about what is felt to be a depersonalizing and dehumanizing consequence of scientific, social and medical practice founded on purely technological assumptions. This may be a very important problem. But it may be more constructively solved by proceeding further in the technical direction rather than not proceeding at all. For example, it seems very important to try to understand how placebos work, what the biological functions of magical belief are, how hypnosis operates, what are the physiological concomitants of feelings of well-being or even religious ecstasy. The claim that a separate realm of experience is unavailable to scientific adjudication is a sorry one; it is finally a dourly pessimistic defensiveness about the liberties nature permits to students of her forms and functions. It also, somehow, implies that the grandeur of natural process, which is appreciable by science, is categorically different from the grandeur of what people make, which at least by extension in this argument is unavailable to science. If not scientists, then available to whom? Poets? Musicians? Dramatists? Painters? Are poets, musicians, dramatists and painters not precise? Not testers of experience and judgers of authenticity? Of course they are, like scientists. The passion for and commitment to understanding the world can be restricted to those outside of science only if one is willing to condemn non-scientists to a universe of relatively imprecise and oceanic meandering in scrutinizing natural and social life.

I am making no apologia for science as a process beyond that it legitimately and with dignity permits an animal concerned with the vulnerability of his own future to make guesses, surmises, predictions, or come to no conclusion about what is going to happen. To rely on those forms of understanding which are congenial because they are general and have worked for centuries is perhaps to be classical in art but conservative if not reactionary in scientific policy-making. Indeed it is curious that scientists are sometimes regarded as technologically austere and somewhat inhuman; in fact theirs is a passionate activity. As Lewis Thomas has written: "The essential wildness of science as a manifestation of human behavior is not generally perceived . . . I don't know of any other human occupation, even what I have seen of art, in which the people engaged in it are so caught up, so totally preoccupied, so driven beyond their strength and resources. Scientists at work have the look of creatures following genetic instructions . . . when they are near an answer, their hair stands on end, they sweat, they are awash in their own adrenalin. . . . There suddenly emerges, with the purity of a slow phrase of music, a single new piece of truth about nature." (Thomas, 1973.) Their committed and hearty skepticism may well provide a more usefully optimistic scheme for intellectual and policy-making work than any sanctified certainties, even ancient ones.

After all, what is the practical alternative? The informed heart of a nervous system governed by an uninformed cortex? Moral sentiment masquerading as ideological certainty? A purge of empiricists on the grounds that they are imperialists? Again, of course not. Presumably, to some people the tool of science is as frightening, glistening and complex as the film of an insect projected onto huge downtown cinema screens. Yet it may be, when all is said and done, the best tool to use to find a remedy to the problems caused by that very tool, science. Let me declare my interest and cue in my violins. It may be the best mechanism for understanding that which existed long before our science-created problems emerged—our human social natures.

Intimacy's Lure: Psychiety's Embrace

Apparently the mirror was not widely available until new ways of producing it were developed in Renaissance Venice. Until then people's senses of themselves largely depended on others, either as painters or talkers. Even Narcissus required a tame, still pond for his self-scrutiny. In the same way that people try to improve how they feel about themselves by honing and tuning their bodies, so also they try to achieve a similar effect by improving the network of their social relations. Certainly in North America traditionally legitimate forms of conduct and legitimate forms of social structure have decreased in their importance for individuals overall. It appears many people are involved in seeking a recuperative exercise technique in terms of which to live and with which they can achieve a sense of contentment about their existence. Dozens of so-called self-help books, sex manuals, grooming manuals, and similar publications purport to provide the insights and codes about the self *which in other social frameworks would come directly from the social framework itself.* Of course the term "self-help" is incorrect since the reader is being helped not by the reader but by the writer. What is overlooked in the frequent criticism of such manuals is that they are in one sense modern versions of the cautionary tale teller, the moral fabulist, the priest's parable. If the modes of self-enhancement in a secular age are secular this is hardly surprising. If the publication of books of sermons has lapsed because of a widespread inattention to what are proposed as God's assertions, then the replacement of these by the claims of men or women or schools of psychology or meditation or what have you is hardly unexpected or surprising. To adapt the McLuhan proposition that the "medium is the message" (McLuhan, 1963), the act of communication is the master pattern of which the facts communicated are incidents and servants. Perhaps it is not the Congregational or Baptist or Orthodox service a person attends but an hour or a weekend in an ashram or an evening in an emporium of strategic conviviality such as Esalen, est, or Arica. The critical underlying feature in all cases is individual people's willingness to accept their frailty and their inability to be completely self-sufficient people and to permit others, whatever their mandate, to offer them guidance, context, or, in the sterner religions or therapies, considerable coercion about what they may or may not do in their lives.

Does not this devout attention to the self cause the bonds of community to break as if—like the caricatured extreme of protestant autonomy—individuals care only for their immortal souls and deal only reluctantly with those of others? Probably not: In fact the act of committing one's own self to a social structuring of the process of living creates interdependencies, expectations and bonds. Selves become mutually invaginated.

People receive "support" from groups of individuals who may have been strangers an hour or a month before but who, using the new rhetoric of self-scrutiny, perforce become forceful members of an individual's community. This is no longer a classical society in which the cement of the community is the social relations expected, conducted, recollected in which people engage. Rather the unit of currency is the psyche. And what we have is a "psychiety." The bonds of community in fact are private renditions, private perceptions, private needs, private strengths, all sketched within a pattern of interdependent other privacies. The shift is quite stunning from a commitment to status to a concern about state. Quite new emphases appear to emerge in what people feel they need, want, have, lack and understand. But, though the participants in the social system may have changed in quite substantial ways, no major structural change in the social system has occurred, except perhaps a modified decline in the importance of kinship systems. So the discontinuity is painful between what people want to use for their private encounters with the social world and what this world is actually made up of.

There have been subtle scattered but notably pervasive consequences of the shift from a belief in the inevitability of political progress to a commitment to the desirability of private therapy. To adopt a cooking term, like optimism itself therapy is a basic sauce which can embellish, enhance, conceal, alter, complement, or fuse the essential flavor of the pattern of behavior in question. When joined to theories of social progress it has produced an increasingly studious attention to the relationship between individual psyche and individual behavior. Thus early Freudians believed that if all people were psychoanalyzed— and certainly if powerful ones were—then the conduct of society would be freer, kinder, more efficient, better. Conversely, the psychohistory school has sought to show how poor psychological condition has yielded a variety of social pathologies when powerful people are untouched by therapeutic insights. Public attitudes on this issue are peculiar. For example, when U.S. Senator Eagleton was forced to step down as the Vice-Presidential candidate in the McGovern campaign because he had psychiatric treatment, surely an important possibility about his treatment was that it was effective and that therefore he was healthier than other candidates who may have had no treatment at all. There remains a serious uncertainty about the value of therapy and how unsettling it is, at least if current attitudes to overt therapy-seeking by politically and economically powerful people is an indication. This does not of course apply to persons in the performing and creative arts in which the self is itself a principal tool of work. Perhaps notions such as therapy, guidance counseling, self-discovery and actualization are available to people in their private lives. But there persists a reluctance to extend to people performing dominating work in the public sphere an open public sanction for private therapeutic exploration. This is curious inasmuch as the same leaders are permitted and in fact rewarded with public acceptance when they submit themselves in prayer and communion with God. Is it mere familiarity with the process which permits this and not the other formula? Or is it in fact the specificity of therapy—the fact that it proposes specific causes, cures, and consequences—which is disturbing? That is, can followers readily accept optimistic leaders who not only know explicitly and in detail what they should and must do but who are subject to an advisor or body of advice rooted in a theory of private life rather than in the norm of public conduct? I think the latter is more reassuring for reasons I have outlined already—that one function of optimism in human evolution was to permit people to come together in communal behavior by agreeing on certain general ideas and principles. Consensus about these seems "easy to learn" from the first family experiences onward, or so it seems. But the rigamaroles and outcomes of therapies are harder to learn for the very reason of their link to the private self. And it is difficult to translate readily from the realm of the private to the realm of the public.

This raises an interesting issue about access to power. As a pure speculation may I suggest that one consequence of a generally upper-middle-class and élite preoccupation with therapy is that persons who are anti-therapeutic or a-therapeutic in either the middle and upper classes or in the working classes will simply acquire those posts which the preoccupied bour-geoisie would normally inherit. As Peter and Birgitta Berger showed so devastatingly, the so-called greening of America proposed by Charles Reich in fact led to nothing more substan-tial in terms of economic and political power than the "blueing of America." (Berger and Berger, 1971.) The normal inheritors of desirable jobs in the industrial, economic and political sys-tems opted out of these systems for reasons of self-discovery (related of course to important social movements and changes of the 1960's) only to be replaced by blue-collar persons and those formerly dispossessed who were ready and willing to fill the desirable positions.

The essential point is that if the pursuit of therapy is in any way an admission of loneliness or of personal imperfection, then it may appear too dangerous for leaders to enjoy, at least in the view of their followers. Leaders must after all be en-meshed in society and therefore not lonely. They must be effec-tive and thus not unfunctional. They must be willing to find peace of mind and certainty of spirit within the conventional-ized definitions of a social moral code. They must do this even if it depends on a nontangible God rather than on a directly supportive connection with a therapeutic person or system which may well be outside the scope of conventional under-standing, if not outlawed. It is quite remarkable that this should be so, given the profound controversies which surround the idea of the nature of God and how best God may be obeyed. It almost seems as if people prefer leaders who are beholden to what cannot be beheld.

Cargo Culture and the World's
Cry of Economic Pain

During the Second World War some air bases were built in areas of Melanesia where aviation and the people involved in it were largely unknown. It occurred to a number of enterprising religious or political leaders of nearby small communities that they might try to profit from this innovation. They noticed that if there were some planes lined up alongside a cleared landing strip this induced other planes to come in and disgorge copious supplies of desirable goods. Without knowing about the world yonder which generated these aircraft and their goods, the little communities cleared runway spaces of their own and erected versions of airplanes to perch alongside the landing strip. The Melanesian villagers were certain this gesture would magically produce the desired airplanes and their desirable goods. The "cargo cults," as these became known by anthropologists and others, were important features of local society and caused predictable unsettlement, passion, confusion and distortion in the social behavior of formerly quite settled communities. The cargo cult phenomenon has become a celebrated anthropological case—and for very good reason. Its origins, dynamics and, most of all, meaning, are quite crystal clear. We all understand.

I've already discussed in some detail the overall question of people's relationship to resources and how symbol-ridden this relationship is, though in matters of food and shelter it is totally real. The cargo-cultural nature of economic existence is highly charged in the context of the implacable reality of scarce or inequitably or ineptly distributed resources. Next to dying itself, the discrepancy between wealth and poverty may be the most discouraging for optimists, but also the most challenging. Can there be enough wealth for everybody? Can it be distributed in such a way that people are reasonably healthy, reasonably comfortable, and at least reasonably content with the social and political circumstances in which their resources are distributed? What is to be done about the remarkable disparity between rich and poor in all countries and between rich countries and poor ones? Do technical means exist for producing enough food, extracting enough fuel, smelting enough metal, fashioning enough clothing so that the world's people can avoid the despair of poverty and life's diminuendo in disease and starvation?

Some years ago (1962) Robert Heilbroner wrote *The Great Ascent*, a reasonably hopeful view for prospects of generalized economic development in poor countries. Years later in *The Human Prospect* (1976) he wrote of a ". . . fear that we will be unable to sustain the trend of economic growth very much longer. . . ." Further he describes ". . . the stunning discovery that economic growth carries previously unsuspected side-effects whose cumulative impact may be more deleterious than the undoubted benefits that growth also brings." (1976:19.) Even such a thoughtfully constructive and sturdy activist/socialist as Michael Harrington records the vivid reality of poverty in poor countries and his own pervasive awareness of the immense difficulties involved in overcoming not simply inequity but even the grossest forms of human want. (Harrington, 1977.)

Perhaps part of what Harrington calls his own "cruel innocence" about the matter of world poverty is the result of an ambient thoughtless optimism which has persisted about economic development certainly since the Second World War and which is the modern and most specific expression of the belief in automatic progress. We will come back to that belief in a moment, but I think it is important first, however briefly, to sketch the context within which the widespread depredations of the Great Depression and then the incalculable convulsion of the Second World War yielded from that time onward a persistent if not altogether formalized belief that somehow wealth would be produced and distributed and human want would be successfully attacked by human skill married to compassion.

The idea has deep roots; it prospered most directly after the economic development of the industrial revolution, and was fertilized by the Darwinian notion—or rather its perversion in social Darwinism—that somehow evolution occurs and more fit forms emerge. The notion of levels of civilization ranging from barbarism to high civilizations is a version of a zoological system of classification. The colonial systems which Europe inflicted upon Africa and Asia contained some notion of elevation of savages to the higher forms—presumably those represented by the metropolitan culture making the arbitrary decisions about who was good, bad, savage and gentle.

The system of classification originated in a trinity composed of varying degrees of political domination, economic superiority and religious conceit. It could and did yield profound psychological results as well (cf. Mannoni, 1956). It produced in many members of so-called savage societies a curious belief that they were in fact inferior as described by the colonial system and that they had to strive mightily to perform the rituals of metropolitan demeanor in order to upgrade their very beings in the desired fashion. The various colonial powers differed in their approach to this blandishment. The British with their indirect rule scheme stimulated some members of local communities to be able to join the British way through education and adoption of the manners of a gentleman, and then to return to their native communities in order to rule on the British model and on Britain's behalf. On the other hand, the French, with Cartesian logic, assumed a complete continuity between overseas France—France *outre-mer*—and the metropolitan culture. Certain Africans became representatives of their territories in the French Assembly and even, as with Léopold Senghor, became important officials—in Senghor's case president of the Assembly. The psychological impact of this scheme was shown to me vividly when I was interviewing a senior black civil servant in the Ivory Coast in connection with a research project I was undertaking in Ghana (I was interested in the way civil service bureaucracies operated in an independent West African country, Ghana, and visited the Ivory Coast for a comparative perspective with a francophone cast). The man I was interviewing spoke with great but unacknowledged ambivalance about the French presence in his country. On one hand he resented and complained about the presumption and exploitation of the system which the French managed. On the other he was clearly rewarded by it and psychologically identified with it. At one point during a particularly heated exposition of his view he reached into his desk drawer, pulled out his passport, a French passport, and snapped it onto his desk. "*Je suis français. Voilà. Je suis un évolue!*" He had made the transition, had evolved into a Frenchman. That this could have been a devolution, a scandal, a betrayal of his own past did not at least overtly concern him, and his pride and assertion were intense at having achieved something which little boys and girls of Lyon or Cavaillon or Calais acquire simply by being born.

The long-term consequences of overcoming the mental set

arising from the experience of colonial domination with its associated poverty, political weakness and racial discrimination is pervasive; rather like the stereotypically nouveau riche member of a metropolitan society who overspends to assert his new status, so many leaders of formerly dependent but still-poor countries spend extremely scarce funds in hectically extravagant ways. A Minister of Aviation's little optimism in buying a 747 may be an effective gesture, but the big optimism of improving his people's welfare may suffer from the confusion of means with ends and from the glamourous magical value rather than real economic productivity of such resources as airplanes, factories, super highways, cloverleaf intersections. Cliché phrases such as "the international demonstration effect," and "the revolution of rising expectations," are all about realities of an intense and evocative kind. They represent an epidemic sweep over virtually the entire globe of a sudden sense of the possible practicality of individual economic optimism. And from fighting the scourge of hunger, the terrors of illness, the incomprehensible fact of thirst, the next step is taken, where it can be, to a transistor radio, some extra gingham cloth, cement blocks at the base of one's hut, a bicycle, a motor-scooter, and at the apogee, a car.

What this requires of the world's limited resources is well known. The possible political and even moral implications of this quest for things and the use of service processes have been gloomily anticipated by Heilbroner (1976) and echoed by Mishan (1978). For whatever it's worth, my own dispirited view is that the crunching encounter of worldwide economic optimism with worldwide economic reality will prove as discouraging to us all as the existence of sin to Catholics, of inequality to Marxists, of disembodied sensuality to Puritans, of executioners to those revering life. The plight of an animal evolved to make use of what it can get suddenly faced with the prospect of getting what it wants—which it may be unable to do—is somehow new. It is almost like a new chemical compound because of the novel pressure of expanded world populations heated and stirred by novel ideas of economic expectations and even entitlements. Perhaps the best we can hope for is that because we are as skilled at predicting disaster—though far less so inclined—as in anticipating good times, the outcome of the race between resource and dream will be less depressing, if also less agreeable than the portents threaten. But even that is not altogether delightful. I must confess I do not believe it is altogether likely, either.

If You Can't Change the World, Change Your Ideas of the World

Perhaps the reality of the prospects for equitable and appreciable improvement in human economic conditions is depressingly unsure. But the theoretical prospect for political and spiritual improvement ·in the human lot remain as beckoning as ever. Earlier I described how the development of civil authority followed from the religious one and how still there is a connection between secular power and ideas about divine order and guidance. The expansion of the role of politics in the twentieth century has been quite unprecedented. Not only does politics refer to constitutions, representatives, legislation, etc., but it has now got to do *inter alia* with sexual behavior, gender roles, the rights of children, the definitions of psychiatry, the protection of the quality of air, and the monitoring and regulation of extremely complex relationships between food and substances added to it for various purposes. Furthermore, in large regions of the world formal religious goals for societies have been abandoned while secular goals frequently founded on one or another version of Marxism now determine how governors and their people act, or think they should act. If there has been a decline in the direct effect of churches in non-communist communities, there remain powerful strains of concern for issues of human rights, proper conduct and desirable social institutions which continue to add forceful moral implications to many political actions. The emerging amalgam of religion with politics has the effect of uniting the final concerns of religion with the contemporary means of politics. People's lives remain affected by the pageant of human social possibilities which religions in the

past have colorfully drawn and which are in the present suffused with a stimulating if less colorful element of realpolitik. If
it is difficult to sustain optimism as one watches starving people die it is easy and perhaps necessary to do so when one
contemplates the necessity of improving the political and moral
conditions under which people live. The happy hunting
ground has been translated; world conferences, Leagues of Nations, United Nations, agencies for development, groups like
Amnesty—all become down-to-earth forces promising soon
what religions could promise in due course.

This is hardly surprising since it is easier, more practical, and
faster to change ideas about the world than to change the world
itself. We can comprehend why, then, there exists a worldwide
urgency about equity, individual dignity and the importance
of a sense of optimism, even for the most miserably poor of the
most over-populated and bereft communities. Rhetoric may
not provide a Gabonese mother yams for her family nor an
economic development proposal any immediate shipment of
tetracycline in rural Pakistan. But somehow the verbal products
find not only willing producers but many unsuspecting or trusting consumers. The reiteration of optimistic rhetoric, even
about the dauntingly difficult problem of economic development, continues.

It is easy for outsiders, particularly sophisticated students of
the political process, to mock and carp at the effortless mono-
logues of politicians as they address the poor about goods and
goodness to come. And yet it is impossible not to understand
or at least sense the power and effectiveness of the interaction
between leader and led as the problem of hope is managed,
even if it is only stage-managed. When I worked in West Africa
I would frequently attend political rallies, and even though
sometimes speeches were in the local vernacular and I could
understand hardly a word, the rhythm, intensity and the point
of the interaction were clear. Even if the politician swept away
from the cheering crowd into the quiet of his cooled limousine
to return to a huge Accra villa built with the proceeds of an
import-export franchise for vital goods registered in his wife's
name—even if the people in the crowds knew all this, which

they did—somehow the interaction as it happened, and perhaps somewhat before and somewhat after, was vitalizing and seemingly appropriate.

Of course in the Ghanaian case the situation turned foul. A country wealthy and sophisticated because of its cocoa forests and expertise in exploiting them, its gold mines, and generally well-articulated social structure embarked on a series of often impractical but symbolically attractive modernization projects. In common with many similar countries, it emphasized the development of new patterns of industrialization rather than the enhancement of existing agricultural strengths. The political messianism of Kwame Nkrumah—a highly infectious and ingratiatingly plausible one—gave way to rancorous disillusion with political promises as cocoa prices fell and the Ghanaian economy began to suffer the consequences of plans for development whose magical component was too high for their practical effect. Now, almost a generation later, Ghanaian currency is nearly valueless, internal economic dislocation is severe, and the brilliant promises of economic wealth wedded to the political glory of African-based social forms has been lost in the stiff peremptoriness of yet another military regime. Needless to say the problems were very great in moving from a dependent colonial system to an independent one, in Ghana and elsewhere, and the blandishments of charismatic leaders were particularly appealing during an historical period of changeover from one system to another. (Tiger, 1964, 1968.)

One general problem which continues to harass optimists convinced of the possibility of human improvement is the corruption of political and economic personnel. A number of factors have stimulated corrupt practice on a large scale in the world: the expansion of world trade, the growth of independent governments, the emergence of classes of local political and economic entrepreneurs to represent their own markets to outsiders and sell their resources to outsiders, the development of international agencies which purport to or actually do effect transfers of aid as well as the secret branches of great power governments willing to subvert local officials. The more integrated and interdependent the world system becomes, the more manipulable it is by those with political power and economic resource. Such corruption is not only demoralizing but wholly treacherous. For example, when food aid was sent to the Sahel nations suffering from drought, much of it ended up for sale on black markets controlled by national and local officials for their own benefit. And there are legion examples of well-connected official or related families who benefit lavishly from direct and indirect theft from projects of construction and other development supposedly given as aid to abet mass welfare, not augment private fortunes.

I happen to believe that corrupt practice in the transfer of unrecorded funds by legal authority is a far greater factor in communal life than usually noted. In a sense it is part of the optimistic principle to be surprised or even shocked when the extent of this becomes known. Where there is considerable social complexity corruption becomes structurally easy. When whole nations are involved, as for example with the sale of Lockheed airplanes to Japan through the allegedly corrupt intervention of the office of the Prime Minister of Japan, corrupt practice becomes the greater and the more lucrative. Obviously siphoning off money from legitimate channels into organizations not under community sanction, or at least survey, must have a grave effect on how successfully communities can govern the use of their resources equitably and/or constructively. It would be hard to argue that the enrichment of criminal organizations or persons with no responsibility to the legal system of a community is cause for satisfaction.

The misuse of resources is cause enough for outrage, yet there is an additional sense of violation which corruption causes. As a psychological phenomenon its effect is possibly greater than any concrete one because of what it does to citizens' notions of propriety, endeavor, and a host of other constructive modes of living which people are widely prepared to employ. Perhaps it's not the money but the principle which is the most salient factor in the process of corruption. After all, even when funds are not involved, the outcry against corrupt practice is sharp—i.e., the convulsive and profound response to Presidential conduct during the re-election campaign of

Richard Nixon in 1972 and thereafter when illegal actions were taken at the very highest level of government. The anger of writers and citizens was understandable. But what was also intriguing about the Watergate episode was that there was an effort to see the exposure of the crimes and their exorcism as a way of revitalizing community morale. For example, in a television interview with New York broadcaster Gabe Pressman on June 9, 1973, Senator Lowell Weicker of the Senate Watergate Committee said that Watergate was "the best thing that ever happened to the nation" because it would permit America to persist for another two hundred years; it had, he suggested, revitalized the institutions of the country and given Americans an opportunity to rededicate themselves to high moral principles. In a similar vein, Henry Steele Commager, writing in *Newsweek*, also saw the redemptive nature of the Watergate matter in the context of the long-range health of American institutions. (Commager, 1974.)

Why conduct oneself responsibly and fairly, according to acceptable practice, when others are stealing, cheating and prevaricating? This is the question posed to the moral order by corrupt practice. The optimistic impulse that social life will either remain decent or become more so is severely violated by corruption. It is significant that the corroding effect of corrupt practice is not total in a social system and that many members, perhaps the vast majority, continue to conduct themselves in ways generally regarded as acceptable and law abiding. Consider, then, how provocative and outrageous was the corruption revealed in the nursing home industry in the New York area. The abusiveness, squalor and venality of the state-franchised system was almost marvelous—the effrontery of the criminals operating the system went beyond even imaginative expectations. The persistent and in essence murderous abuse of old and weak people who should otherwise have been honored or at least made comfortable, in order to grasp sums of money beyond anyone's needs, is presumably as severe a depressant to the social system as selfless heroism is a benign stimulant. Corruption threatens optimism; and as many a crusading politician has discovered, exorcising corruption can lib-

erate optimism and win elections. The fragile symbol of community integrity is surprisingly potent when embedded in a
vivid program promising to restore it.

In social terms corrupt practice is a form of structural sav-
agery. It interferes drastically with the cooperativeness and
congeniality necessary for the effective conduct of complex social relations. In the small-scale communities to which we were
evolved corruption was difficult to conceal. The very size of
social groups assured their members' conversance in anything
of note, particularly knowledge of what resources the community had and how they were used. However, given the large
scale of modern communities, the opportunities for corruption
and affront to the body politic have enormously increased. At
the same time, the relationship between government and citizen has become more complicated through taxation. Because of
the precision of computer-based audits of taxpayer returns and
the decline of cash transactions in economies, individual citizens bear the brunt of governmental assault on corrupt practice.
For example, citizens preparing tax returns of any complexity
are required to produce an array of receipts, schedules, statements, bills, canceled checks and so on; this turns individuals
into accounts of their own existences. In effect such taxpayers
become legal entities in constant connection if not conflict with
an overriding, omnipresent governmental system. This may
turn out in the long run to have surprising consequences for
people's concepts of their reality and their own economy. Already the relationship between the tax structure and such rituals as business lunches has become highly elaborate, and expenditures made against the tax costs are treated as of a
different order than those which exist in economic "real time,"
so to speak.

There is an almost cosmological matter at stake here inasmuch as taxpayers' actions taken today may well be taken in
the context of a tax audit some two or three years hence, and so
the immediacy of even day-to-day existence becomes in a direct
and consequential way affected by possible actions many
months away. Curiously this is the reverse of the traditional
middle-class virtue of practicing "deferred gratification"—the

ability to hold off on the enjoyment of pleasures today in order to receive even more substantial or useful ones later. In some as yet unexamined fashion the psychological inducement toward immediate gratification, given the nature of the tax structure, directly reverses the traditional temperamental practice of bourgeois persons. One may wonder if the bitter complaints frequently expressed about the taxation system betray not only conscious resentment but also confusion created by precisely the shift from deferring gratification to seeking it now because of how the tax system works.

Of course the effort to reduce tax evasion by citizens stimulates more imaginative efforts to evade, which in turn increases preventive measures. The search for tax avoidance benefits has become international—whole countries prosper because they provide systems of taxation which benefit particular citizens or organizations of other communities. It is all very strange, and introduces a peculiar moral dimension into economic transactions where there was none before—between a restaurateur and his patron, between a purchaser of theater tickets and his business "prospect," or among persons who use their domestic places as tax-deductible staging grounds for business forays. An independent system suddenly intervenes in these relationships, with its own rules and its own course of sanctions. A serious anthropology of the ways and meanings of taxation has yet to be undertaken and should be. As a system of authority confidently wedded to the computer machine, modern taxation adds a new and overarching connection with impersonal government into many formerly small-scale or even intimate socio-economic transactions. It is certainly an aspect of the process of bureaucratization of intimacy which is evident in other spheres of life as well.

At the beginning of this book I suggested that optimism is so much part of the ambience of contemporary social life that it hardly receives attention from scholars, certainly not in proportion to its significance in the overall conduct of human groups. I was astonished when I looked into the subject catalogue in the British Museum reading room as I began this project in 1972 to find under "Optimism" about a dozen entries.

The idea of progress is another matter. It has been widely investigated, if only because it so aptly expresses a central impulse in the mechanism of post-industrial revolutionary. thought. Perhaps the pivotal study in the English language is the classicist J. B. Bury's *The Idea of Progress,* which carefully eviscerates the notion of progress through the historical periods following the classical one. (Bury, 1932.) A brief and crisp study is by Pollard (1971), while in my view the extensive and passionate analysis by Wagar provides the most thorough and searching modern conspectus on the subject. (Wagar, 1973.)

A number of other approaches to the problem of the future have been made. First, in the theological tradition, perhaps most obviously the Germans Dietrich Bonhoeffer and, more recently, Jurgen Moltmann have coped with the problem directly. As Moltmann wrote: "There is therefore only one real problem in Christian theology, which its own object forces upon it and which it in turn forces on mankind and on human thought: the problem of the future." (Moltmann, 1967:16.) Psychologists also have written on the subject, though most without direct attention to the possible neurophysiological basis of hopefulness; for example, see Lefcourt (1973), Stotland (1969), Cohen (1956, 1960, 1964) and Tyler (1973).

From still a different perspective, Robert Trivers has written about the possible biological adaptiveness of self-deception; certainly his argument pertains to a variety of other species than the human, and as I have proposed here, perhaps among humans particularly self-deception is a vital feature of psychological experience in its social setting. (Trivers, 1971.)

The notion of progress has stimulated an immense array of writing which need not and cannot be detailed here. The range is striking, through Condorcet, Malebranche, Saint-Simon, Ginsburg, Julian Huxley, Russell, Hobhouse, Spencer, Marx, Comte, and so on. Of course, these and others who struggled with the problem of human consciousness of the future and what to do with this consciousness had no accurate or useful information about human evolution and the various physiological, anatomical and behavioral features of the process. Nor could they know what is now known about the neurophysiology of cognition and the relationship between basic bodily processes and ideas.

Evidently an acquaintance told Samuel Johnson, "I had wanted to be a philosopher, but cheerfulness kept breaking in." However, this did not dissuade the philosophers I have mentioned and many others from reflecting, as less speculative people do, on the forms and functions of agreeable futures. In his startling *A Short History of Decay*, Cioran comments, "Hegel is chiefly responsible for modern optimism. How could he have failed to see that consciousness changes only its forms and modalities, but never progresses? Becoming excludes an absolute fulfillment of goal: the temporal adventure unfolds without an aim external to itself, and will end when its possibilities of movement are exhausted. . . . We are not more conscious than the Greco-Roman world, the Renaissance, or the 18th Century; each period is perfect in itself—and perishable." (Cioran, 1975:146.)

Few philosophers, or indeed members of any other profession, possess the magnificent unsentimentality about human existence and experience of Cioran, and he is probably accurate in identifying Hegel with the beginning of a large philosophical tradition which, when coupled with the Industrial Revolution, stimulated Marxism and its various subforms of progressive optimism. As Robin Fox and I suggested in *The Imperial Animal*, it could be argued that the industrial way of existence was much closer in emotional and social terms to the hunting-gathering way to which we had been adapted in evolution. So *once humans were emancipated both conceptually and actually from the slow recurrence of agricultural production to the complex, natureless, and seemingly almost limitless bounty of industrialization, it was surely inevitable that progressive theory, or at least the certainty of progress, would threaten all less optimistic social theories.*

I have described a variety of the consequences of modernization for still agricultural people in ambitiously modernizing societies, and also for those urban unfortunates who exist on what minimal resources they can acquire in the swelling cities of their countries. Peter Berger has characterized many of the existing plans for modernization as contemporary versions of the "pyramids of sacrifice" on which South American theocracies sacrificed people and placated gods. He says, "The most pressing moral imperative in policy making is a *calculus of pain.*" (Berger, 1976:xiii.) And yet—and this is the bitter complaint of countless commentators on the consequences of modernization—it almost appears that inattention to the "calculus of pain" is as predictable under some human circumstances as the effect of synthetic opiates is on the perception of pain in tested animals. It is tempting, if also perhaps unreal, to draw an analogy between the existence of the internally occurring opiates in the body and the callous blindness or careful inattention of policy makers. In practice there is a certain noticeable equivalent.

As Berger notes, countless politicians have induced numberless subjects to endure manifold hardship in the name of the forthcoming revolution, millennium, purity, triumph of freedom, a particular god. Platoons of Western European Christians vagabonded through Europe and Asia seeking the Holy Grail, apparently persuaded by someone's theory that their brutal crusade was worthwhile. Some of their adversaries sought optimistic refuge in one or another myth of a golden past—some sin-free, trouble-free Eden. They conducted their lives in nostalgia for certainties. The Grail seekers cover ground, the caretakers of the golden age time, but both look ahead many years. They are connected by some equivalent of a nervous system to a body of belief that justifies their behavior in their kind of community.

The analogy between the internal opiates and the external theory or ideology or belief seems less spurious in extreme cases—survivors of concentration camps, grotesque dyscommunity, suicide. There is a dismal literature concerned with the response of people to overwhelming disaster which suggests an organic power which a loss of faith in an acceptable future has on how people act and think. In his remarkably evocative and sympathetic study, *Everything in Its Path,* about Buffalo Creek, an Appalachian coal-mining community devastated by a bursting dam, Kai Erikson comments, "It was once fashionable in the social sciences generally to compare human communities to

living organisms. . . . Science may have gained something
when this analogy was abandoned, but it may have lost something, too, for a community of the kind being discussed here
does bear at least a figurative resemblance to an organism. . . .
It is the *community* that cushions pain, the *community* that provides a context for intimacy, the *community* that represents morality and serves as the repository for old traditions." (Erikson,
1977:193–194.) Discussing "the illusion of safety," Erikson continues: "One of the bargains men make with one another in
order to maintain their sanity is to share an illusion that they
are safe, even when the physical evidence in the world around
them does not seem to warrant that conclusion. The survivors
of a disaster, of course, are prone to overestimate the perils of
their situation, if only to compensate for the fact that they
underestimated those perils once before; but what is worse, far
worse, is that they sometimes live in a state of almost constant
apprehension *because they have lost the human capacity to screen
out the signs of danger out of their line of vision."* (Ibid.: 234; italics
mine.)

At Buffalo Creek the destruction of big optimism saw the
destruction of little as well. Personal demeanor, sexual behavior, familial structures—these and more were marked by a
rapid and troubling deterioration of the standards of the people
of Buffalo Creek. Just as women in concentration camps cease
menstruating, and persons retiring from work face an inordinate risk of illness and death, and those involved in crises of
bereavement, divorce, unemployment suffer or visit blows to
their health, so may a community deprived of the grand illusion
that all is likely to be well experience wholesale deleterious
effects.

Pandora, Pandora

Finally some kind of choice must be made.

Face the worst cases. You have suffered some weirdly punishing, inexplicably general shift in the circumstances of your
life. Your work has been exposed as false or trivial or preten-

tious. You understand that a war will soon start somewhere important to you. In the center of your body is the ache of a love gone awry, away, found dead, or awakened in someone else's bed. Your child informs you that your passion for his or her life is unsupported by any useful knowledge of what the child is, craves and fears. Your remaining parent dies and you are in a foreign country where your friends are all officials. You wait in the hospital while your wife gives birth to a dead baby. You can tell from the matter-of-fact reluctance of your skin to cover you firmly that you've only a couple of decades until you die.

Well then, what then? If you are, in addition to entertaining these charmless problems, also responsible for the sense of well-being of your compatriots or kin or friends, or if you think you can exploit their fear, what then? You can, like Sontag (1978), conscientiously confront the matter of illness or, like Becker (1973), confront the fact of death or, like Trilling, assert the impractical naïveté of a view of life without outright aggression or at least assertion unpleasant to some people. (Trilling, 1973.) Or you can, like T. S. Eliot, escape the nervous system in Anglican cathedrals, and like Aldous Huxley and countless others the banality of what is obvious in gardens of intoxicants and drugs. Perhaps, in times and places as primitive as blood you can seek to cheat the frailty of your own body by watching the bodies of others shot at, teased by lions, taunted by gladiators, or hung in public rectitude. Likewise, there is always the circus with its high-flying speculators, and Houdini chained inside an underwater barrel with just a moment's air.

Or, the matter can be formalized. Better procedures can be created for noting just how the future is to be approached and just who is responsible for correct demeanor in its face. A set of presumptions can be made about what will work and what will not, and a set of rules established to be attended to even while being broken. Funds can be expended for artifacts, of the kind ranging from the great pyramid at Teotihuacán to the glamorous exotica Tutankhamen could afford, to the two cathedrals still being built in Washington and New York, the symbolically major cities of the society which is the model of the modern. Or there are trees to be planted, babies to be conceived, trilogies to be begun; several hours in the gym beckon, a new hairspray, a seance with a posture teacher with an insight into an Oriental trick about the bones of spines. Or sustain the consternation of a complex courtship, or the search for a key to the Cyrillic spy codes of a well-known foe. Or hit a golf ball, build a dinette, marinate corned beef, or teach children about the forest floor.

Something must be done. Perhaps not anything, but certainly something. I have tried to suggest the urgency of the optimistic force and considered how much it was an obligatory feature of the lot of an animal as full of enthusiasm as the human, with its skull so packed with ever-active thinking tissue. When I was completing this book I found myself alone, and exceptionally and appropriately sad, on a Christmas Eve. As I walked through the abandoned streets of my neighborhood toward a too familiar restaurant, I saw on the opposite sidewalk two unsophisticated young women who, perhaps reacting to the solemnity of the occasion or to the evidences of self-satisfaction all around them, were noisy and strident. One of them almost shouted, "And you can see I'm wearing a leather coat." As indeed she was.

How do the tissues of the human being contrive some pleasure out of wearing a leather coat during an angry interchange in an alien neighborhood on a cold night when one is probably far from a humble home inside which one may be quite as lonely as elsewhere? The incident jolted me out of my sanctimonious self-pity. That woman's shout was a gift.

The possibility exists that it is a common human obligation to augment optimism. At the same time I am aware that this is a preposterous intimation. Can it be true that we all share a sentimental responsibility for maintaining an illusion about the graceful hopefulness of wizened old and innocent young? Are we condemned to obligatory optimism, secured this time by the manipulations of biology rather than the certainties of a priesthood? The human species has planted its skins and danced its bones in countless places for thousands of generations, and I have wondered about the possibility that the skill of its brain at estimating its frailty might also have to yield to the power of an almost thoughtless, unpliable, self-energizing conviction that the next move will be to the reassuring rhythm of more music. In the past we have survived the rigors of harder climates, predators more effective, diseases more consuming. We appear to have made effective use of a forlornly hopeful optimistic principle.

Thus it may be unfair to our skill as animals and our vivacity as intellects to do otherwise and to fail to scrutinize carefully what helped make us. The rigorous skepticism of science has made it possible for us to understand what we did not understand about why certain kinds of ideas have certain kinds of impact on certain kinds of people at certain times. We do not know what is inside the walnut of interaction between dream, fear, tissue, birth and death. Yet we have important clues not only from the pageant of our experience and history and the spectre of our dilemma in the future but also from the careful internecine cooperation of scientists of lab and field, who force themselves to be willing to accept that those of their proposals about truth which are wrong may be as valuable as those which are right.

Private optimism is a public resource. Public optimism is a private facility. Both can and have and will become disasters when there is too little fit between the vision and the facts of heat, cold, up, down, fast, slow, rich, poor, old, young, living, dying. It is dangerous to offer entrée to charlatans expert in illusion and big or little demagogues practiced in worthless promise. But perhaps there is a graver danger—because the consequences are almost endocrinological—in accepting that the only responsible commentators are those who by careful austerity have no remaining lust for next year's blooming forsythia, the infant upstairs, a thigh-kiss, or the pointless, joyful melees of birthdays and silver anniversaries.

When in the myth the various forces of life escaped from Pandora's box, one remained at the very bottom—hope. Atlas no longer holds up the world. The Trident is a nuclear submarine. The gods of war are lobbyists and accountants. Cupid is a

February industry. Even if the gods and other such forces have fallen, or become slogans, what Pandora rescued maintains its claim on our attention, if only because where it is dark it is difficult to see.

Bibliography

ABERLE, DAVID. "Religio-Magical Phenomena and Power, Prediction and Control," *Southwestern Journal of Anthropology*, 22:3, Autumn, 1966, p. 101.

ACKERMAN, D. R. "Biological Consequences of Population Control," *International Journal of Fertility*, XVII (1972).

ADORNO, T. W., et al. *The Authoritarian Personality*, New York: John Wiley & Sons, 1964.

ALEXANDER, RICHARD D. Review, *American Anthropologist*, 79:4, December, 1977.

ALVAREZ, ALFRED. *The Savage God: A Study of Suicide*, New York: Random House, 1972.

ANGEL, L. "Early Neolithic Skeletons from Catal Huyuk: Demography and Pathology," *Anatolian Studies*, XXI (1971), pp. 77–98.

ARIES, PHILIPPE. *Centuries of Childhood: A Social History of Family Life*, New York: Vintage Books, Random House, 1962.

ARIETI, SILVANO, ED., *American Handbook of Psychiatry*, 1, New York: Basic Books, 1959.

BANE, MARY JO. *Here to Stay: American Families in the 20th Century*, New York: Basic Books, 1976.

BECKER, G. "Altruism, Egoism, and Genetic Fitness: Economics and Sociobiology," *Journal of Economic Literature*, XIV (1975), pp. 817–825.

BEECHER, H. K. "Placebo Effects of Situations, Attitudes, and Drugs: A Quantitative Study of Suggestibility," in Karl Rickles, ed., *Non-Specific Factors in Drug Therapy*, Springfield, Illinois: Thomas and Company, 1968.

BENSON, HERBERT, and EPSTEIN, MARK. "The Placebo Effect: A Neglected Asset in the Case of Patients," *J.A.M.A.*, CCXXXII, June 23, 1975.

BERELSON, BERNARD. "An Evaluation of the Effects of Population Control Programs," *Studies in Family Planning*, The Population Council, Vol. 5, No. 1, January, 1974.

BERGER, PETER L. *Pyramids of Sacrifice: Political Ethics and Social Change*, Garden City, New York: Anchor Books, 1976.

BERGER, PETER L., and BERGER, BIRGITTE. "The Blueing of America," *The New Republic*, April 13, 1971.

BERGER, PETER L.; BERGER, BIRGITTE; and KELLNER, H. *The Homeless Mind: Modernization and Consciousness*, New York: Atheneum, 1972.

BERNSTEIN, BASIL. *Class Codes and Control*, Vol. I, London: Routledge & Kegan Paul, 1971.

BIERKENS, PETER. "Childlessness and the Psychological Point of View," *Bulletin of the Menninger Clinic*, XXXIX, March, 1975, p. 2.

BIRDSALL, J. B. *Human Evolution: An Introduction to the New Physical Anthropology*, Chicago: Rand-McNally, 1972.

BLURTON-JONES, NICHOLAS. "Comparative Aspects of Mother-Child Contact," in N. Blurton-Jones, ed. *Ethological Studies of Child Behavior*, Cambridge: Cambridge University Press, 1972.

BOK, SISSELA. "The Ethics of Giving Placebos," *Scientific American*, Vol. 231, No. 5, November, 1974.

BOOTH, CHARLES. *Life and Labour of the People in London*, London: Macmillan, 1902.

BOURNE, H. R.; BUMEY, W. E., JR.; COLBURN, R. W.; DAVIS, J. N.; SHAW, D. M.; and COPPEN, S. J. "Nonadrenaline 5-Hydroxytryptamine, and 5-Hydroxyindoleactic Acid in Hind-Brains of Depressed Suicidal Patients," *Lancet*, II (1968), pp. 805–808.

BOWLBY, JOHN. *Attachment and Loss*, New York: Basic Books, 1969.

———. *Separation*, New York: Basic Books, 1974.

BRENNER, MEYER HARVEY. *Mental Illness and the Economy*, Cambridge, Massachusetts: Harvard University Press, 1973.

BRODY, JANE E. Article in *The New York Times*, July 22, 1977, p. 1, col. 4.

———. "Personal Health," *The New York Times*, November 8, 1978.

Bronfenbrenner, Urie. *Two Worlds of Childhood: U.S. and U.S.S.R.*, New York: Russell Sage Foundation, 1970.

Bruce, Harry M. *British Medical Bulletin*, XXVI, 1970, pp. 10–13.

Bury, J. B. *The Idea of Progress: An Inquiry Into Its Origin and Growth*, London: Macmillan, 1932.

Byck, Robert, ed., *Sigmund Freud; Cocaine Papers*, New York: Meridian, 1975.

Campbell, Donald T. "Social Morality Norms as Evidence of Conflict Between Biological, Human Nature, and Social System Requirements," presented to the Dahlem Workshop on Biology and Morals, Berlin, November–December, 1977.

Cannon, Walter B. "Voodoo Death," *American Anthropologist*, Vol. 44, No. 2, 1942.

Carniero, Robert L. "Hunting and Hunting Magic Among the Amahuaca of the Peruvian Mountains," *Ethnology*, 9:4, October, 1970, p. 338.

Casey, K. L. "Pain: A Current View of Neural Mechanisms," *American Scientist*, LI 1973, p. 2.

Caspari, Ernst. "The Biological Basis of Female Hierarchies," in Lionel Tiger, ed., with assistance of Heather Fowler, *Female Hierarchies*, Chicago: AVC, 1978.

Census, Bureau of. Current Population Report, Population Characteristics "Number, Timing, and Duration of Marriages and Divorces in the U.S., June, 1975," Washington, D.C.: Government Printing Office, October, 1976.

Census, Bureau of. "Marriage, Fertility, and Child Spacing: June, 1965, Current Population Reports Series," CLXXXVI, Washington, D.C.: Government Printing Office, 1969, p. 20.

Chomsky, Noam. *Problems of Knowledge and Freedom: The Russell Lectures*, New York: Pantheon, 1971.

Cioran, E. M. *A Short History of Decay*, Richard Howard, trans., New York: The Viking Press, 1975.

Coffman, Richard M., and Painter, Larry J. "The Sex Ratio in Post-Industrial America," presented at the Western Social Science Association Annual Meeting, Temple, Arizona, April 1976.

Cohen, John. *Behavior in Uncertainty and Its Social Implications*, London: George Allen and Unwin Ltd., 1964.

———. *Chance, Skill and Luck—The Psychology of Gambling and Guessing*, Baltimore, Maryland: Penguin Books, 1960.

———. *Risk and Gambling—The Study of Subjective Probability*, New York: Philosophical Library, 1956.

COLEMAN, JAMES S. *Equality of Educational Opportunity*, Washington: U.S. Department of Health, Education, and Welfare, 1968.

COMMAGER, HENRY STEELE. "Learning From the Tragedy," *Newsweek*, August 19, 1974.

COOPER, DAVID. *The Death of the Family*, New York: Pantheon, 1970.

DAVENPORT, BARBARA; SLACK, BOYLAN; and HAMBLIN, CLAIRE. "Psychological Correlates of Childbirth Pain," *Psychosomatic Medicine*, XXXVI, 1974, pp. 215–265.

DAVIES, JAMES C. "Ions of Emotion and Political Behavior: A Prototheory" in Albert Somit, ed., *Biology and Politics: Recent Explorations*, International Social Science Council, Mouton, The Hague, Paris, 1976.

DAWKINS, RICHARD. *The Selfish Gene*, New York: Oxford University Press, 1976.

DESPRES, TERRENCE. *The Survivor: An Anatomy of Life in the Death-camps*, New York: Oxford University Press, 1976.

DEVORE, IRVEN, and KONNER, MELVIN. "Infancy in Hunter-Gatherer Life: An Ethological Perspective" in Norman F. White, ed., *Ethology and Psychiatry*, Toronto: University of Toronto Press, 1975.

DEVRIES, A. B. "Model for the Prediction of Suicidal Behavior," *Psychological Reports*, 22, 1968.

DIAMOND, STANLEY. *In Search of the Primitive: A Critique of Civilization*, New York: E. P. Dutton, 1974.

DICKEMAN, MILDRED. "Confidence of Paternity Mechanisms in the Human Species," mimeo, 1977.

———. "Demographic Consequences of Infanticide in Man," *Annual Review of Ecology and Systematics*, Vol. 6, 1975.

DJERASSI, CARL. "During Behavioral Changes in a Patient with Manic-Depressive Cycles," *Science*, CLXXXIX, 1973, pp. 300–302.

———. "Fertility Limitation Through Contraceptive Steroids in the People's Republic of China," *Study in Family Planning*, Population Council, Vol. 5, No. 1, January, 1974.

DURKHEIM, EMILE. *The Rules of Sociological Method*, Glencoe, Illinois: Free Press, 1950.

EASTWOOD, M. R., and TREVELYAN, M. H. "Relationship Between Physical and Psychiatric Disorder," *Psychological Medicine*, II, 1972, pp. 363–372.

EBLINING, F. J. *Biology and Ethics*, Symposia of the Institute of Biology, No. 18, London, New York: Academic Press, 1969.

EIBL-EIBESFELDT, I. *Ethology*, New York: Holt, Rinehart & Winston, 1970.

EITINGER, L. "A Follow-up Study of the Norwegian Concentration

Camp Survivors, Mortality and Morbidity," *The Israel Annals of Psychiatry and Related Disciplines*, Vol. 11:3, 1973.

ERIKSON, KAI. *Everything in Its Path*, New York: Simon and Schuster, 1977.

FEATHER, BEN W.; CHAPMAN, RICHARD C.; and FISHER, STEVEN B. "The Effect of a Placebo on the Reception of Painful Radiant Heat Stimuli," *Psychosomatic Medicine*, XXXIV, 1972, p. 4.

FEST, JOACHIM C. *Hitler*, New York: Harcourt Brace Jovanovich, 1974.

FIEVE, RONALD R. "The Lithium Clinic: A New Model for the Delivery of Psychiatric Services," *American Journal of Psychiatry*, October, 1975.

————. *Moodswing: The Third Revolution in Psychiatry*, New York: Morrow, 1975.

FOWLER, HEATHER T. "Female Choice: An Investigation into Human Breeding System Strategy," ms., 1978.

FOX, ROBIN. "In the Beginning: Aspects of Hominid Behavioral Evolution," *Man, The Journal of the Royal Anthropological Institute*, 2, 1967, pp. 415–433.

FRANK, JEROME D. *Persuasion and Healing*, New York: Schocken, 1974.

————. "Psychotherapy: The Restoration of Morale," *American Journal of Psychiatry*, March, 1974, 131:271–274.

FREUD, SIGMUND. *The Future of an Illusion*, translated by W. D. Robson-Scott, New York: Anchor, 1964.

FRIED, MORTON. *The Evolution of Political Society*, New York: Random House, 1967.

FRIEDMAN, RICHARD, and IWAI, JUNISKI. "Genetic Predisposition and Stress-Induced Hypertension," *Science*, CXCIII, July 9, 1976.

GABLIK, S. *Progress in Art*, New York: Rizzoli, 1977.

GELLHORN, ERNEST, and KIELY, WM. F. "Mystical States of Consciousness: Neuro-Physiological and Clinical Aspects," *Journal of Nervous and Mental Disease*, Vol. 154, No. 6, 1972.

GINSBERG, MORRIS. *The Idea of Progress: A Revaluation*, Westport, Connecticut: Greenwood Press, 1953.

GODELIER, MAURICE. "Territory and Property in Primitive Society," presented at Werner-Reimers Stiftung Symposium on Human Ethology, Bad Homburg, Germany, 1977.

GOFFMAN, ERVING. *Stigma: Notes on the Management of Spoiled Identity*, Englewood Cliffs, New Jersey: Prentice-Hall, 1963.

GOLDHAMER, HERBERT, and MARSHALL, ANDREW W. *Psychosis and Civilization: Two Studies in the Frequency of Mental Disease*, Glencoe, Illinois: Free Press, 1953.

GOLDING, WILLIAM. *The Spire,* New York: Harcourt Brace and World, 1964.

GOLDSTEIN, AVRAM. "Opioid Peptides (Endorphins) in Pituitary and Brain," *Science,* CXCIII, September 16, 1976.

GOULD-MARTIN, KATHERINE. *Women Asking Women: An Ethnography of Health Care in Rural Taiwan,* Ph.D. thesis, Rutgers University, 1976.

GRANIT, RAGNAR. "Constant Errors in the Execution and Appreciation of Movement," *Brain,* XCV, 1972, p. 4.

GREENE, GRAHAM. *The Lawless Roads,* London: Heinemann, 1939.

GRIFFIN, DONALD REDFIELD. *The Question of Animal Awareness: Evolutionary Continuity of Mental Experience,* New York: Rockefeller University Press, 1976.

HAMBURG, DAVID A. "Evolution of Emotional Responses: Evidence from Recent Research on Nonhuman Primates," *Science and Psychoanalysis,* Vol. 12, 1968:39, pp. 39–54.

HAMBURG, D.; HAMBURG, B.; and BARCHAS, J. "Anger and Depression in Perspective of Behavioral Biology," in L. Levi, ed., *Parameters of Emotion,* New York: Raven Press, 1974.

HARLOW, HARRY F. "Depressive Behavior in Adult Monkeys Following Separation from Family Environment," *Journal of Abnormal Psychology,* 1975, Vol. 84, No. 5, pp. 576–578.

———. "Induction and Alleviation of Depressive States in Monkeys," in N. White, ed., *Ethology and Psychiatry,* Toronto: University of Toronto Press, 1974.

HARLOW, H.; RICHARD, B.; and SUOMI, S. "Induced Depression in Monkeys," *Behavioral Biology,* XII, 1974, pp. 273–296.

HARNAD, STEVEN; STEKLIS, H. D.; and LANCASTER, JANE, EDS. *Origins and Evolution of Language and Speech,* New York: New York Academy of Sciences, 1977.

HARRINGTON, MICHAEL. *The Vast Majority: A Journey to the World's Poor,* New York: Simon and Schuster, 1977.

HARROD, R. F. *The Life of John Maynard Keynes,* Harmondworth: Penguin Books, 1972.

HEILBRONER, ROBERT L. *An Inquiry into the Human Prospect,* London: Calder & Boyars, 1976.

———. *The Great Ascent: The Struggle for Economic Development in Our Time,* New York: Harper & Row, 1962.

———. "Reflections: Boom and Crash," in *The New Yorker,* August 28, 1978, p. 52 *ff.*

HEWITSON, JOHN. "Homeless People as an At-Risk Group," Proceedings of the Royal Society of Medicine, Vol. 68:1, January, 1965.

HEYER, PAUL. *Marx and Darwin: A Related Legacy on Man, Nature, and Society*, Ph.D. Dissertation, Rutgers University, 1975.

HINDE, ROBERT A. "Mother/Infant Relations in Rhesus Monkeys," in N. White, ed., *Ethology and Psychiatry*, Toronto: University of Toronto Press, 1974.

HINDE, R. A., and SPENCER-BOOTH, Y. "Effects of Brief Separation from Mother on Rhesus Monkeys," *Science*, LXXIII, 1971, pp. 111–118.

HIRST, PAUL A. "Morphology and Pathology, Biological Analogies and Metaphors in Durkheim's The Rules of Sociological Method," mimeo.

HOFER, MYRON A. "A Psychoendocrine Study of Bereavement, Part I," *Psychosomatic Medicine*, 34:6 November–December, 1972, pp. 481–491.

HOFFMAN, LOIS WLADIS. "The Employment of Women, Education and Fertility," *Palmer Quarterly of Behavior and Development*, XX, 1974, p. 2.

HOLDEN, CONSTANCE. "New Look At Heroin Could Spur Better Medicinal Use of Narcotics," *Science*, Vol. 198, pp. 807–809, November 25, 1977.

HONIGFELD, GILBERT A. "Non-Specific Factors in Treatment, Part I: Review of Placebo Reactions and Placebo Reactors," *Diseases of the Nervous System*, XV, 1964, p. 3.

HRDY, SARAH B. "Infanticide as a Primate Reproductive Strategy," *American Scientist*, Vol. 65, No. 1, January–February, 1977.

———. "Male-Male Competition and Infanticide Among the Langurs," *Folia Primatologics*, XXII, 1974 (Presbytis Encellus) of Afue, Rajasthan.

HRDY, SARAH B., and HRDY, DANIEL B. "Hierarchical Relations Among Female Langurs," *Science*, Vol. 193, September 3, 1976, pp. 913–915.

HUGHES, DAVID A., and DOWNS, PHILLIP. "A Method for the Investigation of Investors' Mental Processing of Information," *Journal of Business Research*, IV, February, 1976.

ILLICH, IVAN. *Medical Nemesis: The Expropriation of Health*, London: Calder & Boyars, 1975.

JACOBS, MARTIN A., et al. "Parent-Child Relationships and Illness Behavior," *Journal of Consulting and Clinical Psychology*, XXXIX, 1972, pp. 49–53.

JAMES, WILLIAM. *The Varieties of Religious Experience: A Study in Human Nature*, New York: New American Library, 1958.

JAYNES, JULIAN. *The Origins of Consciousness in the Breakdown of the Bicameral Mind*, Boston: Houghton Mifflin, 1977.

KANTER, ROSABETH MOSS. "Interpreting the Results of a Social Experiment," review of *Women in the Kibbutz*, in *Science*, Vol. 192, No. 4240, May 14, 1976, pp. 662–663.

KEHOE, ALICE B. "The Metonymic Pole and Social Roles," *Journal of Anthropological Research*, Vol. 27, 1973.

———. "Rituals and Religion," in *Realm of the Supernatural*, A. Bharati, ed., Chicago: Mouton-Beresford, 1978.

KEYFITZ, NATHAN. "Individual Mobility in a Stationary Population," *Population Studies*, XXVII, July 1973, p. 2.

KLING, A. "Brain Lesions and Aggressive Behavior of Monkeys in Free-Ranging Groups," *Neural Basis of Violence and Aggression*, W. S. Field and W. H. Sweet, eds., Missouri, 1975.

KLING, A., and STEKLIS, H. D. "A Neural Substrate for Affiliative Behavior in Non-Human Primates," *Brain Behavior and Evolution*, 13:216–238, 1976.

KNODEL, JOHN. "Breast-Feeding and Population Growth," *Science*, CXCVIII, December 16, 1977, pp. 1111–1115.

KUNZ, PHILIP R.; BRINKERHOFF, MERLIN B.; and HUNDLEY, VICKE. "Relationship of Income and Childlessness," *Social Biology*, XX, June, 1973.

LABARRE, WESTON. *The Ghost Dance: The Origins of Religion*, New York: Dell Books, 1972.

LAING, RONALD D. *The Politics of Experience*, New York: Ballantine, 1967.

LEBOEUF, BERNIE J.; WHITING, RONALD J.; and GANTT, RICHARD F. "Perinatal Behavior of Northern Elephant Seal Females and Their Young," *Behavior*, XLIII, 1972.

LEE, RICHARD. "What Hunters Do for a Living, or, How to Make Out on Scarce Resources," in R. B. Lee and I. DeVore, eds., *Man, The Hunter*, Chicago: Aldine, 1968.

LEE, RICHARD B. "Subsistence Ecology of Kung Bushman," unpublished doctoral dissertation, Berkeley: University of California Press, 1965.

LEFCOURT, HERBERT M. "The Function of the Illusions of Control and Freedom," *American Psychologist*, May, 1973, pp. 417–425.

LEISS, WILLIAM. *The Limits to Satisfaction: An Essay on the Problems of Needs and Commodities*, Toronto: University of Toronto Press, 1976.

LEOPOLD, C. A. and ARDREY, R. "Toxic Substances in Plants and the Food Habits of Early Man," *Science*, May 5, 1972, pp. 512–514.

LÉVI-STRAUSS, CLAUDE. *The Savage Mind*, Chicago: University of Chicago Press, 1968.

LLINAS, RUDOLFO. "La Forme et la Function des Cellules Nerveuses," *La Recherche*, 43:1975:240, p. 50.

LORENZ, KONRAD. *On Aggression*, New York: Harcourt, Brace & World, 1966.

———. *Behind the Mirror: A Search for a Natural History of Human Knowledge*, New York: Harcourt Brace Jovanovich, 1977.

LUCHTERHAND, ELMER. "The Gondola-Car Transports," *The International Journal of Social Psychiatry*, Vol. XIII, No. 1, 1966–67.

———. "Survival in the Concentration Camps: An Individual or a Group Phenomenon," in B. Rosenberg, I. Gerver, and F. W. Howton, eds., *Mass Society in Crisis: Social Problems and Social Pathology*, New York: Macmillan, 1964.

LUKER, KRISTIN. *Taking Chances: Abortion and the Decision Not to Contracept*, Berkeley: University of California Press, 1975.

LURIA, GINA, and TIGER, VIRGINIA. *Everywoman*, New York: Random House, 1977.

LURIA, RICHARD E. "The Validity and Reliability of the Visual Analogue Mood Scale," *Journal of Psychiatric Research*, XII, 1975.

LURIA, RICHARD E., and McHUGH, PAUL R. "Reliability and Clinical Utility of the 'Wing,' " Present State Examination, *Archives of General Psychiatry*, XXX, June, 1974, pp. 866–871.

McCLELLAND, DAVID. *The Achieving Society*, New York: Free Press, 1967.

McCLINTOCK, MARTHA. "Menstrual Synchrony and Suppression," *Nature*, Vol. 229, January 22, 1971.

McHUGH, PAUL R.; MORAN, TIMOTHY H.; and BARTON, GEORGE J. "Satiety: A Graded Behavioral Phenomenon Regulating Caloric Intake," *Science*, CXC, October 10, 1975.

MACLEAN, PAUL. "A Mind of Three Minds: Educating The Triune Brain," in National Society for the Study of Education, *Education and the Brain*, Chicago: University of Chicago Press, 1978.

MACLEAN, PAUL D. *A Triune Concept of the Brain and Behavior*, ed. V. A. Knol and others, Toronto: University of Toronto Press, 1973.

McLUHAN, MARSHALL. *Understanding Media*, New York: McGraw-Hill, 1963.

McNAIR, DOUGLAS N. "Anti-Anxiety Drugs and Human Performance," *Archives of General Psychiatry*, November, 1973.

MALCOLM, ANDREW I. *The Pursuit of Intoxication*, Toronto Addiction Research Foundation, 1971.

MANDELL, ARNOLD J. "Neuro-Biological Barriers to Euphoria," *American Scientist*, LXI, October, 1973, p. 5.

MANNONI, O. *Prospero and Caliban*, London: Methuen, 1956.

MARKS, GENE L. "Neurobiology: Researchers High on Endogenous Opiates," *Science*, CXCIII, September 24, 1976.

MARLER, PETER, and HAMILTON, WILLIAM J. *Mechanisms of Animal Behavior*, New York: John Wiley & Sons, 1966.

MARRIS, PETER. *Loss and Change*, New York: Pantheon Books, 1974.

MARSHACK, A. *Form in Indigenous Art: Schematization in the Art of Aboriginal Australian and Prehistoric Europe*, ed. by Peter J. Ucko, London: G. Duckworth & Co., 1977.

———. "Implications of the Paleolithic Symbolic Evidence for the Origin of Language," *American Scientist*, March–April, 1976.

———. *The Roots of Civilization*, New York: McGraw-Hill, 1971.

———. "Ukrainian Upper Paleolithic Symbol Systems: A Cognitive and Comparative Analysis of Complex Ritual Marking," *Current Anthropology*, 1979.

MASON, W. "Determinants of Social Behavior in Young Chimpanzees," in A. Schieir, H. Harlow and F. Stollnitz, eds., *Behavior of Non-Human Primates*, New York: Modern Research Trends, Academic Press, 1965.

———. "The Social Development of Monkeys and Apes," in I. DeVore, ed., *Primate Behavior*, New York: Holt, Rinehart & Winston, 1965.

MATLIN, MARGARET, and DAVID STANG, "The Pollyanna Principle," in *Psychology Today*, March 1978, pp. 56, 59, 100.

MEIERHOFFER, MARIE. "Problems Relating to the Development of Babies and Young Children in Institutional Care," International Conference on Health, Douglas, Isle of Man, September, 1972.

MELZACK, RONALD, AND CHAPMAN, RICHARD C. "Psychological Aspects of Pain," *Post-Graduate Medicine*, LIII, 1973, p. 6.

MENDLEWICZ, J.; MASSART-GRIOT, T.; WIMOTT, J.; and FLEISS, J. L. "Blood Groups in Manic-Depressive Illness and Schizophrenia," *Diseases of the Nervous System*, XXXV, January, 1974, pp. 39–41.

MENDLEWICZ, J.; TIEVE, R. R.; RAINER, J. O.; et al. "Affective Disorders on Paternal and Maternal Sides: Observations in Bipolar (Manic-Depressive) Patients With and Without a Family History," *British Journal of Psychiatry*, 122, January, 1973, pp. 31–34.

METZ, ROBERT. *The New York Times*, October 22, 1975.

MICHAEL, R. P., and KEVERNE, E. B. "Pheremones in the Communication of Sexual Status in Primates," *Nature*, CCXVIII, pp. 746–749.

MICHAEL, RICHARD P. "Hormonal Steroids and Sexual Communication in Primates," *Journal of Steroid Biochemistry*, VI, 1975, pp. 161–170.

MILLER, G.; GALANTER, I.; and PRIBRAM, K. *Plans and the Structure of Behavior*, New York: Holt, Rinehart & Winston, 1960.

MISHAN, E. J. *The Economic Growth Debate: An Assessment*, London: George Allen and Unwin, 1978.

MOLTMANN, JURGEN. *Theology of Hope: On the Ground and Implications of a Christian Eschatology*, translated by James W. Leach, New York: Harper and Row, 1967, p. 16.

MONOD, JACQUES. *Chance and Necessity: An Essay on the Natural Philosophy of Human Biology*, New York: Knopf, 1971.

MONTAGU, ASHLEY. *Man's Most Dangerous Myth: The Fallacy of Race*, Fifth Edition, New York: Oxford University Press, 1974.

MURPHY, JANE. "Psychiatric Labeling in Cross-Cultural Perspective," *Science*, Vol. 191, March 12, 1976.

NOWLIS, GEOFFREY H., AND KESSEN, WILLIAM. "Human Newborns Differentiate Differing Concentrations of Sucrose and Glucose," *Science*, XXCI, February 27, 1976, pp. 865–866.

PARK, LEE, and COVI, L. "Nonblind Placebo Trail—An Exploration of Neurotic Patients' Placebo When Its Inert Content Is Disclosed," *Archives of General Psychiatry*, XII, April, 1965, pp. 36–45.

PATTERSON, KIP E., and SEAY, BILL. "Resistance to Pathopsychology in Adolescent Monkeys *(Macaca fascicularis)* Reared with Mothers and Peers," *Journal of Abnormal Psychology*, LXXXIV, No. 5, 1975, pp. 524–530.

PATTISON, E. M.; LAPINS, N. A.; and DOUR, H. A. "Faith Healing: A Study of Personality and Function," *The Journal of Nervous and Mental Disease*, CLVII, December 1973, p. 6.

PENFIELD, WILDER. *The Mystery of the Mind*, Princeton: Princeton University Press, 1975.

PIAGET, JEAN. *Genetic Epistemology*, New York: Norton, 1971.

POLLARD, SIDNEY. *The Idea of Progress*, London: Penguin Books, 1971.

PORTER, JOHN. *The Vertical Mosaic: An Analysis of Social Class and Power in Canada*, Toronto: University of Toronto Press, 1965.

PRICE, J. "The Dominance Hierarchy and the Evolution of Mental Illness," *The Lancet*, Vol. 2, July 29, 1967, pp. 243–246.

PRITCHARD, MICHAEL. "Dimensions of Illness Behavior in Long Term Haemodialysis," *Journal of Psychosomatic Research*, XVIII, 1974, pp. 55–67.

———. "Prophylactic Efficacy of Lithium in Manic-Depressives," *Archives of General Psychiatry*, XXVIII, 1973.

RACKOFF, VIVIAM M. "The Family: An Ethological Imperative," *Social Research*, Summer, 1977, Vol. 44:2.

REDMOND, D. E., JR.; HINRICHS, R. L.; MAAS, J. W.; and KLING, A. "Behavior of Free-Ranging Macaques After Intraventricular 6-Hydroxydopamin," *Science*, CLXXXI, 1973, p. 202.

RICHARDS, JAMES J., JR. "Some Psycho-Social Consequences of a Change to a Replacement Birthrate in the United States," *Journal of Applied Psychology*, LIX, 1974, p. 1.

RICHTER, CURT P. "On the Phenomenon of Sudden Death in Animals and Man," *Psychosomatic Medicine,* Vol. 19:191–198, 1957.

RICKELS, KARL, ED. *Non-specific Factors in Drug Therapy,* Springfield, Illinois: Charles C. Thomas, 1968.

ROETHLISBERGER, F. J., and DICKSON, W. J. *Management and the Worker,* Cambridge, Massachusetts: Harvard University Press, 1961.

ROHNER, RONALD P. *They Love Me, They Love Me Not: A Worldwide Study of the Effects of Parental Acceptance and Rejection,* New Haven: Human Relations Area Files Press, 1975.

ROSENBLATT, P. C.; WALSH, R. P.; and JACKSON, R. A. *Grief and Mourning in Cross-Cultural Perspective,* New Haven: HRAF Press, 1976.

ST. JOHN, NANCY. "Mothers and Optimism: Congruence of School Related Attitudes," *Journal of Marriage and the Family,* August, 1972.

SAHLINS, MARSHALL. *The Uses and Abuses of Biology,* Ann Arbor: University of Michigan Press, 1976.

SAMUELSON, PAUL A. "Maximizing and Biology," mimeo, 1977.

SEAY, B.; HANSEN, E.; and HARLOW, H. F. "Mother-Infant Separation in Monkeys," *Journal of Child Psychology and Psychiatry,* III, 1962, pp. 123–32.

SELIGMAN, MARTIN E. P. *Helplessness,* New York: W. H. Freeman, 1975.

SCITOVSKY, TIBOR. "The Place of Economic Welfare in Human Welfare," *Quarterly Review of Economics and Business,* XIII, No. 3, Autumn, 1973.

SHAPIRO, ARTHUR K. "The Placebo Effect in the History of Medical Treatment: Implications for Psychiatry," *American Journal of Psychiatry,* CXVI, 1959, pp. 298–304.

SHAPIRO, JUDITH. "I Went to the Animal Fair . . . The Tiger and Fox Were There," review of *The Imperial Animal,* by Lionel Tiger and Robin Fox, *Natural History,* LXXX, October, 1971, pp. 90–98.

SHEPARD, PAUL. *Thinking Animals: Animals and the Development of Human Intelligence,* New York, Viking, 1978.

SHIPLER, DAVID. *The New York Times,* January 28, 1978.

SHORTER, EDWARD. *The Making of the Modern Family,* New York: Basic Books, 1975.

SHUVAL, JUDITH; ANTONOVSKY, AARON; and DAVIES, A. MICHAEL. "Illness: A Mechanism for Coping with Failure," *Social Science and Medicine,* VII, 1973, pp. 25–26.

SKLAR, RUTH. "The American Birthrate: Evidences of a Coming Rise," *Science,* CLXXXIX, 1975, pp. 693–700.

SLATER, MARIAM K. "Ecological Factors in the Origin of Incest," *American Anthropologist,* Vol. 61, 1959, pp. 1042–1059.

SMITH, PHILLIP. "Stone-Age Man on the Nile," *Scientific American*, Vol. 235:2, August, 1976.

SNYDER, S. "Opiate Receptors and Internal Opiates," *Scientific American*, pp. 236:5, September, 1976.

SNYDER, SOLOMON. "The Brain's Own Opiates," *Chemical and Engineering News*, 55(48):26–35, 1977, pp. 266–271.

SONTAG, SUSAN. *Illness as Metaphor*, New York: Farrar, Straus & Giroux, 1978.

SPEER, ALBERT. *Inside the Third Reich*, New York: Macmillan, 1970.

———. *Spandau*, New York: Macmillan, 1976.

SPENCER-BOOTH, Y., and HINDE, ROBERT A. "Effects of Six Days' Separation from Mother on 18-to-32-Week-Old Rhesus Monkeys," *Animal Behavior*, Vol. 19, 1971, pp. 174–191.

———. "The Effects of 13 Days of Maternal Separation on Infant Rhesus Monkeys Compared with Those of Shorter and Repeated Separations," *Animal Behavior*, 19, pp. 559–605, 1971.

SPINETTA, J., and MALONEY, J. "Death Anxiety in the Outpatient Leukemia Child," *Pediatrics*, Vol. 56, December, 1975, pp. 1035–1037.

STEIN, LARRY. "Norepenephrine Reward Pathways: Role in Self-Stimulation Memory Consolidation and Schizophrenia," Nebraska Symposium on Motivation, 1974.

STEINHOFF, PATRICIA A.; SMITH, RAY A.; and DIAMOND, MILTON. "Characteristics and Motivations of Women Receiving Abortions," *Sociological Symposium*, VIII, Spring, 1972.

STEPPACHER, ROBERT C., and MAUSNER, JUDITH S. "Suicide in Male and Female Physicians," *J.A.M.A.*, CCVIII, April 15, 1974, Vol. 228.

STOTLAND, EZRA. *The Psychology of Hope—An Integration of Experimental, Clinical and Social Approaches*, San Francisco: Jossey-Bass, 1969.

STRUVE, F. S.; KLEIN, D. F.; and SARAF, K. S. "Electroencephalographic Correlates of Suicide, Ideation and Attempts," *Archives of General Psychiatry*, 27, 1972.

TELEKI, GEZA. "Group Response to the Accidental Death of a Chimpanzee in Gombe National Park, Tanzania," Switzerland: S. Karger, *Folia primat.* 29:81–94, 1973.

THEISSEN, D. D. "A Move Toward Species-Specific Analysis in Behavior Genetics," *Behavior Genetics*, Vol. 2, No. 2–3, 1972.

THOMAS, C., and GREENSTREET, P. "Psychological Characteristics in Youth as Predictors of Five Disease States: Suicide, Mental Illness, Hypertension, Coronary Heart Disease and Tumor," *Johns Hopkins Medical Journal*, 132, January, 1973.

THOMAS, LEWIS. "Natural Science," *The New England Journal of Medicine*, 288:307, 1973.

————, cited in J. Bernstein, "Profile," *The New Yorker*, December, 1976.

TIGER, L., and FOX, R. "The Zoological Perspective in Social Science," *Man*, (n.s.) Vol. I:1, 1966.

————. *The Imperial Animal*, New York: Holt, Rinehart and Winston, 1971.

TIGER, L., and SHEPHER, J. *Women in the Kibbutz*, New York: Harcourt Brace Jovanovich, 1975.

TIGER, LIONEL. "Somatic Factors and Social Behavior," in Robin Fox, ed., *Biosocial Anthropology*, New York: John Wiley & Sons, 1975.

————. "Bureaucracy and Charisma in Ghana," *Journal of Asian and African Studies*, 1 (1), 1964.

————. "Bureaucracy and Urban Symbol Systems," in Horace Miner, ed., *The City in Modern Africa*, New York: Praeger, 1968.

————. "Ions of Emotion and Political Behavior: Notes on a Proto-theory," commentary in A. Somit, ed., *Biology and Politics*, Mouton: International Social Science Council, Paris.

————. "Live Animal in a Machine Age," *The New York Times Week in Review*, May 14, 1978.

————. "The Male Bond," *The Observer*, June 29, 1969.

————. *Men in Groups*, New York: Random House, 1969; London: Thomas Nelson, 1969.

The Times of London, July 3, 1973.

TINBERGEN, NIKO. "Ethology and Stress Diseases," *Science*, July 5, 1974, Vol. 185, pp. 20–27.

TRILLING, LIONEL. "Aggression and Utopia: A Note On William Morris's 'News from Nowhere,' " *The Psychoanalytic Quarterly*, Vol. XLII, No. 2, April, 1973.

TRIVERS, R. L. "Parent-Offspring Conflict," *American Zoologist*, XIV, pp. 249–64, 1974.

TRIVERS, ROBERT L. "The Evolution of Reciprocal Altruism," *The Quarterly Review of Biology*, Vol. 46, No. 4, March, 1971.

TURNBULL, COLIN M. *The Mountain People*, New York: Simon and Schuster, 1972.

TVERSKY, A., and KAHNEMAN, D., "Causal Schemata In Judgements Under Uncertainty," in M. Fishbein, ed., *Progress in Social Psychology*, Hillsdale: L. Erlbaum Associates, 1977.

————. "Intuitive Prediction: Biases and Corrective Procedures," *Management Science* (forthcoming).

TYLER, LEONA E. "A Design for a Hopeful Psychology," *American Psychologist*, December, 1973, Vol. 28(12), 1021–1029.

UDRY, RICHARD J.; BAUMAN, KARL; and CHASE, CHARLES L. "Population Growth Rates in Perfect Contraceptive Populations," *Population Studies*, XXVII, No. 2, July, 1973, p. 158.

VESSEY, STEVEN. "Night Observations of Free-Ranging Rhesus Monkeys," *American Journal of Physical Anthropology*, 38:2, March, 1973, pp. 613–619.

WAGAR, WARREN. *Good Tidings: The Belief in Progress from Darwin to Marcuse*, Bloomington: Indiana University Press, 1973.

Wall Street Journal, The, October 20, 1975.

———. July 18, 1977.

WATTERS, W. *Compulsory Parenthood,* Toronto: McClelland and Stewart, 1976.

WEISS, KARL S. "Marital Status and Risk Factors for Coronary Heart Disease: U.S. Health Exam. Survey of Adults," *British Journal of Preventive and Social Medicine*, XXVII, February, 1973, p. 1.

WEISSMAN, MYRNA, et al. "Symptom Patterns in Primary and Secondary Depression: A Comparison of Primary Depressives with Depressed Opiate Addicts, Alcoholics, and Schizophrenics," *Archives of General Psychiatry*, July, 1977, Vol. 54.

WEISSMAN, MYRNA; FOX, KAREN; and KLERMAN, GERALD L. "Hostility and Depression Associated with Suicide Attempts," *American Journal of Psychiatry*, 130:4, April, 1973.

WEISSMAN, MYRNA; KLERMAN, GERALD L.; PAYKEL, EUGENE; FRENCH, NANCY; MARK, HAL; FOX, KAREN; and PRUSOFF, BRIGITTE. "Suicide Attempts in an Urban Community, 1955 and 1970," *Social Psychiatry*, 8, 1973, pp. 82–91.

WESTOFF, CHARLES F. "The Decline of Unplanned Births in the U.S.," *Science*, CXCI, January, 1976.

WESTOFF, CHARLES F., and RYDER, NORMAN B. *The Contraceptive Revolution*, Princeton: Princeton University Press, 1977.

WHELAN, ELIZABETH M. "Illegitimate and Premaritally Conceived First Births in Massachusetts, 1966–1968," *Social Biology*, XIX, March, 1972.

WHELAN, ELIZABETH. "The Temporal Relation of Marriage, Conception and Birth in Massachusetts," *Demography*, XCII, August, 1972.

WHITE, A. A. "The Intentional Exploitation of Man's Known Weaknesses," *Houston Law Review*, IX, May 1972.

WILKINSON, RUPERT. *The Prefects: British Leadership and Public School Tradition*, London: Oxford University Press, 1964.

WILLIAMS, B. J. "Investigations of a Little-Known Way of Life," Review of *Kalahari Hunter-Gatherers*, by R. B. Lee and I. DeVore in *Science*, 196:4291, May 13, 1977, pp. 761–763.

WINOKUR, GEORGE. "Genetic Aspects of Depression, Separation and Depression," *A.A.A.S.*, 1973, pp. 125, 137.

WINTROB, RONALD. "The Influences of Others: Witchcraft and Rootwork as Explanations of Behavioral Disturbances," *Journal of Nervous and Mental Disease*, Vol. 156:5, 1973.

WOODHAM-SMITH, CECIL. *The Great Hunger*, New York: Signet Books, New American Library, 1962.

WHYTE, WILLIAM F. *Street Corner Society*, 2nd ed. Chicago: University of Chicago Press, 1955.

YOUNG, LAURENCE D.; SUOMI, STEPHEN S.; HARLOW, HARRY F.; and McKINNEY, WILLIAM T. "Early Stress and Later Response to Separation in Rhesus Monkeys," *American Journal of Psychiatry*, CXXX, April, 1973, p. 4.

ZIHLMANN, A., and TANNER, N. "Gathering and the Hominid Adaptation," *Female Hierarchies*, ed. L. Tiger with assistance of Heather Fowler, Chicago: AVC, 1978.

ZYLMAN, R. *Journal of Traffic Education*, October 20, 1972.

Index

Art (*cont.*)
  assertion and, 79–80
  biology and, 32
  cave, 71–79
  progress and, 25
Ashanti, 226

Baby boom after Second World
    War, effects of, 127–33
Bane, Mary Jo, 97–98
Barchas, J., 153
Barton, George J., 240
Beauty care, 257–59
Becker, G., 199, 281
Beecher, H. K., 175
Behavior
  animal, 28–29, 51–52
  chemicals and, 151–55, 165–68,
    172–74
  contraceptive pill and, 139–42
  elements of, 17–18
  ethological study of, 28–29
  fertility and, 139–44
  genetics and, 27, 35, 51–52
  neurochemicals and, 172–73
  stop-go systems of, 52, 173
Being and Nothingness, 23
Benignness (benignity)
  family influences on, 101–2
  of future, 51
Benson, Herbert, 178–79
Berelson, Bernard, 126, 127
Berger, Birgitta, 265
Berger, Peter, 265, 278–79
Bernstein, Basil, 104
Bernstein, J., 177
Biology
  antithetical perception of,
    politics and, 31–32
  behavior and, 29–31, 34–35
  economics and, 199
  Freud on, 45–46

future and, 30
human nature and, 31–33
religion and, 40–42
society and, 29–30, 34–35
uniqueness of human culture
    and, 32–33
Birthrates, 110
  employment of females and,
    136–37
  governmental control of, 125–
    127
  reduction in, 122
  after Second World War,
    effects of, 127–33
  sexual promiscuity and, 135–36
  socio-sexual effects of, 127
Blei, Barbara, 244
Boarding schools, 104
Body, human, 237
  dieting and, 238–39, 243–45
  exercise and, 245–46
  food and, 238–48
  self-administered substances
    for, 257–59
  shape of, implications of, 242–
    243
Bok, Sissela, 178, 179
Bonhoeffer, Dietrich, 277
Bonus, cost of living, 205, 206
Books, self-help, 262
Boom-bust cycles, 222
Boorstin, Daniel, 228
Booth, Charles, 33
Boredom, travel and, 227–28
Bottle-feeding, 137–39
Bowlby, John, 85
Brain
  ancient processes of, 49, 155–
    156
  chemical effects on, 151–55,
    159, 171–72
  consciousness and, 48–49